MOUNTAIN DAYS

MOUNTAIN DAYS

A Journal of Camping Experiences in the
Mountains of Tennessee and North Carolina,
1914-1938

Paul M. Fink

FOREWORD BY KEN WISE

HUNTER LIBRARY AT WESTERN CAROLINA UNIVERSITY

Original manuscript copyright © 1960, Paul M. Fink, Jonesboro, TN.
This edition copyright © 2019 Hunter Library at Western Carolina University. All rights reserved.

A different version of this work was published in 1975 as *Backpacking Was the Only Way: A Chronicle of Camping Experiences in the Southern Appalachian Mountains* by East Tennessee State University Press, Johnson City, TN.

This work is licensed under a Creative Commons CC BY-NC-ND license. To view a copy of the license, visit http://creativecommons.org/licenses.

Suggested citation: Fink, Paul M. *Mountain Days: A Journal of Camping Experiences in the Mountains of Tennessee and North Carolina, 1914-1938.* Cullowee, NC: Hunter Library at Western Carolina University, 2019. DOI: https://doi.org/10.5149/9781469651859_Fink

ISBN 978-1-4696-5184-2 (alk. paper)
ISBN 978-1-4696-5185-9 (ebook)

Cover image: Paul Fink in the Black Mountains, 1920.

TABLE OF CONTENTS

vii   FOREWORD

xix   PREFACE

1   **AUGUST, 1914**
Big Bald Mountain

11   **AUGUST 19-22, 1915**
Unaka and Roan Mountains

19   **MAY 27-30, 1916**
Big Bald Mountain

27   **SEPTEMBER 22-26, 1916**
Le Conte

37   **JULY 14, 1918**
Roan Mountain

41   **SEPTEMBER 19-23, 1918**
Clark Creek, Rich Mountain and Roan Mountain

49   **JUNE 9-19, 1919**
Eastern End of the Great Smokies

73   **SEPTEMBER 5-7, 1919**
Big Falls of Clark Creek

79   **JUNE 15-24, 1920**
Black Mountains

101   **JUNE 2-12, 1921**
Le Conte and Vicinity

125   **JUNE 10-12, 1922**
Roan Mountain

131   **AUGUST 10-16, 1922**
Western End of the Smokies

151   **NOVEMBER 4, 1922**
Great Smoky Mountains

159   **JUNE 14-18, 1923**
Rich Mountain, Big Butte and Westward

173   **JULY 13-21, 1924**
Balsam Mountains and the Great Smokies

199   **AUGUST 6-12, 1925**
Great Smokies

215   **JULY 20-26, 1927**
Central Portion of the Great Smokies

225   **AUGUST 9-14, 1929**
Eastern Portion of the Great Smokies

237   **AUGUST 11-16, 1930**
Eastern Part of the Great Smokies

251   **SEPTEMBER 17-20, 1938**
Roan Mountain

259   **WATCH THAT AXE**

263   **OUTFITTING**

265   **CLOTHING**

267   **SHELTER**

269   **SLEEPING COMFORT**

271   **FOOD**

275   **MISCELLANEOUS**

FOREWORD

One of the foremost documents pertaining to early twentieth century exploration in the Great Smoky Mountains and the Unaka Range along the border of North Carolina and Tennessee is a journal kept by Paul Fink, an inveterate adventurer from Jonesborough, Tennessee with a genuine appreciation for wilderness terrain. In 1960, after nearly a lifetime of exploring the mountains, Fink organized his journal notes into a manuscript, *Mountain Days: A Journal of Camping Experiences in the Mountains of Tennessee and North Carolina, 1914-1938*. The manuscript, arguably the most substantive early written account of exploration into the remote recesses of the Smokies backcountry, particularly its eastern end, remained unpublished until 1975 when the Research Advisory Council at East Tennessee State University in collaboration with Fink issued it in a limited edition under the title *Backpacking Was the Only Way: A Chronicle of Camping Experiences in the Southern Appalachian Mountains*. In the interim, Fink's book has become a scarce item.

While the image of Paul Fink that emerges from the pages of his manuscript is that of a fearlessly adventurous young man well-liked by his hiking companions with whom he enjoyed light-hearted comradery, its author was nonetheless a serious observer whose knowledge of the interior of the Smokies was unmatched by all but a very few contemporaries. As early as 1919, even the noted chronicler of Smoky Mountain life, Horace Kephart, had come to recognize the twenty-seven-year-old Fink as a superior authority on the mountain's topography as well as a fellow sojourner in the quest to establish a national park in the Smokies. The two began exchanging letters on some of the more arcane landmarks in the Smokies and at one juncture, realizing Fink's enthusiasm for a park in the Smokies, Kephart off-handedly suggested that he start "a propaganda to have the Government buy up the best forests here before they are destroyed."[1] The remark would prove prophetic. Within a few years, Fink would find himself not only immersed in the mechanisms of the park movement, but also in the efforts to determine the course of the newly proposed Appalachian Trail (AT). Both endeavors would come to rely heavily on his intimate knowledge of the topography of both the Unakas and the Great Smokies.

Fink's involvement in both movements had their origins in his relationship with Harlan Kelsey, president of the Boston-based Appalachian Mountain

Club, an organization committed to promoting wilderness conservation. In 1920, Kelsey invited Fink to join the club after having learned that the young backpacker from Tennessee was the foremost authority on the mountains along the North Carolina-Tennessee border. Though the two had yet to make a personal acquaintance, Kelsey was confident in seeking the young Fink's opinion on the feasibility of an ambitious new proposal. On January 16, 1922, Kelsey forwarded to Fink a copy of "An Appalachian Trail: A Project of Regional Planning," an article published by Benton MacKaye in the October 1921 issue of the *Journal of the American Institute of Architects*.[2] Kelsey was intrigued by MacKaye's proposal for a recreational trail spanning the length of the Appalachian Mountains and began engaging Fink in regular correspondence concerning possible routes for such a trail. Later, in a letter to MacKaye, Kelsey, referring to Fink, commented that "there is no better person in the south to give advice regarding the Unaka or Smoky Mountain route."[3]

At the same time Kelsey was working to gain traction for MacKaye's AT proposal, he had also become involved in the most recent movement proposing the establishment of a national park in the Southern Appalachians. Kelsey had grown up listening to proposals for a national park practically all of his life, but none had come to fruition. In a letter to Fink on December 2, 1924, Kelsey recalled his childhood in western North Carolina forty years earlier and listening to his father tell stories of those who purported to know the origin of the idea for a national park in the Great Smoky Mountains. "It is one of those things" Kelsey wrote Fink, "which anyone who claims to be the originator of, is either a fake or a fool."[4] Kelsey's comment to Fink was likely prompted by a flood of unsolicited letters recommending various locations for the national park which Kelsey had been receiving since having been appointed earlier that year by Hubert Work, Secretary of the Interior, to the Southern Appalachian National Park Committee, an ad hoc group charged to "undertake a thorough study of the Southern Appalachian Mountains for the purpose of selecting the most worthy site in that range as a national park."[5]

Prior to the authorization of the Southern Appalachian National Park Committee and his own appointment to it, Kelsey intimated in a letter to Harrington Moore, director of the Council on National Parks, Forests, and Wild Life, that Fink would be a good candidate for the proposed committee. "Paul Fink as you have rightly stated has a very clear idea of what is really needed and he would be an excellent member of such Board of Survey. All signs point to the Smoky Mountain Range, yet certainly the matter cannot be decided without really carefully worked out reports."⁶ A year earlier, as interest in a park began gaining momentum, Kelsey had requested Fink's opinions concerning the necessary criteria for a national park as well as his thoughts on whether the Smokies were a suitable candidate.⁷ Fink not only confirmed Kelsey's impressions of the Smokies, but, in a response to Work, assured him that in accordance with the National Park Service's established criteria for a national park, the Smokies' "qualifications, both of geological formations, forest coverage and animal life, will fill the needed requirements."⁸

Notwithstanding Kelsey's recommendation, Fink was not considered for membership on the Southern Appalachian National Park Committee. Fink's lack of prominence and visibility within the greater political realm was likely perceived to offer little reinforcement in lending heft to the committee's mission. In spite of his superior knowledge of the Southern Appalachian Mountains and his tireless efforts in the park movement, Fink's contributions to the success of establishing the Great Smoky Mountains National Park would always remain in the shadow of others.

Fink's *bona fides* as an authority on the Southern Appalachians resided in his boots-on-the-ground experience in the mountains. In 1914, at the age of twenty-two, Fink made his first backpacking trip into the Unaka Mountains. Two years later, in the company of a childhood companion from Jonesborough, Walter Diehl, he completed his first extended excursion into the remote backcountry of the Great Smoky Mountains, an exercise that would become a life-long avocation. As Fink and Diehl quickly learned, "those who know the eastern end [of the Smokies] intimately are few and far between. Not many of the natives are familiar with that welter of ridges and ravines, where getting lost is far easier than staying on the right route."⁹

Like Kephart, Fink had, from the time of his earliest acquaintance with the mountains, engaged in the practice of recording in a journal the details of his travel experiences in the Smoky backcountry. As he later admitted, he was interested in exploring mountains of "untouched and primeval wilderness, where there was only the barest evidence of man's presence." How he became aware of Fink's journal is unknown, but Fink's "untouched and primeval wilderness" apparently met Col. David Chapman's criteria for a national park. Chapman, who, as vice president of the Great Smoky Mountains Conservation Association (GSMCA), would become the single most relentless force in steering the park movement to its successful end, requested that Fink share his journal with Milton Ailes, a Washington D.C. banker, ostensibly in the hopes that the journal would enlighten outsiders to the suitability of the Smokies as a national park.[10]

Chapman, like Kelsey, had learned to rely on Fink's first-hand knowledge of the mountains. In a letter dated July 25, 1924, Chapman informed Fink of an upcoming visit to the Smokies by members of the newly formed Southern Appalachian National Park Committee. The visit was of critical importance to Chapman as it represented the best and possibly only opportunity for him to promote the Smokies as the premier location for the proposed new park. Chapman was planning to take the Committee on an overnight excursion to Mount Le Conte and insisted Fink join the party to help sell committee members on the superiority of the Smokies as a wilderness area.[11] Harlan Kelsey would be in the visiting party and Chapman clearly understood that Kelsey had utmost respect for Fink's opinions.

The Committee ultimately concluded that the Great Smoky Mountains and a range of the Blue Ridge Mountains flanking the Shenandoah Valley offered the best prospects for new national parks in the Appalachians and immediately set forth a report that soon put the legislative gears in motion. Although the initial congressional bill identified the proposed park as the Smoky Mountains National Park, Kelsey petitioned for the more general name, Southern Appalachian National Park. Chapman, however, was insistent on the more specific designation—Great Smoky Mountains National Park. He thus dispatched Fink to persuade Kelsey to drop his demand and convince the legislative committee to add the word "Great" to the proposed name.[12] The details of what subsequently transpired were apparently unrecorded; nevertheless, the park did come to be known as the Great Smoky Mountains National Park.

By 1925, Fink's expertise was in great demand by those engaged in the AT project as well as by Chapman in his efforts to complete the national park. In March, Fink was appointed to the Board of Managers for the newly formed Appalachian Trail Conference, a body organized to determine the course and organize construction of the trail. Prior to this appointment, Fink had been encouraging the Smoky Mountains Hiking Club to take control in determining the course of that section of the AT projected to follow the main divide of the Smokies and to initiate construction of the trail. In a letter to Fink, MacKaye expressed his satisfaction with this arrangement, "I am glad to know that the Smoky Mountains Hiking Club is interested in putting through the Appalachian Trail in that section."[13] Fink would later be elected as the Club's special vice president for trail building, a responsibility he took seriously.[14] In the 1929 *Handbook of the Smoky Mountains Hiking Club*, he contributed a brief treatise, "Let's Make Some Trails in the Smokies," outlining the best practices for constructing the AT through the Smokies.[15]

At Chapman's instigation, Fink was appointed as a director of the Great Smoky Mountains Conservation Association.[16] Fink stepped up to serve in a pivotal role as solicitor of major gifts to purchase land for the new park.[17] As political interest grew and public donations accumulated, Fink began outlining possibilities for the optimal land area that should be purchased for the park. Chapman once asked of Fink, "What do you think is the ideal 150,000 acres we should have?"[18] Fink would later represent the GSMCA in accompanying counterparts from the National Park Service as they traversed the Smokies to determine possible boundaries for the park.

By September, 1928, Chapman was sounding Fink on the necessity of convening a nomenclature committee for purposes of determining and codifying the names of the streams, peaks, ridges, gaps, and other major landmarks within the Tennessee side of the proposed park area.[19] As there were dozens of Mill Creeks, Big Creeks, Low Gaps, and other commonly shared place names scattered throughout the mountains, much of the committee's work would involve elimination of duplicates and identifying substitutes. Following ten months of correspondence, the two agreed that membership on the committee should include artist Robert Lindsay Mason, photographer Jim Thompson, university professor Hodge Mathes, and Knoxville businessman Brockway Crouch with Chapman insisting that Fink act as chairman.[20] Under Fink's leadership, the Tennessee Nomenclature Committee launched immediately into the work of identifying, verifying, and documenting the names of the major physical features on the Tennessee side of the mountains. To insure nomenclature coherence throughout the mountains, Fink took the initiative of enlisting Mark Squires, a state senator from Lenoir, to organize a corresponding North Carolina Nomenclature Committee, a group that would include Horace Kephart and George Masa, a photographer and close hiking companion of Kephart's.[21]

The laurels of public recognition accrue to those whose accomplishments are most visible to the public eye, but often elude those in the background whose knowledge and hard work drive the engines of progress and success. The latter instance is certainly the case for Paul Fink. While others have been recognized as pioneers of the AT, this trail, without Fink's efforts, would likely have not been routed along the spine of the Smokies, a wilderness area he identified as "probably the wildest and most rugged piece of country east of the Rocky Mountains."[22] As it is, the Smokies afford some of the most spectacular scenery along the entire length of the trail.

Both Chapman and Kelsey understood that no one in the country possessed a deeper knowledge of the Great Smoky Mountains than Fink and very few were more committed to the idea of a park or worked harder to insure its establishment. For one brief moment, it appeared that Fink's contribution to the park effort would be memorialized in the naming of a Finks Gap along the main divide of the Smokies. Citing conflict of interest in his role as chair of the nomenclature committee, Fink immediately squelched the effort. Whether publically recognized or not, Paul Fink has unquestionably earned his place in the pantheon of notables whose efforts brought the Great Smoky Mountains National Park into existence.

Paul Fink's greatest legacy is his manuscript. Certainly, other outsiders had visited the Smokies before him and left accounts of their observations. Local Smoky mountaineers ventured into the highlands to hunt bears, herd cattle, or practice moonshining, and the occasional timber ranger surveyed the slopes for the lumber companies, but typically the mountaineers and rangers did not keep written records. On planning his first visit to the Smokies, Kephart later confirmed that even after the most diligent search, he "failed to discover so much as a magazine article, written within this generation that described the land and its people." Kephart's claim is a deliberate exaggeration, nevertheless it hints at the rarity of Fink's chronicle of early Smoky Mountain exploration. Though his manuscript was not published until 1975, it does, however, afford a remarkable glimpse into the largely unexplored wilderness of the Great Smoky Mountains prior to the advent of the national park and the establishment of the AT.

* * *

We are both fortunate and grateful that Paul Fink's manuscript was preserved by his daughter, Sara, with instructions from her father to keep the manuscript carefully "so that when Beth, John, and Sally come to mature years they can get an idea of the joys of exploring our mountains in days and ways then gone forever." Through the graciousness of his grandson, John F. Boschen, the original manuscript now resides in the Betsey B. Creekmore Special Collections and Archives at the University of Tennessee.

Working from this manuscript, the Hunter Library at Western Carolina University here reissues Fink's collection of Unaka and Smoky Mountain backpacking adventures under its original title, *Mountain Days: A Journal of Camping Experiences in the Mountains of Tennessee and North Carolina, 1914-1938*. The manuscript is illustrated with nearly thirty photographs that were omitted from *Backpacking Was the Only Way*, and furthermore, the book contained eight photographs not found in the manuscript. In an effort to make this reissue of Fink's book as informative as possible, yet preserve the integrity of the original manuscript, the eight additional photographs are included as a group at the end of this foreword.

Publication of this book was made possible with a grant from the Thomas W. Ross Fund and completed under the editorial direction of Elizabeth Skene Harper, Special and Digital Collections Librarian at Western Carolina University. A special acknowledgement of thanks is extended to Allison McKittrick, Library Assistant in Special Collections at the University of Tennessee, who, through sheer diligence, compiled the first draft of the book's manuscript by comparing the digital scan against the original document, verifying accuracy, inserting changes where necessary, and then, formatting the entire copy. This book is a faithful rendering of Fink's manuscript. His spelling of place names and unique use of language has been kept intact, and images have only been slightly modified from scans of the original photographs. Completion of the book would not have been possible without the conscientious expertise of Lucas Rogers and Jenny McPherson, both at the Hunter Library at Western Carolina University, who digitally prepared the photographs illustrating the text. And a special thanks to Anne Bridges, Associate Professor Emeritus at the University of Tennessee Libraries, for having first broached the idea of republishing Fink's manuscript and for contributing sound advice to the book's foreword.

KEN WISE, 2019

We change trains at Kona.

Registering at the tower.

The Cabin at Le Conte Crossing.

Myrtle Point.

Gatlinburg—Getting Ready to Start.
W.P. Davis, D.C. Chapman,
Russell Hanlon, Loye W. Miller.

The Tower on Top.

Looking the Mountains over.
Front row—Paul M. Fink, Harlan P. Kelsey,
Gen. Frank Maloney, Dr. H.C. Longwell.

On Myrtle Point.
Left to right: Dr. Roy Sexton, Bill Ramsay,
Horace Albright, Dr. H.M. Jennison, John T. Moutoux.

References

Unless indicated otherwise, all citations are from the Paul Fink Papers, McClung Historical Collection, Lawson-McGee Library, Knoxville.

1. Horace Kephart to Paul Fink, 28 Jan, 1920, folder 111, box 15
2. Harlan Kelsey to Paul Fink, 16 Jan, 1922, folder 28, box 4
3. Wood, Loren M. *Beautiful Land of the Sky: John Muir's Forgotten Eastern Counterpart, Harlan P. Kelsey.* p. 221
4. Harlan Kelsey to Paul Fink, 2 Dec, 1924, folder 110, box 15
5. Quote from Daniel Pierce, *The Great Smokies: From Natural Habitat to National Park.* P. 53
6. Harlan Kelsey to Harrington Moore, 6 Feb, 1924, folder 110, box 15
7. Harlan Kelsey to Paul Fink, 15 Nov, 1923, folder 110, box 15
8. Paul Fink to Hubert Work, 19 Feb, 1924, folder 110, box 15
9. Paul Fink to Myron Avery, 27 Apr, 1929, folder 29, box 4
10. David Chapman to Paul Fink, 14 Jun, 1924, folder 103, box 14
11. David Chapman to Paul Fink, 25 Jul, 1924, folder 103, box 14
12. David Chapman to Paul Fink, 16 Feb, 1925, folder 103, box 14
13. Benton MacKaye to Paul Fink, 31 May, 1925, folder 39, box 5
14. Paul Fink to Arthur Perkins, 11 Feb, 1929, folder 29, box 4
15. Paul Fink to Arthur Perkins, 7 May. 1929, folder 29, box 4; *Smoky Mountains Hiking Club Handbook*, 1929, p. 60-61
16. David Chapman to Paul Fink, 29 Dec, 1925, folder 103, box 14
17. David Chapman to Paul Fink, 12 Nov, 1925; Dec 1, 1925, folder 103, box 14
18. David Chapman to Paul Fink, 11 Jan, 1927, folder 103, box 14
19. David Chapman to Paul Fink, 21 Sep, 1928, folder 103, box 14
20. David Chapman to Paul Fink, 29 Jul, 1929; Paul Fink to David Chapman, 29 Aug 1929, folder 103, box 14
21. Paul Fink to Mark Squires, 23 Sep, 1929, folder 103, box 14
22. "The Great Smoky Trail" in *Briefs of Proceedings of the ATC*, folder 39, box 5

PREFACE

It may well be that my fondness for the outdoors is an inherited trait. My father was a great camper, hunter and fisherman, and among my earliest memories are those of playing with his camping gear, and listening to his stories of experiences in the open, in Florida, as well as among our own mountains. Books on outdoor life were always in our home—that old classic, Nessmuck's *Woodcraft*, the works of Dan Beard, Ernest Thompson Seaton, and others.

When I was about grown I began to put into practice some of the things I learned from books and word of mouth. Though I did a little hunting, my main interest was in woodcraft, the way of living in the woods. I much preferred to spend my time in the open observing the birds and animals as they went about, rather than killing them. I had read the accounts of the Long Hunters and others of the old frontiersmen; how they lived comfortably in the wilderness making do with what little they carried on their backs and the much they had in their heads. I craved to do likewise, insofar as present-day conditions permitted.

I'd done a little camping near home, when my friend, Walter S. Diehl, then at the University of Tennessee, fired my ambition further by fascinating accounts of trips he had made into the Great Smokies with school friends from Knoxville. His description of that country was so wonderful that I wanted to see it too. Under his guidance I did. Soon other expeditions into the big mountains became a regular part of our plans, seldom omitted for many years. These trips were preferably into the more rugged, wilder and least known regions.

On many of these tramps, mostly with Walter, a few with others, I kept field notes of our journeys, rewritten and expanded on returning home. It is from those notes that the following accounts have been drawn. They cover only a part, by no means all, of my backpacking adventures among the Mountains.

We wanted most to visit the wildest, most primitive sections, where no one lived, roads were non-existent and trails were very few and faint. On some of our first visits to the Smokies, we would travel for days and see no trails, blazes, or any other evidence that man had ever been there before. The country was just as untouched as any Daniel Boone had ever visited. There were no maps worthy of the name, no means of transportation nor any source of additional supplies; and we were entirely dependent for food and shelter on our knowledge of woodcraft and the outfits we carried on our backs.

Things were pretty rugged at times. More than once we were lost for days at a time, not even knowing—or caring—just what state we were in. Jungle-thick vegetation slowed our progress to a crawl and almost stopped us. Storms, rain, and clouds plagued us, but we always finally won through, without any serious complications. Our plans were seldom adhered to, and generally much altered en route. That mattered little to us, for all our needed supplies were in the packs on our backs; we could make camp in one place just as well as in another.

In pursuing these accounts, let the reader remember the notes were not made solely as a record of our experiences, both enjoyable and temporarily disagreeable. They were also to serve as guide data, preserved for hoped-for future visits. If the writer seems preoccupied by clouds, rains, and the daily search for water and suitable campsites, those things loom large in the thoughts of a wilderness camper. Their presence or absence spell all the difference between a pleasant and an onerous trip. But do not let anyone think that the days and nights on end when one's clothing was never dry, the laurel and briar-choked trails, cliff-dotted mountain sides, and a score of such-like troubles meant that any particular expedition was not a success. While we may have heartily deplored all these discomforts at the time, in retrospect those were the most enjoyable trips, the ones longest remembered. No matter what obstacles Nature and the weather used in an attempt to defeat us, we knew we had what it took to win through.

In conclusion, I acknowledge my obligation to Walter Diehl, companion on hundreds of miles of wilderness trails, without whose presence many of these trips might not have been made. Childhood playmate, consummate woodsman and finest of camp-fellows, we have enjoyed half a century of close, uninterrupted friendship.

PAUL M. FINK, 1960

DATE: AUGUST, 1914

DESTINATION: BIG BALD MOUNTAIN.

OBJECT: EXPLORATION.

WEATHER: FAIR.

PARTY: WALTER S. DIEHL, JAMES MCNEIL, ALEX MCNEIL, PAUL M. FINK.

For two or three years Walter had been firing the imaginations of several of us with accounts of his backpacking trips into the Great Smokies with the Bain brothers and others from Knoxville. Now we wanted to do a little of the same. We'd done some camping close to home, all very easy stuff, and there was a lot we didn't know. Just how much we didn't imagine—yet. Proper clothes and shoes—tents and sleeping gear—the right foods and how to prepare them—how to care for ourselves in the woods—there were a thousand things of which we were totally ignorant.

After one of his Smoky trips in 1914, Walter agreed to take us out for a few days. For our destination we chose Big Bald Mountain, on the state line in Unicoi County. Probably the choice was because my father had been there many years before and had told us of the wonderful view from its big, open top. Maybe the name "Bald" intrigued us. None of us had been there, but we had the U.S. Geological Survey topographic maps and were supremely confident of our ability to find our way.

Walter's equipment was what he had used elsewhere, but the rest of us had to depend on whatever we could pick up around home. We must have been very optimistic about the weather, for all the shelter we took was a single army pup tent and a small rubber blanket. These were wrapped around our blankets, spare clothing and other outfit, and carried as a blanket roll slung over the left shoulder and across the body. Our cook kit was rudimentary, and we started with most of our food in paper bags carried in our hands. What a fix we would have been in if a sudden shower had caught us! Wool shirts we wore, but the rest of our clothing, save for sweaters carried in the blanket rolls, was about the same as our usual daily garb in the middle of the summer.

Blithely we start

First Day

Blithely we started toward Clark Spring afoot. No other type of transportation was available for us, nor did we care, for the loads were light and all were accustomed to much walking.

For a long time Clark Spring had been a popular resort of the rustic type, much in favor with the people of the surrounding country, who would come to spend a week or two in the cool mountain air and drink quantities of the iron-sulphur water. About the Spring a number of cottages had been built.

At the old frame hotel a group of Jonesboro girls were camping, chaperoned by Mrs. J. T. Whitlock. We arrived late in the afternoon and were given a cordial welcome, and more to the point, a real supper.

Some time after dark a local fiddler or two come strolling up the hollow, and soon a country square dance was under way, on the open dance floor under the trees. The fact we had walked fifteen miles that afternoon was no hindrance, and soon we were in the middle of it.

When the dancing was over and all had quieted down for the night, we rolled up in our blankets on the plank floor of the hotel porch, with the little stream murmuring and chuckling almost under us—chuckling, no doubt, with fiendish amusement at the kind of night we would spend.

First it was the punkies, the black gnats that bred by the millions in the muck by the side of the brook. We had brought nothing like flydope to repel them. All we could do was slap, rub and scratch, poor ways to cope with such pests. Finally, we gave up fighting and covered up, heads, necks and ears, in our blankets, believing the stifling heat more easily endured than the burning, itching bites of the gnats. Tight as we wrapped ourselves, enough still got in to remind us they were still on duty.

We were tired enough to sleep anywhere at first. Before long we began to realize that a pine floor is a poor substitute for a Beauty Rest mattress, and that a board simply will not adjust itself comfortably to the contours of the human frame. All night long we rolled, twisted and squirmed, trying to ease the pain of each aching joint and to find a softer spot. It couldn't be done, at least for more than a few minutes at a time. At the first faint light of day we were ready to turn out.

Second Day

The tiny creek at the Spring, where we washed our dishes after breakfast, was simply crawling with crawfish, from tiny ones up to those four inches long. For amusement we caught about a quart, and then some inventive mind suggested a fine use for them, as a substitute for alarm clocks.

The hotel had been very simply built. On the second floor, all the sleeping rooms were open to the roof above, with the partitions separating them from the hall only eight feet high.

Carrying our precious crawdads safely in old tin cans, we stole silently into the hotel, where everyone was still sound asleep, and crept up the stairs to the second floor. Then, guessing as best we could, the location of the beds in the various rooms, we began distributing the crawfish over the partitions. We tried to play no favorites but to give to each room its fair share.

Some we could hear hit the floor with a moist "splat," a clean miss and a crawdad wasted. Others, better aimed, landed with muffled thumps, and we sat tight and awaited developments.

They were not long coming. First a sleepy voice or two, inquiring, "What was that?"

Then someone found out, and delightful shrieks lifted the roof echoing from numerous rooms as startled girls found more varmints on their beds or flopping on the floor. Our mission accomplished, we very discreetly and hurriedly left out, not to return for some hours after the excitement had time to die down and injured feelings cool off.

Of course, we couldn't have come that close to the Sally Hole, for years a favorite picnic spot, without going in for a swim. Then some time was devoted to snake hunting, both with rifle and by hand. The stream was full of brown watersnakes, taking their siestas on rocks in the creekbed. As we came close they slipped off into the water, usually whipping under the same rock or one close by.

Three of us armed with stout sticks would stand waiting, while the other lifted the rock or turned it over. Before the snake could escape it was pinned to the bottom with a stick. Then one of us would reach down, catch it by the tail, swing the writhing serpent through the air and crack its head on a rock. So plentiful they were we must have killed a score in that way.

Maybe we were more tired that night. Maybe the punkies were not so voracious or maybe a single night's exposure to a bare board bed had toughened us a bit. At any rate, while our slumbers were not entirely peaceful and untroubled, we did sleep much more soundly.

Third Day

A long trek was before us if we hoped to reach our major objective, Big Bald, that night. We were up, fed, packed up and ready for the trail before the camping party came to life, with no assistance from crawfish this morning. A native had told us the starting route, a plain, well-used trail up Clark Creek, past the Sally Hole, and on to turn left up Sill Branch. The going was fairly easy until we started the hard pull from the head of Sill Branch to the top of Rich Mountain. Here we had to stop and blow a number of times before we emerged into the open, cultivated fields on top, to get our first clear view of Big Bald, across the valley of South Indian Creek. It would be a long way down and a longer way up before we would be able to call it a day.

If we had but known it we could have found a road of sorts, with reasonably good going, down Mill Creek to the valley. Ignorance as usual was costly. We stayed on top of the mountain a couple miles to Chestnut Knob, then dropped down a steep open field and a wooded slope to Lower Higgins Creek.

It was on the way down that I was forcibly impressed with the fact that

On Rich Mountain

street shoes, the rather sharp-pointed ones in vogue then, and light socks are not fit footcovering for woods tramping. Every downward step on the steep hillside jammed my toes forward into the front of the shoe. The thin socks had no cushioning effect whatsoever. Before long the constant rubbing made the tops of the toes tender, and blisters began to form. The heels were loose and ill-fitting and the rubbing there made for more blisters. To make it worse, men at that time were vain about small feet and fitted their dress shoes tight. That was bad enough in town, but under the constant pounding on the trail the feet spread. In a few miles the shoes grew too tight in places, to bind and rub.

At this late day it is impossible to trace our exact route in our approach to the Big Bald. As we went along, we asked for directions from the natives but they either misunderstood or couldn't follow the route given. Shortly after the steep portion of the climb began, the trail we were on petered out. Optimistically, we started up the side of the mountain, on the theory that so long as we were going up, all would be well eventually.

That was a sad error, particularly as the ridge we were climbing chanced to be the steepest, roughest buttress of the whole mountain. Overgrown with laurel we had to crawl under or bull our way through, strewn with loose boulders and set with cliffs and rock ledges, every foot upward we gained was at the cost of most strenuous effort.

Walter had brought along his .22 rifle, in hope of bagging a squirrel or grouse. As he led the way up one particularly stiff spot, the stock came loose

Big Bald, from South Indian Creek

from the barrel, unnoticed, sliding down the mountain side until caught by a lucky grab by one following.

At one point we came out on the rocky crest of the ridge. It was more open, seemed to offer easier going, and we essayed to follow it. The idea wasn't too good a one. When a giant copperhead snake disputed passage and almost ran over one of us barring entrance to his den, we gave up and dropped back to the bushgrown, less rocky side of the ridge.

It was by far the most rugged going I'd ever encountered, and after an hour or so of it I was getting disgusted, not to say pooped. To pep us up, Walter kept telling us of much wilder country in the Smokies, where he'd been a few weeks before. (Though now he admits this was about as bad as what Smoky had to offer.) He takes a lot of pleasure in telling that every now and then, after pulling up some especially bad spot, I'd ask,

"Are the Smokies worse than this?"

To boost my morale, he'd answer, "Lots worse."

Then in bitter, disgusted tones, I'd consign the Smokies to the depths of the Bottomless Pit.

The August sun was blistering hot in the valley, and in the dense tangle there was no breeze to temper the heat. Our canteens were soon dry and our throats parched. Long before we reached the top we were suffering from thirst and couldn't even "spit cotton."

Even the worst of things can't last forever. Just before sunset we could tell we were nearing the top. The grade grew less steep, the rhododendron and thick underbrush gave way to an open beech and birch forest, and we came to a tumbling brook of clear, cold water. Throwing our loads aside, we dropped down on our stomachs to drink our fill. Never did water taste better. An excess of cold water after the hard climb was too much for Walter, with resulting nausea.

Exhausted, we went no further. Firewood and good water in plenty, level grass under the trees for a campsite—what more could one ask? I can't recall what we had for supper, but I'll bet not a single crumb was wasted.

One thing we hadn't taken into consideration when outfitting was the fact that though the lowlands might be swelteringly hot, the night air at an altitude of over a mile could get very chilly. This we began to realize after nightfall, when a light breeze began to make. The one pup tent wasn't big enough to shelter all four of us. We made use of it instead as a cover. The rubber blanket was spread to protect us from the damp earth, a single blanket on it, and the rest on us, covered by the tent and some thick, leafy branches on top of that. A night fire helped some, mainly because the man whose turn it was to replenish it hourly, sat by it a while and got himself well warmed, while the rest of us were shivering in bed. Tired as we were neither cold nor discomfort would keep us entirely from sleep.

Fourth Day

A light frost lay on the grass—and us—as we rolled out early. After breakfast we packed up and followed the stream to its source, the Yellow Spring, on the north side of the mountain at the edge of the bald area. Some two or three hundred feet below the summit, even in the driest of weather it runs an unfailingly abundant flow of coldest water. There are other sources in a marsh swale close by, but the Yellow Spring is the best water on the mountain. For many years it has been a favorite camping spot for hunters, herdsmen and other visitors. Close by it we laid our packs and pushed on.

The top of the mountain is entirely bare of trees, with a luxuriant growth of rich grass, where much livestock from the valleys below is driven every summer to pasture. Level and a hundred yards in diameter, it is the highest point in twenty miles and one of the very few mountain tops from which one has an uninterrupted view of 360 degrees. Here, someone had erected a rude pole tower. Up it we climbed for a good look-see. The sky was cloudless and the air fairly clear, and we could look out over a welter of mountains in every

The top of Big Bald

direction. From here we had our first glimpse of the Black Mountains, with Mt. Mitchell in the center.

The day was spent in exploring the top of the mountain, in delightful loafing and in catching up on our sleep. No breeze this night, the air a bit warmer, and we had little need for a night fire.

Fifth Day

The route down from the mountain led eastward across Little Bald. This Mountain did boast a bare top then, but the timber was closing in and on another visit twenty years later the forest had completely reclaimed it.

All along there was a fair trail, followed with little difficulty, save from that given by our feet, showing more blisters daily. The night before we had undertaken to bandage the raw spots, wrapping each toe separately. We had no medical preparation to keep the bandages from sticking to the raw surfaces. The only substitute we could turn up was gun grease. Maybe it wouldn't be recommended by the doctors, nor could it be found in the pharmacopoeia, but it certainly served its purpose that time.

The roads, trails, etc., in that country have been so totally changed since this trip was made that one cannot tell exactly how we got down to Spivey Creek, or from that to Granny Lewis Creek. It wasn't cross country, though, but along well travelled trails, just as it was from Granny Lewis to Unaka Springs, via Burnt Hill Gap and Mine Branch.

We look them over

At the time Unaka Springs was quite a popular little summer resort, with a number of cottages belonging to people of Johnson City, Bristol, etc., and a rustic hotel operated by H. M. Deaderick, an old friend of my family. Conversation with him brought out the fact that he had built the lookout tower we found on Big Bald, in order to make a panoramic picture of the mountains. Our camp was on a sand bar beside the river. For the record, a sand bank can be a very poor bed, especially for those like ourselves who hadn't learned the trick of scooping out depressions to fit the shoulders and hips.

Sixth Day

It was a long twenty miles home, any way we figured it, a discouraging prospect for folks with feet like ours. There was no other good way of getting there, so on we plodded—or limped, crossing the river on the railroad bridge to Chestoa and down the track to Erwin, thence along the wagon road to Embreeville.

I was due to go back to work, but the others wanted to return to Clark Spring for a few days more in the mountains. They went on down the river, while I hobbled ten painful miles on in to Jonesboro. Rather, it would have been ten miles, if the driver of a passing farm wagon hadn't taken pity and given me a lift part of the way.

At home I made a careful survey of my person and found a total of thirteen blisters and skinned toes on my feet, with countless chigger bites scattered over the rest of my body. In some ways this, my introduction to mountain backpack camping, had been a rough trip, a hard trip. But the memory of the wide views from the mountain tops, the pleasure of living in the open and the companionship of congenial friends far outweighed all the discomforts and hardships along the way, so much so that I craved more and more of it. In preparation for the future, that there might be less of the bitter and more of the sweet, I set about learning all I could of ways to take some of the toil and trouble out of camping and make it more efficient and enjoyable.

DATE: AUGUST 19-22, 1915

DESTINATION: UNAKA AND ROAN MOUNTAINS.

OBJECT: EXPLORATION.

WEATHER: RAIN AND FAIR.

PARTY: JAMES AND ALEX MCNEIL, JOHN M. TURNER, HENRY PATTON, DAVE WILSON, PAUL M. FINK.

A tenderfoot gets big ideas early. The year before, Walter Diehl had taken James and Alex McNeil and me to Big Bald Mountain, on our first backpacking trip. After that one experience, in our deep ignorance and great self-confidence, we fancied ourselves seasoned explorers, capable of caring for ourselves anywhere. The fact that we came through our first trip alone, with a minimum of trouble and no real difficulties, was due more to the watchful care and protection of the Red Gods than to any great capacity on our part.

The start was not too auspicious. Alex and Jim, John and I went by train to Unaka Springs, Henry and Dave joined us at Unicoi. Our plan had been to strike into the mountains at once, but a succession of brisk showers brought a decision to stay at the Springs overnight, with an early start in the morning. At the hotel we met a couple of young fellows from South Carolina camping close by and accepted their invitation to spend the night in their tent. As a hospitable gesture they brought out a bottle of "Old Zeke," the kind of rotgut corn liquor selling then for about seventy-five cents a quart. None of us was inclined to partake anyway, but the fiery impact of a drop or two on our tongues made evident the advantages of total abstinence.

August 20, 1915

Across the Nolichucky River from Unaka Springs were the remains of an old, never-used railroad bed, blown from the side of the mountain many years previously by the Southern Railroad, in a vain attempt to bluff off or block a predecessor of the CC&O Railway from building a railroad through the mountains into North Carolina. Crossing the bridge, we started up the river along the old road bed, after two or three miles turning eastward toward Unaka Mountain, along a U.S. Forest Service trail.

Almost every hollow between the ridges had a tiny stream trickling down it, on its way to the river below. One of these, unnamed insofar as we knew, tumbled and fell for three hundred feet over the boulders, in a series of beautiful cascades, through the midst of which the trail passed.

Across the deep gorge of the river clouds were gathering on Flat Top. About noon they reached us, driven by gusts of heavy wind. No rain was falling, but in a very few minutes we were more than merely damp, from moisture congealed on our clothing. The dense mist cut off our vision beyond fifty feet. Travelling in a cloud was a new and rather disturbing experience to us. We were too far out from Unaka Springs to return. There was no place to go for shelter, so we plodded steadily on the muddy trail to the top of the ridge that we fondly hoped would turn out to be the state line. When a break in the clouds let us see Buffalo Mountain to the northward we took compass sights that indicated that we were only a short distance west of Indian Grave Gap, and about where we had hoped to be. How proud we were of our engineering ability when after passing over the next knob, we came to the road crossing through the Gap from Tennessee to North Carolina.

The cloud closed in on us again as we moved on, a mile or two further, out of the timber into a grassy clearing. When some shadowy shapes looming up in the mist were identified as haystacks we knew we were at the Beauty Spot and still right on course. Henry had been here before, coming up from Unicoi, and knew the rest of the way on to the top of Unaka Mountain.

The greater part of the mountain had been logged, and the maze of skidways and old railroad beds were very confusing. One of the logging camps had been located right here at the top, but all the buildings had been burned except a small stable. "Any port in a storm," said we, and moved in without further ado. It wasn't the most desirable camping spot in the world, but it did give shelter from the fog and drizzling rain. All the wood we could find was sodden, and the fire we finally got going on the stable floor was far more efficient in filling the shack with smoke than it was for the purposes of cooking supper and drying wet clothing. Finally we were fed, warmed and dried, and began to settle down for the night. I fear there was no great amount of slumbering done by anyone. I know that once I waked from a fitful nap and saw John sitting by the door, staring out into the mist.

Too pretty not to be named

August 21, 1915

The sun was rising in a clear sky when we came to life, to gather outside and look down on the valleys below, all filled with cloud, another new experience for us. Cooking breakfast was just as smoky a business as at supper the night before, but we finally completed preparation of the simple camp menu of flapjacks, bacon, eggs and coffee, and made up our packs for the day's march. Henry and Dave left us here, going back down the mountain to Unicoi. The rest of us turned our faces toward Roan Mountain, now filling the horizon to

Going down

the East. For a while an old railroad grade took us down to the wagon road that passed through Iron Mountain Gap to Magnetic City (now Buladean). For many years this road had been one of the main routes crossing from one state to the other.

The old stage road, once used by a hack line from Jonesboro to Cloudland in the heyday of the hotel there, left the valley and turned up the mountain at Magnetic City. Time, erosion and a dense growth of bushes had obliterated it in places, and we were lost often as not, usually striking straight up the mountain side when we realized the situation.

Once I nearly came to grief at a place where the earth had totally washed away, leaving only a bare, steeply slanting rock, ending in a thirty foot precipice. As my foot slipped I fell and began to slide on my back toward the edge. There was nothing to grasp to stop me, and the others were too far away to help. Just in time my hobnails caught on a rough spot, holding me until I could very cautiously turn over and crawl to the far side, out of danger.

Unaka Mountain, from Iron Mtn. Gap

On the southwest end of the long flat top of the mountain the old roadway passed Sunset Rock, with one of the finest views in the country. The Black Mountains, with Mt. Mitchell in their center, the far Blue Ridge, Unaka, Big Bald, and scores of other peaks and ridges were all there to be seen. More than an hour we stayed, time partly spent in identifying the mountains by the map, partly simply looking at them.

Cloudland, the summer hotel built some thirty years before by Gen. John T. Wilder, stood a mile further along the mountain. An enormous three story frame structure, it was never a great financial success and had been abandoned for about a decade. The ravages of wind, and weather were already evident— glassless windows, leaking roofs, sagging floors and a general atmosphere of decay.

A short inspection of the old hotel, and we hunted a campsite for the night. The needs of the hotel had been supplied by a free-flowing spring two hundred yards in front, and there we set up our night's lodging amid the balsams. The sky was clear, with no prospect of rain, and we did not bother to pitch the tent, a decision we were to regret in the morning, when the heavy mountain dew had us as wet as a light shower would have done. The lush grass was as fine a mattress as we could have asked. Our blankets were spread, heads uphill, on a gentle slope. To keep from sliding out of bed we pegged up an old plank as a footboard. It served that purpose all right, but the next morning our feet

Cloudland Hotel

and legs were as tired as if we had been walking for a day. Gravity, continually pulling us downhill, had kept our feet pressing hard against the plank all night.

The stage road ran along the top of the mountain, between our camp and the hotel. As we sat around the campfire after supper, we heard horse's hoofs coming from the west and pulling to a stop above us. Then came a voice:

"What are you doing down there?"

"Camping," we answered.

"Come up here."

"Can't do it. You come down here."

Silence a few moments, then the demand came again.

"Come up here!"

"If you want to see us, you come down here."

Again the short silence, then the "Bang!" of a pistol shot, and a bullet clipped through the balsam boughs close by.

It was one of the few times I've carried any arms on a mountain trip. Thinking that if we were in for trouble, it had better be in the open than to be shot at by firelight from under cover of the balsams, I snatched my pistol from my pack and started up the hill toward the road. Before I was well under way there came the most welcome sound of galloping hoofbeats, and there was no further disturbance during the night.

Next morning we found a freshly emptied whiskey bottle by the roadside, leading us to believe the shot of the night before was only a bit of drunken bravado.

Carvers Gap

August 22, 1915

Our first plan had been to travel on eastward along the state line, past Hump Mountain and on to Grandfather, but now we could see that it would take longer than we had provisioned for. Too, the clouds beginning to build up in the west promised more rain and another wetting. So, after a climb to Roan High Knob, loftiest point on the mountain, we started along the road descending the north side of the mountain, opposite the way we had come. There was a short stop to enjoy the peaceful beauty of Carvers Gap, with sheep grazing in the open bald, then down the washed-out road to Burbank and Roan Mountain Station, on the ET&WNC Railway, where we hunted up an old friend, Dulaney Maher, grandson of Gen. Wilder, builder of Cloudland Hotel.

There were no bathing suits in our packs, but Dulaney knew a secluded pool in Doe River, safe from view. A good dip freshened us up, ready for the train trip home, through the Doe River Gorge. Now we rode in stage, on the platform of a Pullman observation car, though I am afraid our battered, smoke-redolent clothes weren't quite in keeping with the vehicle and its other occupants. Home from Johnson City by late train.

DATE: MAY 27-30, 1916

DESTINATION: BIG BALD MOUNTAIN.

OBJECT: EXPLORATION.

WEATHER: FAIR-THUNDERSTORM.

PARTY: HENRY W. PATTON, PAUL M. FINK.

May 27, 1916

It was already dark when we stepped off the train in Erwin, with a four mile walk to Unaka Springs ahead of us. Permission had been granted us to sleep on the beds in the Whitlock cottage, but we were unable to find the custodian of the keys. Tests of the windows showed them too securely fastened for entry by that route. All the sleeping quartets left for us was the porch floor, and we soon rolled up in our blankets there.

A plank floor is fine for certain things, but as a mattress it has very positive limitations. All night we rolled from side to side, lying first on our backs, then on our stomachs, no position comfortable for more than a few minutes. What time we were not twisting and turning, hunting a softer spot on the boards, we were busy combatting a horde of blood-thirsty mosquitoes. All in all, it made for a very poor night's rest.

May 28, 1916

It was barely daylight when we rolled out, with aching bones and drowsy eyes, to drag slowly down to a sand bar by the misty river. All the driftwood we could find was damp, hard to start and harder to keep burning, but finally we managed to cook a breakfast of eggs, bacon, and flapjacks. These washed down by a cup or two of scalding coffee, black and strong, waked us up and gave us energy enough to hit the trail.

The way led along the railroad to Mine Branch, up that to Burnt Hill Gap and down to Granny Lewis Creek. There had been some changes in the road since my visit three years before and we made a false turn down the creek, misguided, intentionally or not, by a passing native. An hour of time and a couple of miles of distance were lost here. Lunch was at a little spring close

Granny Lewis Creek

Temple Hill and No Business Knob, from Granny Lewis Creek

beside Spivey Creek, where I'd stopped, coming down, on a previous visit. It was all new country to Henry.

The morning had been fair and hot. Clouds began to gather as we climbed, and we could hear the rumbling of thunder above and ahead, growing louder and louder all the while. As we topped out on the divide, in the swag between Little Bald and Big Bald, we met the storm head-on. There was no place we could go for shelter. All we could do was take it and plod on.

We were neither above nor below the cloud but squarely in its middle. The rain came in blinding sheets from nowhere or no direction in particular, and in a jiffy there wasn't a dry spot on either of us. The lightning hissed and crackled all around us, so close we might easily have reached out and caught a bolt as it passed. There was nothing near from which the thunder could echo, and its sound was dull and flat. There was nothing comfortable in our situation, but there we were, and there was little we could do about it.

Through the cloud and falling rain we could see only a few feet, but the footway of the trail to our right, toward Big Bald, was plain, and along it we sloshed, through pools of rainwater at times to our shoetops. After half an hour the storm abated, the cloud passed on and the sun shone brightly. The temperature of the air dropped smartly, making us shake and shiver in our soaking clothes.

After such a downpour the matter of firewood was no small problem. Luck was with us. Near the Yellow Spring on Big Bald we found a large fallen wild cherry tree, uprooted by some violent windstorm only a few months before. It's smaller limbs, still sound and free from contact with the sodden earth, offered excellent fuel. Getting it cut and ready for the fire was not so easy. Our fingers were so stiff and numb from rain and cold we could scarcely hold axe or knife. Finally we got a little blaze under way and thawed out sufficiently to get the pup tent up. Our situation began to look a little brighter.

Fire burning, we set about drying out. Every stitch of clothing we wore was soaked. Only our sweaters in our packs were dry. Our blankets, carried in oilcloth cases on top the packs, had only a few damp spots. Henry won the toss and retired first to the shelter of the tent, clad only in his sweater and rolled up in both blankets. I undertook to keep the fire going and rigged up around it a series of stick frames, hanging his clothes on them to dry before the blaze. The heat of the fire and the exercise of chopping wood dried me a tiny bit and stopped some of the shivering. The late afternoon sun was bright, but the mountain air was more than cool.

The Camp on Big Bald

From the summit of Big Bald

Constantly turned before the fire, Henry's clothes finally dried, he dressed and we changed places. I must have been pretty well worn out, for as soon as I grew comfortably warm in sweater and blankets I dropped off to sleep, not to wake until after dark, when all my clothes were dry and Henry had supper cooked and ready.

There was no supply of browse close at hand to make a good bed, but our ground cloth kept us from contact with the wet ground, and that was all we asked. We were far too weary to pay much attention to minor discomforts, and soon were sleeping peacefully.

May 29, 1916

The storm of the day before, and more threatening this morning made us think better of our original plan to go home via South Indian Creek, over Rich Mountain to Clark Creek, and decide to return the same route we had come.

Big Bald is one of the few mountains I know from which one may see in every direction. Its whole top is bare of timber, as the name indicates. The summit is roughly circular, about a hundred yards in diameter, with a deep, spongy turf, dotted with many tiny mounds filled with a spongy, moss-like growth.

The haze was too heavy to see much more than the closest mountains and ruled out very successful photography. While lazing on the soft grass of the flat, open peak we were joined by a tall, lank native. Giving the name of John Sprockins of Bee Log, N. C., he was ostensibly on the mountain to salt the cattle grazing on the lush grass of the high pasture. An hour was spent in talking of this and that, during which he asked a number of pointed questions as to who we were, where from, why we were on the mountain, etc. When a letter to him, enclosing some pictures, was returned, marked "Unknown," the thought came to our mind that his real mission might have been to look us over, suspecting us of being spotters for the "revenuers" hunting some of the illicit stills reputed to be operating thereabouts.

Leisurely we tramped back to Unaka Springs, missing the afternoon train by a few hundred yards. Our calculations as to the amount of food we would need had been in error, and our supplies were about exhausted. Leaving our packs at the hotel, we crossed the river on the railroad bridge and walked a quarter of a mile down the tracks to Chestoa to a store. Carrying our lunch back, we stepped out onto the top of one of the big piers in the middle of the bridge and sat down to eat, just as one of the mile-long coal trains of the CC&O Railway approached. Laughingly I remarked, "It would be just our luck for that train to break down on the bridge, tie us up here, and then another rain come and drown us the second time."

The words were hardly spoken when the train pulled in two up the track, the rear end grinding to a halt on the bridge. While we were laughing at the coincidence a brisk shower came up. To save a wetting we clambered up on the train, intending to walk over the cars and so off the bridge. A hard-hearted brakeman tried to chase us off, with no success. No sooner were we under shelter than the rain stopped, and five minutes later the train was coupled up and gone.

Our friend of the peak

The remainder of the day was spent renewing acquaintance with the Deadrick family at the hotel. That night we slept on a mattress in one of the vacant cottages, a far more comfortable bed than the one we had rested (?) on two nights before.

May 30, 1916

An early breakfast and a long walk to Erwin to catch the 7:00 A.M. train, but we made it with five minutes to spare. Home by the Southern Railway by 10:00 A.M.

DATE: SEPTEMBER 22-26, 1916

DESTINATION: LE CONTE.

OBJECT: EXPLORATION.

WEATHER: FAIR.

PARTY: WALTER S. DIEHL AND PAUL M. FINK.

For several years Walter had been visiting the Great Smokies in company with the Bain brothers and others from Knoxville, and had been singing to me praises of their beauty and their wild ruggedness. All this was at a time when one could seldom find a single person who had even so much as heard of those mountains, much less visited them. His stories had whetted to a keen edge my craving to see for myself what was there. He agreed to take me on a personally conducted tour to Le Conte, a peak even more unknown than the mountain range itself. So the night of September 21, 1916, found us in his room in Knoxville sorting out our gear and making up our packs. He, the more experienced, was using a duffle bag and pack harness, while I still depend on the old Army issue knapsack, with blanket in a waterproof roll on top.

September 22, 1916

No motor roads penetrated the Smokies that early, and if they had, we had no car to ride over them. Easiest access was by rail, so we rode the K&A Railroad to Walland and then the Little River Railroad to Elkmont. This road had been built by the Little River Lumber Company, that for more than twenty years had been cutting timber on the northwestern slopes of the Smokies. It entered the mountains along the twisting, tumbling Little River, up a canyon so constricted that often the road had to be blown out of the faces of cliffs dropping sheer to the waters edge.

Riding the rear platform for a closer look at the scene, we grew curious as to why the rails over which we were riding were wet. Querying the flagman, we learned that a tiny stream of water from the tender dampened the rails, to muffle the high-pitched squeal of flange against rail as the wheels rounded the abrupt curves. Otherwise, he said, "You couldn't hear your ears."

We first saw LeConte

Shouldering our packs at Elkmont, we followed first an old trail built by the U.S. Forest Service to the Huskey Gap, on Sugarland Mountain. Here I had my first glimpse of Bull Head, with the massive bulk of Le Conte behind it. A few minutes look, to get an idea of its immensity, and down the side of the mountain we went, dropping to the West Prong of the Little Pigeon River. The trail was steep as the very devil, but we didn't fully realize it yet. We were only going *down* it then.

Our plan had been to make our camp at Bear Pen Hollow or the Grassy Patch, using it as a base of operations. But, a severe cramp in one of my legs brought us to a halt just across the stream from its junction with the Road Prong, coming down the defile from Indian Gap. Hemlock browse and thick moss in plenty made a luxurious bed in our pup tent. A comfortable night's lodging assured, we lost no time in cooking and eating a real meal. The rockihominy and chocolate we had for lunch supplied energy enough to finish the day's march, but by no stretch of the imagination could it have been called a feast.

September 23, 1916

I'd done a little fishing elsewhere, but never for trout. Today, Walter planned to initiate me into that sport. The stream was full of fish, rainbows in the lower and more open reaches, and speckles in the upper, smaller pools and reaches.

Our business was with this latter species, and we didn't wet a line until we reached the Grassy Patch, at the confluence of Alum Cave Creek and the Walker Camp Branch. Above here were the best pools, that scarcely an angler a year would visit, and the fish not so wary as in the more heavily fished waters. The streams were low and crystal clear, conditions no-wise favorable for trout fishing, and the day's catch was nothing to brag about, Walter twenty-five and I seven, the largest about eleven inches long. Walter was very kind, saying mine was a better haul than he had made on his first trial, but that was poor consolation. I'd not yet learned how wary those fish were, how one had to "Injun up" on a pool and, hidden behind a rock, drop his line in beyond it.

Regardless of who did the *catching*, I did my humble best to *eat* my part, my maiden experience with camp-cooked trout. Fried to a crisp brown, sided by bit of flapjack flavored with a hint of woodsmoke, seasoned with the zest of a day in the open—even kings can command no better.

Eating seated on opposite sides of the campfire, I noticed Walter stare fixedly for a moment past my shoulder, then, without shifting his gaze, grope behind him for his rifle. Imagining nothing less than a bear about to breathe down my neck, I cleared the fire in a single leap, landing almost in his lap. To my chagrin, the intruder was only a "boomer," the red squirrel of the higher levels, sitting peaceably on a stump by the trailside.

Putting a "mess" of beans on to soak for the morrow's dinner, our pipes were fired up and we settled down onto our browse bed to swap a few yarns before going to sleep.

"Babbling brooks" is a trite old saying, but the stream by our camp talked the whole night through. The voices in the water were so plain and distinct we could almost follow the conversation. As the river tumbled over the rocks there was the illusion of a wagon, jolting slowly up the rough old road. An old mill wheel seemed to rumble and creak in the distance. There was even the chirping of birds.

September 24, 1916

The rest of the trout made a hearty breakfast. Dishes washed, we hung the bean pot over the fire, and long before the sun reached our camp in the depths of the valley, we set out for the top of Le Conte.

The only trail of which we had heard was the rudimentary one up Bear Pen Hollow, leaving the river and turning left up a little hollow a few hundred yards

Our first view of Cliff Top

Close-up of the Cliff Top

above Cold Branch. For the first eight or nine hundred feet—altitude—the grade was easy and the going good, but after leaving the top spring of the little brook the sides of the ravine closed in and grew much steeper. Thirty degree slopes were the usual thing, and forty-five degree ones were common. There were occasional blazes, and at times a faintly marked footway, and there was little trouble following it. That is, there was little trouble *finding* it. *Following* it was something else entirely. The man who blazed that trail was much more concerned about finding the *shortest* way to the top, rather than the *easiest* way of getting there.

When we finally clambered out of the ravine to the crest of the ridge we had our first view of the Cliff Top of Le Conte. The top of the ridge was a real knife edge, a bare few feet wide, choked with bushes and with precipitous slopes on either side. A native had told us that just about here a new and better trail turned off to the right, its beginning marked by a spruce tree decorated with many tin tobacco tags tacked onto the bark. This trail, as he phrased it, "surrounded the top", saving considerable climbing and rough going.

This was one of the only trips I carried a rifle, slung from my shoulder. With it was a spare shirt, should there be chilly breezes on top. Either or both was a clear invitation to trouble, when pushing through dense growth.

Walter, leading the way, delights to tell how he missed me from close behind and called back to see what was detaining me. A big clump of bushes shook violently, and out of it came my voice:

"Be there in a moment."

All this was repeated at short intervals, with more and greater bush shaking, and still I didn't appear. Just as he turned back to investigate the delay, there came a final convulsion and I staggered into view, with half the bushes in the clump, torn from their moorings, trailing after me, hopelessly entangled with my gun, spare shirt, etc. All the time there had been a strange, sulphurous blue haze hanging around the thicket, with peculiar sounds coming from the midst. Just how true all the details of his story may be I cannot say, but I do recall very distinctly being hung up several times on that ridge.

The trail swung around to the North side of the Cliff Top, where a lone ascent was feasible, passing through thick balsam and up moss covered ledges to the open top, this covered with waist-high rhododendron to the very brink of the cliffs. At the edge of the timber Walter searched a moment, then showed me, carved perpendicularly on a balsam tree, the legend, "W. S. Diehl, '14, '15." While he was adding "16" to the list of dates, I registered on a tree close by.

Pushing through low hanging balsam boughs, we stepped into the open. There, suddenly as a picture flashed on the screen, was a scene so grand it almost took my breath.

Beyond the cliff-rimmed gorge of Huggins Hell at our feet, and stretching away into the distance as far as one might see, were peaks innumerable, with sharp, high ridges and deep ravines everywhere. Chief feature on the skyline from East to West was the main divide of the Great Smokies, from Mt. Guyot

Clingmans Dome and the Main Divide

to Thunderhead. The air was clear, far more so than usual, and we could easily distinguish many details of the landscape ordinarily invisible. Far beneath us, in the valley of the river, were the Chimney Tops, that only a few hours before had towered twelve hundred feet above our camp. Now they were a mere minor detail of the scene. Faint as a whisper, hardly to be distinguished from the sighing of the breeze in the balsams, came up the sounds of the stream three thousand feet below.

It was easy to realize why all this had been called the roughest and wildest region east of the Rockies, for it would be hard to conceive a timbered country more rugged. Spots hardly a rifle shot apart were separated by chasms so abysmal that it would require hours to make way from one to the other, even if the timber and laurel were not present to frustrate the traveler. Every ridge was like the edge of a gigantic saw. Cliffs were rare, as is usually the case in mountains as old as these. Where they did occur, they were almost masked by a lush curtain of bushes.

Only the urge to push on to the High Top dragged us away from the rugged majesty of the scene. The mountain top between the two peaks is a hundred yards wide, mantled with as dense a stand of balsam as one might hope to find. A storm a few years before had levelled many trees here. The fallen trunks and jutting branches formed a veritable *cheval-de-frise*, made more difficult by a rampant new growth sprung up among the fallen timber. A short, fruitless struggle with this showed we could not hope to push through in the time available and reluctantly we returned to the Cliff Top for a long last look before staring down off the mountain. Later we were told that other than being able to say that we had reached the highest point on the mountains, there was little to be gained, for the High Top was so densely timbered there was no good lookout.

Starting down, we took what we rashly believed was the upper end of the Tag Tree Trail. In a few hundred yards it "petered out", involving us in such impassible tangles of rhododendron that we gave up the attempt and pushed through only slightly less difficult brush, back to the top of the ridge and the route up which we had come. Grouse were plentiful all over the side of the mountain, but so thick was the undergrowth we couldn't get a shot.

Inspection of the bean pot at camp showed them still too hard to eat. There were plenty of other things to devour, and we did, leaving the beans still simmering over the fire. The climb had been a wearying one, so we rolled into our blankets early and were drifting off to sleep before the last rays of the evening sun had left the Chimney Tops above us.

September 25, 1916

The thought for the day had been to clamber up the precipitous sides of the Chimneys, but we gave it up as a bad idea and decided to try something easier—to fish awhile, and then visit the Alum Cave. Both of us fished the Walker Camp Branch and though the water was still low and clear, each of us caught more in less time than on a couple of days before. Trout were in every pool, and under reasonably favorable circumstances a good fisherman should have been able to make an unbelievable catch.

Half a mile above the mouth of Alum Cave Creek, a dim old trail we had been told dated back to Indian days turned to the left up the side of Le Conte. For a thousand feet it pushed upward through the laurel, at times so steep we were forced to cling to the bushes to make our way. It was almost like a tunnel through the growth, and we were almost at the Cave before we realized we were even nearing it.

In the true sense of the word, this is not a cave but an enormous jutting ledge near the top of the ridge, altitude about 5,000 feet. From the level of the floor to the outer edge of the overhang is a hundred feet or more, the projection about sixty feet and the length of the whole formation greater than a

Alum Cave

hundred yards. At the back where the sun never penetrates, the dust is shoe-mouth deep, rising in tiny puffs from under the feet as one strides along. Encrusted on the rocks were crystals of pure alum, leached out by ground water. The shale rocks, stained red by iron oxide, are soft enough to be scratched by a knife.

Tradition says that centuries ago the Cherokee Indians took alum from here. During the Civil War the Cave was a source of minerals for the Confederacy, and we were told that until only a few years ago it was still possible to find traces of the log vats and try-works.

The beans were finally edible that night. We cooked and ate a meal that for variety and quantity would have popped the eyes of the folks at home—soup beans, stewed apples, and apricots, trout, bacon, flapjacks, and coffee, together with anything else to be found around camp. We had the appetites and capacities of youth, heightened by strenuous exercise in the open air and tried nobly to finish everything in sight.

September 26, 1916

Strange to say, our appetites were not any too keen this morning, but we put away the rest of the trout, with bacon, flapjacks, and coffee. We would have liked to have stayed longer, but work was calling and we had no choice but to pack up our gear and hit the back trail.

There was all the time in the world, our packs were light by now, and we proceeded leisurely down the river. All very good until we started back over Sugarland Mountain to Elkmont and then the work began. It hadn't seemed too bad coming in, but we were going downhill then. For eight hundred vertical feet we panted up the side of a steep pine-covered ridge, than which, under a blazing sun, nothing is hotter. At the summit, in the Huskey Gap, we lay down to rest, more exhausted than when we reached the top of Le Conte. A couple more miles mercifully down hill brought us to the railhead at Elkmont, to laze in the shade until the train pulled out for Knoxville and home.

Grub List (no amounts recorded)

Meal	Bacon
Flour	Powdered eggs
Rice	Powdered milk
Beans	Erbswurst
Coffee	Baking powder
Cocoa	Dried apples
Oatmeal	Dried apricots
Sugar	Rockihominy
Lard	Sweet chocolate

DATE: JULY 14, 1918

DESTINATION: ROAN MOUNTAIN.

OBJECT: OUTING.

WEATHER: FAIR.

PARTY: LENA S. FINK, PAUL M. FINK.

Ever since my first trip there several years before, I had been telling Lena of the beauties of Roan Mountain. It may be I wanted to inoculate her with a bit of my own interest in the mountains. But whatever the reason, or the inducements presented, at last I persuaded her to make a trip there with me.

At one time there had been a carriage road to the top of the mountain, but years of disuse and neglect had rendered it impassable to any vehicle, and the top could be reached by foot only.

We owned no car then. If we had, there was no highway to take us to the little town of Roan Mountain Station, from which our ascent would have to begin. But the trains of the "Narrow Gauge" (the ET&WNC RR) passed through the village, to get us there.

To enjoy the scenery through Doe River gorge we rode the observation car. As we entered the foothills above Elizabethton, Lena would point to some nearby ridge and ask:

"What's the name of that mountain?"

"I suppose those knobs have some local name, but I don't know it."

"Don't tell me those are only *knobs*. They're mountains."

"Just wait. You'll see some real mountains before we get back."

So it went, she claiming them to be veritable mountains, I just as certain they were only minor elevations.

Comfortably situated at the rambling frame Roan Mountain Inn, between Doe River and the railroad, we found a hack that would take us as far as Burbank, a tiny settlement at the northern foot of the Roan. Bright and early on Sunday morning, well fortified by a real breakfast, we set out.

Beyond Burbank the road was not negotiable by vehicle and there the hack was to await our return. From here the old road ascended by a long series

Resting in the Gap

of curves and switch-backs, on an easy grade that made climbing no task at all. First it passed through mingled small farms, pastures and cut-over brush, by log cabins and tiny frame houses, then plunged into the timber. Steadily upward it went, first along the side of a wooded ridge, then crossing a deep, shaded hollow, with a crystal brooklet tumbling over mossy boulders, on to another slope, continually doubling back on itself to gain altitude.

A little too optimistic as to my knowledge of the way, I essayed to make a shortcut between switch-backs too soon and succeeded in getting us lost. A needless hour was lost, aimlessly pushing through brush, crossing a steep potato patch and a mucky swale before we regained the road. Lena wasn't anyways pleased with the inauspicious start, justifiably so.

Once more straightened out on our way, we stuck pretty close to the road thereafter, unless the upper end of a shortcut was in plain sight.

To one not used to mountain climbing, a winding trail to a high summit seems interminable, to have no end. So Lena found this one. For an hour or two all was very well, then the trail through the timber, with no lookouts, grew monotonous. The growing altitude and the accompanying shortness of breath began to have its effect. I tried to pep her up with vivid descriptions of the beauties of Carvers Gap and Cloudland, but ere long even these lost their appeal.

"Is it really beautiful in the Gap," she asked.

On the road to Cloudland

"Sure is. It's the prettiest place you ever saw."

"It must be if it's worth all this."

Finally, patience completely exhausted, she sank down on a log beside the trail and refused to go a single step further, adding that never again would I inveigle her into the solitude of the mountains. By that time I could tell by the change in the kind of timber, it's thinning and the general character of the mountain side, that we were almost in Carvers Gap. A little high-powered persuasion and a promise to turn back if we hadn't reached the Gap in five more minutes, and she reluctantly consented to start on once more.

Well within the last limit we left the timber and, rounding the last bend in the road, came out into the open grassland of Carvers Gap, with its scattered gray boulders and the balsam trees bordering the higher slopes. The sky was a cloudless blue, and sheep were placidly grazing on the rich green turf.

For at least five minutes Lena sat on a convenient log, saying not a word, content to drink in the quiet beauty of the scene. Finally there came the question:

"How long can we stay?"

"About an hour or so, I suppose."

"Can we come back next year?"

The Roan had made another convert.

Time was wasting, and we pushed on upward from the Gap, following the rocky, washed-out old stage road, through balsam trees nearly closing in the narrow lane, around the northern shoulder of Roan High Knob and on to the old Cloudland Hotel. Badly enough deteriorated when I saw it three years before, it was in far worse shape now. The right side of the front had caved in, much of the roof had fallen victim to winter wind, and it was evident that in a short time nothing would be left on the site but the rough stone foundation.

We would have been happy to have had hours to spend wandering over the broad, park-like open top of the mountain, but it was long past noon and we couldn't tarry. With a long, last look at Cloudland as we rounded the High Knob, we hurried on, with a few minutes time out to enjoy a second glimpse of Carvers Gap and a drink of icy water at the spring trickling out at the edge of the timber.

Down the mountain we hurried, much faster than we had climbed it. Going down, shortcuts between switchbacks were more easily seen, and we took advantage of every one, steep though they might be. The hack was waiting at Burbank, to bring us back to the hotel, tired but amply repaid for our efforts. One can imagine we did ample justice to the supper that night.

Everything in life is relative. As we rode the train home next day, Lena looked with disdain at the low ridges near Elizabethton, and said:

"I know now why you called them knobs."

She had been initiated.

DATE: SEPTEMBER 19-23, 1918

DESTINATION: CLARK CREEK, RICH MOUNTAIN AND ROAN MOUNTAIN.

OBJECT: EXPLORATION.

WEATHER: RAIN, COLD, FAIR.

PARTY: HENRY W. PATTON, PAUL M. FINK.

We never needed an excuse to go to the mountains, just the opportunity. This time, as usual, our plans as to itinerary were ambitious, considering the time involved. Also as usual, such things seldom work out according to plan, and this was no exception. We had some discomforts, but a most enjoyable trip, regardless.

September 19, 1918

We had the luxury of motor transportation (a rare thing those days) as far as Conklin, then started on afoot. The master plan had called for the night to be spent near Devil Fork on Clark Creek, but black clouds gathering showed the advisability of making camp shortly above the Sally Hole. Well enough we did, for the tent was barely up when a steady rain began. Steady is the right word, for it rained steadily the rest of the afternoon, and all night. We couldn't see any advantage in getting soaked, hunting firewood for a fire we probably couldn't have started anyway, and our supper was a cold, if not dry one. Our lullaby was the constant drip, drip, drip of water on our tent from the trees above.

September 20, 1918

It was still raining when we waked, and we could see that one part of the trip, a hunt for the Big Falls, was very definitely out. Nor was there any chance for having a fire, so we settled down to pass away the time as best we could, always hoping for a break in the weather.

A baker tent, 6 x 7 feet, too low in the ridge to allow one to stand erect, may be admirable for sleeping quarters, but it's too cramped quarters for any length of time by day. There was little we could do to speed up the passing of the hours. Dawdling over a cold breakfast, and later, a cold dinner, consumed a little time. We spun all the yarns we knew and even invented some, discussed everything of importance (and some things not), and still it rained. Looking out the open front of the tent, we could see an old rail fence close by and laid plans to steal a few rails for firewood, if and when the rain slackened.

After lunch someone suggested that if we had a deck of cards that might help, but no cards. Finally we hit on the scheme of tearing up a note book and making cards of the pages. They were very crude, the pencil markings not too legible and they were hard to shuffle and deal, but they did prove a great help. Hedging against more rains in the future, I afterward added a miniature deck of cards to my outfit but can't recall ever having used them.

Toward the latter part of the afternoon the rain ceased for a while. Just as we were about to start a raid on the rail fence, Jake Phillips, living at the last house along the creek, came by and stopped for a little chat. Naturally we kept our hands off the fence while he was there. As he started to go, he glanced about, then said,

"If you boys need any firewood, just help yourselves to a few of those old rails."

He never knew how close he came to having his fence stolen.

Our tent was a baker model, homemade of cotton drill and waterproofed with paraffin. Evidently I'd made a poor job of it, for under the continual downpour it developed leaks in several spots. Emergency repairs were in order. Heating a tin plate over the fire, it was applied again and again until the leaking areas were thoroughly dry. Lard was then rubbed in, and the hot plate used again to melt it into the fibers of the cloth. A crude way of doing the job it may have been, but it shed the water perfectly until the whole tent was done over a couple of years later.

The rain gave us only a brief respite. Supper was hardly over before it started again, and was still falling when we went to sleep, with the haunting fear that this was one trip destined to be rained out from the beginning.

September 21, 1918

During the night the rain ceased, and the crack of dawn found us out of our blankets getting breakfast. Before the sun was well up we were packed and starting on the trail along Sill Branch, toward the top of Rich Mountain. So long as it followed close to the stream the grade was easy. As we started up the mountain it grew steeper and steeper, the last three or four hundred feet about as abrupt a grade as any equally well-travelled trail I've ever seen.

Hoof-prints proved that horses had been ridden, or more probably led, over the mountain along it. Right now mud from the previous day's rain made the steep trail very treacherous going.

Just at the top of the mountain we found the "improvement", where George Copeland had cleared a large acreage for a grain and stock farm, with barns and other buildings in the saddle between the two tops of Rich Mountain. From these a graded but rough and rocky road led down Bald Creek to South Indian Creek. Here was a much better road to the Nolichucky River at Chestoa, some four miles above Erwin.

Our rapid pushing along was rewarded by reaching the railroad in plenty of time to catch the morning passenger train, riding it up through the spectacular gorge of the Nolichucky River and on to the village of Toecane, N.C., where the Toe and the Cane Rivers unite to form the Nolichucky.

Toecane was the nearest rail point to Roan Mountain. About 1:30 P.M. we left the river, intending to cross Pumpkin Patch Mountain to Little Rock Creek. After an hour's walk and no sign of crossing a mountain we began to sense something wrong, and hailed the driver of a passing wagon, asking where we were. His reply, "Three miles from Bakersville," showed we had missed the road and were some four miles out of our way. Taking pity on us, he told us to climb on the wagon, took us to Bakersville, where he put us on another road to Little Rock Creek and Glen Ayre. The net result of the misadventure was two hours lost time and a mile further to walk.

Our friend the driver had a spite against the town of Bakersville, and took great delight in telling a sure landmark to keep from becoming lost around there. Pointing to the pallid moon in the late afternoon sky, he laughed,

"So long as you can see *that* there's no reason in getting lost. The man in the moon always has his face pointed *from* Bakersville."

Above Glen Ayre we asked a Mr. Freeman if we might sleep on the hay in his barn. He refused, but told us to go on a couple of miles further up the Mule Trail toward Carvers Gap to an old sawmill site and gave us permission to burn anything we wanted out of the old slab pile.

Before long we were overtaken by a horseman, who plied us with questions as he rode alongside. As was our custom, part of our clothes were Army issue, and our packs and canteens bore the U. S. brand, though of obsolete issue.

First we were asked what Army camp we were from—this was in the middle of World War I. When we denied being in the army, he wanted to know why we were wearing uniforms. Then he questioned us about the U.S. markings on our gear, etc. From the way he kept coming back to these same things in his rambling talk we could see he wasn't at all satisfied with our answers. Finally he turned aside into a barnyard, and before we had gone much further we saw him riding back down the road.

We found the old sawmill, almost beneath the top of the Roan, at an altitude of 4,500 feet. The slab pile was big as a house, so there was no lack of good firewood for cooking supper or keeping us warm.

The joker was the wind. It blew in hard gusts from every known direction, including straight up and straight down.

Keeping a decent cooking fire was a difficult task, and here it was that Henry first found his patent revolving smoke cloud, that followed him around, no matter which side of the fire he sat upon. A night fire was utterly out of the question. If built close enough to warm us in the least, it would have burned the tent over our heads in five minutes. Browse, ferns, or long grass for a bed was nowhere in sight, so we scooped depressions in the sawdust, and curled up as nearly in the lee of the slab pile as we could tell by the shifting breeze. I had only a single light army blanket, Henry a heavier blanket and a down quilt. With this bedding he slept fairly warm, but I almost froze. An hour or two of sleep was all I could manage to get. The rest of the night I spent shivering and shaking.

The moon and stars were brilliant when we turned in, and the sky was clear. The only cloud in sight was on the peak above us, where it had been resting all afternoon.

September 22, 1918

As soon as it was light enough to see I rolled from my blanket and quick as I could built a fire to thaw out by. It was easy then to tell why I'd been so cold during the night. Spewed up out of the damp sawdust all about us were long "rabbit's ears" of frost. On the margin of the tiny stream nearby was a thin skim of ice, proof positive that the thermometer had dropped well below thirty degrees, the coldest night I'd ever spent in the open. As the sun rose the cloud lifted from the top of the Roan, the wind died away and the sky was clear, portents of warmer weather ahead of us.

As we slowly plodded along up the trail toward Carvers Gap we were joined by Mr. Freeman, bound for the top of the mountain to see about some livestock grazing on the high meadows. Hanging from his watch chain was the biggest Masonic emblem I ever saw. I immediately made myself known as a member of the fraternity, told him who we were, where from, and what we were doing there. When he was thoroughly satisfied, we told him of the man who had so closely questioned us the afternoon before, and how mystified we had been by his conduct. Mr. Freeman laughed,

"I know all about that, and I'll set it all right when I get back. You see, some deserters from the army are supposed to be hiding out around here, and he suspected you might be two of them. There's a $50.00 reward for every one caught. If he had been sure he might have brought the sheriff up to get you. You'll not be bothered now, though."

Mr. Freeman told us many interesting stories of the region, the building of Cloudland Hotel, etc. Like ourselves, he was curious as to the cause of the many "natural balds" scattered throughout the Southern mountains, of which the Roan is such an outstanding example. Concurring with our own ideas, he believed the balds the result of some natural causes, rather than of human agency. In boyhood he had been told by his grandfather, one of the earliest settlers on Little Rock Creek, that at the time of his arrival the Roan had been as bare as it is today, and that the Indians living thereabouts had no traditions telling of a time when the summit had been wooded.

From Carvers Gap on to the top there was much evidence of the presence of the cloud that had hung about the heights all the evening and night before. The boughs of the balsams were white with hoar frost congealed from it. On the weather side of the rocks and the tree trunks it had formed in angel feathers three inches long. There was no snow on the ground, but on the balsam fans the frost was so heavy we raked it up by handsful for a snowball battle. Ice on tiny pools by the roadside was half an inch in thickness.

The frost speedily melted under the bright sun, and the air warmed up comfortably. The day was spent in wandering over the broad top of the mountain, from end to end, and in exploring the Cloudland Hotel now fallen almost into ruins. The spring that had supplied water for the hotel was found some two hundred yards in front of it, hidden among the trees.

Close to the spring we found something else that pleased us no end—a tiny shelter probably built by hunters, the rock fireplace in front complete with chimney made from old drain pipe looted from the hotel. No sooner was it found than we took possession. With vivid recollections of the discomforts of the night before, we began making arrangements for a much more pleasant

Frost on the balsams

The ruins of old Cloudland

evening to come. All the old browse bed was cleaned out and replaced with fresh, thatched in and covered over with the tent, for a ground cloth. On this springy mattress our beds were made, each man in his own blanket bag, and the down quilt spread over all. No Beauty Rest could have surpassed our bed in sleeping enjoyment, the fire in front dissipated the chill of the air, and a more pleasant night we never spent in the mountains.

Our snug haven on the Roan

September 23, 1918

As it began to grow gray in the East I turned out and walked back up to the top, to see the sunrise from the upper windows of the old hotel. A wonderful enough sight from there when the sun peeped up over the rim of the world, a better place from which to view it would have been Roan High Knob.

A few thin bands of low cloud turned slowly from gray to pink, then to gold, and then the sun seemed to fairly jump from below the horizon before a single ray touched any one of the dozens of ridges and peaks. One moment it was gray dawn, the next full day was upon us. It was the first sunrise I'd ever seen from a mountain summit. Usually our camps were located a little further down the slope, close to water, and my chronic laziness worked to keep me from climbing out on top early, then dropping back down to camp for breakfast.

There was yet a day or two of time at our disposal. As we had been forced to eat dry rations while holed up by rain at the start, we had plenty of food left to let us go on east along the range, to the Hump and then drop down at Elk Park. Folks are funny, though, and nothing would do us but that we start back home at once, by way of Carvers Gap and the old carriage road to Burbank and Roan Mountain Station. From there the "Narrow Gauge" Railway took us through the spectacular gorge of the Doe River to Johnson City, and thence by the Southern Railway home.

DATE: JUNE 9-19, 1919

DESTINATION: EASTERN END OF THE GREAT SMOKIES.

OBJECT: EXPLORATION.

WEATHER: GENERALLY FAIR, SOME RAIN.

PARTY: WALTER S. DIEHL, PAUL M. FINK.

When Walter and I had stood on the Cliff Top of Le Conte in the summer of 1916 and looked out at the rugged eastern-half of the Smokies, he had fired my imagination with stories of their untouched and primeval wilderness, where there was only the barest evidence of man's presence. We had laid tentative plans then to visit this section the next summer. Little did we think that a world war was so close in the making, and that three full years would intervene before we would have the chance to be together in the mountains again. When the war ended in the fall of 1918 our plans were immediately revived, and when summer came again we were on our way.

June 9, 1919

A train running late in leaving Jonesboro made for a very tight connection of only a few minutes with the K&A Railroad in Knoxville. It had been our idea that this train ran all the way to Elkmont, our jumping-off place.

This was our error, for it went only to Townsend, the mill town of the Little River Lumber Co., in Tuckaleechee Cove, and stopped there for the night. The superintendent of the company most kindly put his gasoline car at our disposal, and we finished the trip on our special train, up through the deep, rocky gorge of the East Prong of the Little River. It was after dark when we reached the Wonderland Park Hotel, and after supper. Through the kindness of the cook that was remedied, and we were soon in bed, impatient to be on our way on the morrow.

June 10, 1919

This was to be a long trip, with not a single opportunity to replenish any of

Starting from Elkmont

our supplies en route. We would be dependent entirely on what we could carry on our backs—food, shelter, and everything else. This called for heavy packs, weighing about sixty pounds apiece as we left the hotel.

Previously I'd been using an old issue army knapsack, with blanket roll atop, but that kind of gear was not commodious enough to hold a full outfit, nor were the shoulder straps suitable for the heavy load I'd have to carry. During the past year I'd made myself a combination pack-harness and tumpline, designed to my own ideas, using a Navy seabag to hold my outfit. It had proven very satisfactory in a light trip near home, and now I was anxious to find out how comfortable and efficient it would prove under the strains of heavy loads in any kind of weather. It simply *had* to work, comfortable or not, for there would be no changing it after we were under way.

Our tent, too, was new, a Compac, that had the great virtue of being lightweight, but was very cramped quarters for two men. Walter soon dubbed it our "sleeping sock," and said we put it on rather than get into it. We didn't mind sleeping a bit crowded, but it gave no shelter for cooking in the rain or for other purposes.

The cabin at Grassy Patch

The starting trail was the same one we'd used en route to Le Conte, through the Huskey Gap of Sugarland Mountain, and down the steep path to the West Prong of the Little Pigeon River. The road along the stream was no better than it had been before, its upper portion hardly fit for anything but a sled. The morning had begun bright, but clouds gathered early, and several light showers forced us to take shelter wherever we could find it. The heaviest caught us just as we arrived at the house of Davis Bracken, an old friend of former trips, and we were happy to accept his invitation to come in. Well do I recall his greeting to Walter:

"I'm shorely glad to see ye. I heered you'd gone to the war, and I was afeered you'd been destroyed."

Bracken's home, last house but one up the river, stood where one caught his first glimpse of the Chimney Tops, two spectacularly sharp peaks on a hogback ridge on the north flank of Sugarland Mountain. We'd planned to get some pictures from his porch, but now the outlines were partially veiled by rain and mist, and we had to give up the idea.

Bracken was custodian of the Champion Fiber Company's possession cabin at the Grassy Patch, where Alum Cave Creek and the Walker Camp Branch unite to form the West Prong. Finding we planned a few days fishing and general physical hardening before starting for the high tops, he suggested we stay at the cabin, and offered us the keys. Not a minute did we delay in accepting.

This first day of travel under heavy pack had been wearing on men fresh from office work. A quick supper, and we were in bed by dark. In no time at all the sound of our snores was mingling with the gurgling of the stream, and frightening the hootowls from their perches in the hemlocks.

June 11, 1919

Hopes that the showers of the day before had been heavy enough to render the stream murky weren't bourne out. As usual, the water was low and clear, and the trout weren't having any—at least not much—of what we had to offer. When we quit trying early in the afternoon and came back to the cabin we found Davis Bracken and his teenage son Richard there.

Eked out by a lot of other food, there were enough fish to go 'round. After all had stowed away a good meal, a smudge of rotten wood was built to hold at bay the swarms of blood-hungry "punkies" (black gnats), and we settled down for a long chat.

Bracken, a man of fifty-odd years, living his whole life in the mountains, was a very intelligent person and far above the average native in his knowledge of things of the outside world. He was an entertaining talker, and from him we added a great store to our knowledge of mountain ways. One of his sayings in particular was so apt that it has stuck in my memory ever since: "Lots of city people think the mountain folks ain't no better'n varmits."

In the conversation some mention was made of Horace Kephart's book, *Our Southern Highlanders*. It developed he had read it, loaned him by a teacher in the school further down the Sugarlands. I sought his opinion of the book as an accurate delineation of the mountain people and their ways. His answer, "Well, I don't guess any man could've writ it better," raised the book to an even higher place in my estimation than it had formerly held.

Bracken was later to meet Kephart and, under the name of Jasper Fenn, to appear in Chapter X of the 1922 edition of the book.

June 12, 1919

Among other things that we had learned from Bracken was that above the Chimney Tops, where the stream was rougher, more shaded and the water consequently colder and more aerated, only speckled trout were to be found. Then for a mile or so down the valley, as it began to widen and the timber be more open, one might expect to catch both speckled and rainbows. Below that, when the water had warmed a little as it ran more slowly among great boulders absorbing a bit of heat from the sun, only rainbow trout lived. As the speckles had proven so reluctant to bite for us the day before, we decided to fish downstream this day, and see what our luck would be with the rainbows.

It wasn't a bit better—worse, in fact. When in disgust we called it quits at noon there were only two in the string, one speckled and one rainbow, each of respectable size and both of Walter's catching.

Rain caught up on us about Fort Harry. Fortunately, there was a shelving rock by the side of the road, too low for standing under but plenty high for sitting, and we "holed up" under its protection while a good old mountain rain poured outside for an hour. Our modest lunch of raisins and rockihominy was just enough to make us realize how hungry we were. Someone came up with the bright idea of cooking our fish. A store of dry leaves and twigs under the ledge furnished the kindling, a dead rhododendron bush just outside gave bigger fuel, a couple of forked sticks served as cooking utensils, and before long we were munching crisply broiled trout. From lack of salt they were not too palatable, but the experiment convinced us that trout broiled over the fire could be equally delicious as those fried in the pan.

In the long run it did us little good to have ridden out the rain in the shelter of the ledge, for the bushes beside the trail had us thoroughly wet long before we reached the cabin. There our clothes were soon dry, and a big dinner made us forget the privations of midday.

June 13, 1919

The Brackens started home early, leaving us in possession of the cabin, and with a warm invitation to come again and stay as long as we wished. To our regret, we were never able to accept it as frequently as we might wish.

The water was a little higher and slightly milky from the rain of the day before, but the fish were still not in the mood to bite. True, we got about as many as we wanted to eat, but that was no string at all on a stream where under good conditions one might hook a hundred trout a day.

All afternoon we lazed around, collecting the scattered bits of our outfit and getting everything shipshape, ready for the long, hard pull to begin on the morrow.

Just under the crest of a spur of Le Conte opposite the cabin, locally known as Hole-in-the-Rock Mountain, are two holes completely through the ridge, plainly in sight from the cabin yard. A story we had heard on a previous trip was that no one had ever gone through them, and that more than one curious investigator had disappeared, never to be heard of again. Richard Bracken explored that legend, telling of several trips he had made to them. By his account, the larger hole is some fifteen feet high and easy of passage, though the climb up is rugged and difficult.

Running up to the apex of another ridge facing the east and just across the river from us, was a great "slick," of kalmia or "mountain laurel," just then coming into full bloom. In the early morning, while night still hung about our cabin in the depths of the valley, the first rays of the rising sun fell full upon this enormous bed of kalmia, turning the whole mountainside into a glowing mass of shell pink, one of the most glorious floral displays I've ever been fortunate enough to see. All up the valley, particularly on the Walker Camp Branch, the rhododendron maximum was blooming in great profusion. Clumps big as a house were so heavy with blossoms as to resemble a snowbank. No other place have I ever seen the white rhododendron bear such masses of bloom.

June 14, 1919

From the Grassy Patch the trail to the top of the mountain at the state line led first over the boulders and through the mire beside the Walker Camp Branch for about a mile (distances are deceptive and hard to estimate correctly), turning to the right up the tiny Newfound Gap Branch. Here, close by the side of the main stream, was a little spring, flowing water so cold it rattled our teeth.

The trail, faint enough at the mouth of the branch, soon dwindled away to an occasional blaze or a clipped bush, with no discernable footway. These we chose to disregard and pushed straight on up the ravine, knowing that so long as we were climbing we were on the right way. The ascent was toilsome, over rocks and ledges and through waisthigh bushes. These thinned out as we neared the top, the last two or three hundred feet up a steep, grassy bank, shaded by stunted beeches and an occasional balsam. The whole climb from the river, some fifteen hundred feet, was on a grade of full thirty degrees, in places much steeper than that.

At Newfound Gap, the first gap east of Mt. Mingus, we met our first balsam forest, not to leave it until our descent from Mt. Guyot. All the way we would

Le Conte, from near Newfound Gap

be on or near the state line, between North Carolina and Tennessee, winding in every direction as it followed the main divide of the Smokies. The general trend would be toward the northeast.

Newfound Gap is a little lower than Indian Gap, on the opposite side of Mt. Mingus, where for centuries an old Indian trail crossed the mountain, on a route a wagon road, of sorts, later followed. The approach to Newfound Gap from either state, however, is not as favorable as at Indian Gap. The name is of long usage. In his name list, Arnold Guyot mentions it as "New or Righthand Gap."

For a mile or two the top of the mountain was fairly broad and the faint trail wound along a grassy ridge, set with large spruce and birch timber. Soon we began to notice a characteristic feature of the topography that would persist the length of the trip. In fact, it is evident along the whole state line. Though the slope is steep on both sides, it is particularly so on the north—Tennessee—side. Often it is precipitous. The cliffs, though, are rarely bare, but covered with a solid mantle of green bushes and stunted trees, rooted in every crevice.

On the southern—North Carolina—slopes, the dense forest reaches to the very top. As a result, the traveler along the eastern half of the Smokies seldom catches more than a glimpse of what lies to the south of him. Every good lookout faces the ridges and valleys of Tennessee. Through the greater part of this trip, the triple fanged peak of Le Conte, standing out north of the main chain, dominated the scene. Mt. Collins (now Mt. Kephart) was long another outstanding feature of the landscape.

The Smokies can be very confusing to the visitor, in that the buttressing ridges, at their junction, are often higher than the main divide. Especially when the clouds are resting on the mountains, the traveler, resting on the assumption that the watershed is always the highest, can be far from his course before he realizes his error.

We were the victims of this just before reaching the main top of Mt. Collins. At a fork in the trail, the seemingly best way turned to the right up a short ridge and then took us down five hundred feet, along a steep, rough trail cut through a laurel slick, before we could look back and, seeing the higher mountains to our left, realize our mistake. Losing the way was nothing to worry about. It was the hard pull back up, under heavy pack that galled us.

A few hundred yards further on we found the true lead, marked with a large H blaze on a big balsam. Here the true trail turned sharply right down a steep, bushy slope, rather than continuing on to the Jump-off, at the end of Mt. Collins.

Walter had been there before, but wanted to see it again, so our packs were dropped by the side of the trail while we walked a little way out the knife-edge ridge connecting Mt. Collins with Le Conte.

Emerging suddenly from the timber screen at the Jump-off, we were perched on the rim of a gigantic bowl, broken in half, its sides the northeastern end of Mt. Collins and the main Smoky range. From beneath our feet the mountain side fell away precipitously for a thousand feet and more before sloping sharply down to the headwaters of Porters Creek. The sides of the chasm are not stark bare rock, but shielded by trees and shrubbery growing in every crack and cranny in the rocks. The stones we threw out disappeared from sight long before we heard them, faintly, crashing into the timber below. (Note: the spectacular Charlies Bunion was created near here by a cloud burst a few years after this visit.)

This enormous gulf was not shown on the existing maps. Only a fairly steep slope was indicated. That was no surprise to us, for we already knew full well they could not be relied upon. Admittedly reconnaissance maps, they were only good enough to get lost by.

The first night's camp atop the Smokies was half a mile east of Mt. Collins. There was no spot in sight level enough for a decent campsite, so our tiny Compac tent was set up right on the state line, where Walter and I, sleeping

The Sleeping Sock

side by side, lay in different states, he in Carolina and I in Tennessee. Water was unusually close to the top, a tiny trickle running scarcely a gallon an hour, but sufficient for our needs.

Several times during the day we had been puzzled by recent blazes, with now and then a surveyor's stake. We could think of no explanation, unless some lumber company might have been running a boundary line. Bear sign had been seen by the trail, and ruffed grouse were common.

Making camp, we flushed a hen grouse, with her brood of young. They were not yet able to fly, but there was nothing wrong with their ability to run, or their protective coloration. They would scuttle a yard or two among the leaves, stop, squat motion less on the ground, and instantly were invisible. The old grouse kept up a constant clucking in the bushes, so finally we retired to let her call together her scattered flock and lead them out of danger.

This was to prove our most strenuous day on the trail. The long, steep pull from the cabin up to Newfound Gap had been a heartbreaking task.

June 15, 1919

A light shower just before dawn bothered us not a bit. We had intended making it an easy day, so slept late, spending a good part of the morning puttering around camp. Our shoes were showing some signs of disintegration, the constant wading when fishing not helping them. We had greased them thoroughly, but leather can take only so much water before the stitches begin to give way. With a rock for a last and the poll of the axe for a hammer, we nailed the soles back on. Not too workmanlike a job, I fear, but one that held out until right at the end of the trip.

The air seemed to be clearing a bit toward noon, and we hurriedly packed up and pushed on. The scenery along the Sawteeth just ahead of us is the most spectacular on the whole range. We had hoped to cover this part of the itinerary under light conditions favorable for photography, for the ever present haze is a great obstacle to successful picture making.

Between our camp and Porters Gap we had no high mountains to climb, but the going was even more difficult. Here, along the Sawteeth, is the most rugged portion of the whole Smoky range. The name is most apt, for the divide resembles nothing so much as the blade of a titanic saw, the teeth a succession of sharp peaks rising two or three hundred feet above the gaps between, all at an altitude of six thousand feet above the sea.

For a distance of over two miles the crest of the ridge will average scarcely three feet in width with many places barely wide enough for a foothold. On either side, particularly on the north, the sides drop nearly straight down. But for the protection afforded by the dense bushes it would be a hazardous undertaking to attempt passage. Even as it is, the trip is not free from peril of falling.

The scenery from the Sawteeth is magnificent, the grandest we were to see, with the possible exception of the view of Mt. Guyot from Sharp Top. All along the way are outlooks giving a panorama stretching all the way from Mts. Mingus and Collins to Laurel Top. Le Conte was a dominant feature, we would catch occasional glimpses of Clingmans Dome and Guyot. Range ranked behind range until the misty blue of the distant mountains merged imperceptibly into the haze of the horizon. A wilder and more rugged country I never hope to see.

Scattered here and there throughout the forest cover we could pick out great patches of laurel and rhododendron, hundreds of acres in extent. To the natives these are known as "hells," "slicks" and "Woolly patches." From a distance they might easily be mistaken for open fields or smooth green lawns. In reality, their iron-hard shrubby growth is so impenetrable that even the hardy black bears fail to push their way through.

In the valleys far below us there were no clearings or cabins to be seen. Save

A lookout on the Sawteeth

for occasional blazes along the state line there was little to show that man had ever been this way before.

In Porters Gap was the explanation of the recent blazes we had seen some distance back. This was a surveyor's stake, with the faded date of September 1918, and giving the distance to the Cocke County line at Mt. Guyot as eleven miles. The discovery was of value to us, for thereafter the sight of an occasional blaze was proof we were on our true course and not strayed off on some tributary ridge. In a few rare instances the survey party had made the going easier for us, when they had chopped out their line through some particularly mean bit of laurel. That made for an easier passage than on one of Walter's former trips, when his party had the option of swimming through the brush or of floundering along on the top of it.

It was very dry on top, and this evening we had to descend more than a thousand feet on the south side in search of water. Part of the way we involuntarily slid, for each of us had lost the heel off a shoe in the rough going of the day. On fairly level trails this would bother us little, if at all. But descending

Le Conte, from the Sawteeth

Rough country near Porters Gap

steep grades, where one depends on his boot heels for braking, one or the other of us was continually slipping and hitting the earth with a thud, usually dull and sickening, as all thuds in literature are supposed to be, with his pack on top of him. Then the whole tangled mess would roll downhill 'till some friendly tree stopped it. Fully half the descent was made in this fashion.

Finally a tiny seep of water was found, oozing out from under a ledge, and camp made on the bottom of a deep, narrow ravine. There was no level place big enough to pitch our tent. Moving rocks and pulling up bushes by the roots at last gave a spot big enough for our beds. At that, our heads were under the overhang of one big rock, and our feet stuck out into space. The earth was dry, but above us, on the sides of the ravine and on the trees were distinct evidences of very highwater in the past.

Shortly after we wrapped up in our blankets, clouds began to drift over the moon and we could hear the faint growling of thunder in the east. It rolled closer and rumbled louder, and we grew much concerned about our situation. In fact, we were much more than simply concerned—we were scared. A heavy rainstorm on top could fill that gorge with a roaming torrent, as we knew had happened before, and wash us and our kit all the way down to the Oconaluftee River. In the darkness there was no hope of gathering our things together, or of climbing the steep banks with them. Even if we ourselves escaped without injury, we would have been in a serious predicament. To be afoot in the depths of the Smokies with no food or other outfit would be no laughing matter.

To make the best of a threatening situation, each of us picked out a sizable tree, and determined that if the flood came we would climb high as we could, tie ourselves on safely with our packstraps, and let the rest go as it might.

The thunder rolled nearer and louder. When a light shower began to patter down we were on the verge of putting our plans into effect, and clambering up to our perches. Fortunately for our peace of mind, the dripping rain lasted only a few moments, and the thunderstorm lost itself somewhere around Laurel Top. The reverberations grew fainter and fainter, and had died away entirely by the time the moon broke through the clouds again. Then we gave a deep sigh of relief, and went to sleep in peace.

June 16, 1919

Any long climb under pack is bad enough, but facing it the first thing in the morning, before one is limbered up and before the strengthening effects

Porters Gap

of breakfast begin to show themselves is a discouraging prospect indeed. The steep pull back to Porters Gap this morning was a heartbreaking one: To make matters worse, Walter, who must have swallowed some kind of bug when eating, lost his breakfast and developed nausea and a burning thirst that clung to him all day.

This was one of the very few times we ever had a pistol in our outfit, a long barrelled .22 Colt automatic Walter had brought, should we run across any small game. In Porters Gap it seemed that all the "boomers" in the mountains were celebrating Old Home Week, dozens of them, by far the greatest concentration I'd ever seen. They were so plentiful and so devoid of all fear of man that I knocked down a couple, and could easily have gotten more if we had wanted to stay longer.

All the way across Laurel Top to Hughes Ridge we made slow progress, travelling as easily as the rugged and precipitous terrain would allow. My canteen had sprung a leak—evidently I'd sat down on it too hard in sliding down from Porters Gap—and soon was empty. To quench Walter's thirst, a number of times I left my pack and dropped down three or four hundred feet on either side, looking for water. The hot weather had dried up all the top springs and not a drop could I find. Profuse perspiration from the work of heavy packing dehydrates one quickly, and with only one canteen of water between us, our

Looking west toward Laurel Top

mouths were parched and we were spitting cotton long before the end of the day.

We had been eagerly looking forward to reaching Hughes Ridge (now Peck's Corner), for we had been told of a spring very near the top. Again we were disappointed. All to be found was a small damp mudhole beside the remains of an old surveyor's camp, evidently that of the party whose blazes we had seen.

The afternoon was almost spent. The prospect of a dry camp was a dismal one, and we separated in search of a water supply large enough for our modest needs. The beds of all the little trickles were dry, and we hunted vainly for some little time before we could locate a promising spot. Water was finally gotten by scooping out a pool in the muck, letting it slowly fill, then bailing it out time and again until the water seeping in ran clear.

In all our years of camping together Walter and I had fallen into a way of dividing the work. Usually he found the firewood and water, and gathered the browse, ferns, etc., for our beds. I built the fire and cooked the meals. Together we put up the tent. Tonight he was still sick and weak from the day's packing without food and with little water. Most of the evenings work fell to me, and it was well after dark before we at last rolled into our blankets.

The woodsfolk are plentiful enough in the Smokies, but they are wary and shy, and are not frequently seen by travelers such as we. Today they had been much more in evidence than is usual. Many varieties of small birds were in the bushes and trees, the slate-colored junco especially numerous. Several times we flushed ruffed grouse, and once found the dropped feathers and dusting places of wild turkeys. At Hughes Ridge we both saw and heard ravens, resident only on the higher mountains of the South. Strangely, the only boomers we saw were in Porters Gap, but there were plenty of signs of bears all along the way.

The black bear has a way of making his presence known in the neighborhood by rearing on his hind legs beside a balsam tree, then reaching back over his shoulder, tearing off a strip of bark with his teeth. Often he will add a stroke or two with his front claws. Maybe the height of the marks above the ground is his way of telling other bears his size, and warning the smaller ones to watch their step. Not infrequently a larger bear will chance by, and tear off a bit of bark higher than the first. On this day we saw a score of trees bearing marks of teeth and claws, even three on a single tree.

June 17, 1919

When Walter attacked his breakfast with accustomed zest I could see he was himself again. We moved along leisurely, for barring some mischance we now had plenty of time to finish the trip, and were disinclined to hurry. Our hearty appetites had lightened our loads greatly, and hard work had toughened our muscles. Packing was no longer the drudgery it had been at the start.

The going from Hughes Ridge to the junction of Smoky and the Balsam range, locally known as "The Ledge," was easy, as compared with what we had been traversing. The top of the mountain was broader and more open, neither rough nor steep, with the exception of the last peak west of the Balsam. This had no name, either on the map or known to us. For purposes of reference we spoke of it as High Top (now Mt. Chapman).

All the eastern end of the Great Smokies, at an altitude about five thousand feet, is mantled with a virgin forest of balsam fir. In this particular section it grows more densely than in any other spot we had seen. Often one cannot see beyond a hundred feet for the boles of the trees.

Their tops are so closely interwoven that the direct sunlight hasn't reached the forest floor in a thousand years. Undergrowth is sparse and the ground is carpeted with a deep moss of yellowish-green hue. Scattered over the moss are a myriad of oxalis. Only a dim light filters down from above, and the whole aspect is gloomy and funereal.

Late in the afternoon we reached the summit of High Top. Pushing for a

Cliff east of Hughes Ridge

few yards through breast-high bushes, we came to an open lookout, with one of the grandest views of a single mountain I've ever seen.

Beneath the rock where we stood, the side of High Top dropped sharply away two thousand feet to the Buck Fork of the Middle Prong of the Little Pigeon River. Beyond the stream it rose as steeply to the summit of Mt. Guyot, second highest of all the peaks of the Great Smokies.

It would not be hard to convince one, standing here and looking across to the vast bulk of this gigantic mass of earth and stone, two miles away, by direct line across the abysmal gorge, that Guyot is the largest, if not the highest mountain in Eastern America.

For a few minutes we stood speechless, awed by its wild and rugged beauty. Our first thoughts were of our Kodaks, that we might be able to show others a faint impression of its majesty. Unnoticed, clouds had been gathering and

A balsam forest

Mt. Guyot, from Sharp Top

the light had become too poor for successful photography. Unfortunately, that day and many others, films and lenses did not have the wide latitude for light conditions that they do today.

Rain was close at hand. With a last look at the wonderful scene we reluctantly shouldered our packs and took to the trail again, in search of a good campsite. We found it in Balsam Gap.

We rushed frantically, trying to get everything under shelter, but before we could open our packs and pitch the tent the shower was upon us. In attempt to stay dry ourselves we snuggled down and pulled the waterproof ground cloth over us. It may have been waterproof once, enough so to protect us from ground moisture, but it had no virtue in keeping off rain. The falling water gathered on its upper surface, then came through on us in streams. Taking the rain in the open was preferable to this. The groundcloth was pitched aside, and each of us hunted a leaning tree, for what little protection it might afford. By a rare coincidence, three years before, to the day and almost to the hour, Walter and a party were caught by rain in the same gap, and holed up under the identical trees that were now sheltering us.

After wetting us thoroughly, the elements relented and the rain stopped. Water in plenty was close to the top, standing, dead and partially dry balsam was located, and before long the savory odors of cooking food were mingling with the acrid tang of the balsam smoke.

In an effort to dry out and keep from sleeping in our wet clothing, (no new experience, by the way), our soaked shirts, etc., were hung on a rack before the blaze, and the woven puttees we wore rolled and laid on the ground close beside the fire. Soon I caught the stench of scorching wool, and looking across the fire, saw Walter's "putts" smouldering. Snatching them up in response to my yell of warning, he saw mine in the same condition, and I joined the rescue brigade. The leggings were already sadly picked out and frayed by all the brush we had struggled through. The burning evened up the ragged edges and proved more of an advantage than otherwise.

Lying in that blissful state that precedes the slumber of a well-fed but tired body, when one is cognizant of what goes on but is too drowsy to do anything about it, I heard a faint noise and furtive motion close beside me, but outside the tent. Putting my hand against the tent wall, I felt something move. Too sleepy to investigate, I supposed it a bush shaken by the breeze, dismissed it from my mind, and dropped off to sleep. Next morning there was no bush to be seen. Then I thought I'd dreamed the whole thing, and said nothing to Walter about it.

A few months later, talking the trip over with him, I mentioned the dream. He replied:

"I heard it too, coming from close to where we had cooked supper. I slipped my gun from its holster into my blanket, with the idea that if anything came close to the tent I could take a shot at it. I heard no more, and must have dropped off to sleep before it came close to the tent."

All we could figure was it must have been a young and unsophisticated bear, attracted by the odors of our cooking. Had it been any smaller animal, as a bobcat, fox, coon, etc., my hand would have been too high on the tent to have touched it. Bear we knew were plentiful thereabouts. Only a few yards from our camp were trees freshly marked with tooth and claw.

June 18, 1919

Our maps showed only a very small depression in the ridge between the knob at the end of the Balsam range (now Tricorner Knob) and the top of Mt. Guyot, a sad error, for when we surmounted the knob we could see a climb on the opposite side of at least seven hundred feet.

Here at Balsam we encountered the first evidence of logging operations since we had left Mt. Collins. A great shock it was to us, to travel for days through a magnificent, truly virgin forest, where there was only the very faintest, scattered evidence man had ever been there before, and then step suddenly into the utter devastation the spruce logger leaves behind him.

In the years just gone the whole basin of Big Creek, draining the eastern ends of the Smokies and the Balsams, had been cut over. Everything of any size had been taken, for the paper mills can handle anything above sapling size. Then, as usual, fire had gotten out into the slash and completed the devastation, burning everything, even the organic matter in the forest floor, leaving the bare soil to erode and wash away under the heavy rainfall. A few straggling bushes of firecherry, laurel and blackberry were making a feeble effort to cover over the scars.

Our packs were left on the end of Balsam and we pushed rapidly on to the top of Guyot. The main reward was the right to say we had been there, for the whole top of the mountain was densely timbered and there was no lookout. Even climbing trees was little help. We searched for, but couldn't find, the trees on which Walter and the Bain boys had registered in 1916. While we were carving our names and the date on others, wisps of clouds began to drift through the timber and the mutter of thunder came up the ridges to the east. We had no craving to be caught in a thunderstorm on top, and hurried back to our packs.

My name, carved then on a tree, nearly caused that knob to be called for me later.

When the publicity began that ended in the creating of a National Park in the Smokies, some friends of mine in Knoxville made the long trek along the stateline to Guyot. Finding my registration on Balsam, which at the time had no title on the map, they began referring to it as the "Paul Fink Knob" to identify the spot. The appellation was already gaining some little use when I heard of it, and promptly took steps to squelch it.

As we regained the top of this knob we could hear another thunder shower coming up the Balsams. Things didn't look too comfortable, with storms approaching from two sides. Without a bit of delay we picked up our packs and left there, the quickest way down from the top. At the lowest point of the Gap we wasted no time hunting for a possible trail, but turned straight down the mountain side, knowing that before long we would strike some little stream that would lead to Big Creek and the logging railroad.

For at least three hundred feet the descent was as steep as anything we had negotiated on the whole trip. Often we had to lower ourselves by clinging to bushes, and at times had to slide a short distance. To add to our discomfort, the two rains we had heard met overhead, and in a trice soaked us to the skin, for there was no sign of a shelter.

Luckily the downpour lasted but a few minutes. Soon we found the upper end of an old skidway and followed it to the railroad, where Camp #12 of the Champion Lumber Co. had stood. Steel had been pulled on the road the fall before, fire had gotten into the slashings, and all the camp buildings and railway trestles had been burned. The old grade remained to lead us out, and we followed it for twenty miles to Crestmont, where the saw mills had stood. Our packs were stored at the depot and we were taken in for the night by T. M. Clapp, in charge of closing out the company's operations at Crestmont.

Grimy and trailworn as we were, shoes wrecked beyond repair, clothes half torn off by the clutching fingers of the brush and with two weeks growth of beard on our faces, Clapp and his wife treated us royally, and really made us feel at home. Plenty of hot water and a cake of soap apiece finally got us pre-

On the old grade on Big Creek

sentably clean. As we sat and talked on the porch, Mrs. Clapp stepped into the house and brought out a plate of home-made candy. It disappeared in a moment, and never did candy taste so delicious.

Whatever was on the table that night for supper was delicious to us, and how good a real bed felt, after more than ten days of sleeping on browse and even bare, wet ground.

June 19, 1919

Home by train and bus, via Newport and Greeneville, stopping for a shave, so the folks at home would recognize us. All a prosaic ending for the longest and hardest mountain trip I had yet taken.

Grub List

Bacon	3 lb.	Corn meal	3 lb.
Ham	3 lb.	Rice	1 lb. 8 oz.
Dried beef	8 oz.	Oatmeal	1 lb.
Bouillon cubes	4 oz.	Baking powder	8 oz.
Dehydrated soup	1 lb.	Dry beans	2 lb.
Canned cheese	1 lb.	Coffee	1 lb.
Crisco	1 lb. 8 oz	Cocoa	8 oz.
Powdered milk	1 lb.	Tea	4 oz.
Powdered eggs	1 lb.	Sugar	4 lb.
Flour	8 lb.	Raisins	2 lb.
Rockihominy	1 lb.	Salt, pepper, etc.	1 lb.
Evaporated fruits	2 lb.	Sweet chocolate	2 lb.
		Total	42 lb.

This list was calculated for two men for two weeks, and would have been right for that time. The substitution of one pound each, flour for rice and oatmeal, might have been of advantage, for those foods serve well in place of bread. We might have done with less Crisco. As it was, we forgot and left the whole can at the cabin at the Grassy Patch and didn't miss it. It would have been needed if we had gotten much game.

DATE: SEPTEMBER 5-7, 1919

DESTINATION: BIG FALLS OF CLARK CREEK

OBJECT: EXPLORATION.

PARTY: WALTER S. DIEHL, HENRY W. PATTON AND PAUL M. FINK.

For some years the Big Falls of Clark Creek had been almost an obsession with me. Friends living along the Creek and others who had visited them had told me of their great beauty and height, with guesses running all the way to five hundred feet. Getting to them was no simple matter, though, for they were at the very headwaters of the creek, on a tiny side branch. They were only eight or nine miles above a favorite picnic spot, the Sally Hole, (then the end of wheeled transportation), but these were long miles, hard ones, too. For a couple of miles above Devil Fork the going wasn't too bad, along a trail that followed the remains of an old tram road, built about 1890 when a portion of the timber was cut. Above that one had no choice but to follow the bed of the creek. Rough and rocky the whole way, it was laurel choked and often blocked with fallen timber. The sides of the ravine were too steep to go around, and one must climb over and push his way through. It was truly a primitive forest, full of enormous poplar and hemlock trees, where neither axe nor saw had ever been seen.

I'd made at least half a dozen attempts to reach the falls with different companions, but something always occurred to defeat the attempt. Twice Henry Patton had cut himself with the axe. Other times, rain or threatening rain stopped me or something else intervened. Truly the God of Bad Luck had been standing between me and the falls, 'til I'd begun fearing I'd never get to see them, and was thinking of them as the Falls of Doubt.

When Walter wrote he was coming down from Washington for a few days, Henry and I decided he might carry some good luck charm or "conjure bag" that could dispel the evil influence, and that by his guidance and under his care we might at long last pin down the elusive cataract. Always willing to give a sympathetic ear to anything like a trip into the woods, without an instant of hesitation he agreed to use his magic powers to lead us on a successful search for the falls.

September 5, 1919

A car—a novel approach to Clark Creek for us in those days—dropped us about a mile upstream from Chucky River, where we shouldered our packs and pushed on. An old house formerly stood at the Mill Hole, just below Sill Branch, and about the ruins were a dozen aged apple trees. The fruit wasn't choice by any means, but the opportunity was too good to be passed up, so we picked up about a peck and took them with us.

Squaring away for camp that night in the first clearing above Devil Fork (the clearing now—1958—has a fine stand of second growth timber) we felled an eight inch black or sweet birch for firewood. Sweet birch, incidentally, had few superiors as fuel. It burns slowly with plenty of heat, about as well green as dry, and gives off an aromatic smoke that imparts a delicious tang to any food broiled over it.

Henry was one of the best of camp cooks. He delighted in preparing dishes just a little differently from the way it was ordinarily done, and often served us foods we seldom otherwise saw in camp. This night he proposed making some of our apples into applesauce. All very well, but then came the problem of seasoning it. We never carried anything like spices. Sugar was all we had. After a bit of pondering over the question, he took a stick of birch from the wood pile and shaved a double handful of the spicy inner bark into the stewing apples. It did take a bit of straining to get all the slivers of bark out of the sauce, but the result was delicious.

One of the most delightful times on a camping trip comes in the evening, when all the chores are done and stomachs are amply filled, and congenial souls can stretch out on the ground around the camp fire and shoot the breeze to their hearts' content. So it was tonight, and it was a late hour indeed when we finally rolled into our blankets and ceased talking.

September 6, 1919

As we sat by the fire eating our breakfast an old friend, Jake Phillips, who lived at the Sally Hole, chanced by and stopped for a chat. As he admittedly made moonshine liquor at times, it may have been that he was operating a still in the neighborhood and was keeping an eye on us. One of us asked how long he aged his whiskey before selling it. His answer was that he sold it direct from the still. When we argued that we had always understood it should be aged at least two years before it was fit to drink he scoffed at the idea:

"Why, if a feller kep' hit fer two years, hit'd be so - - - - good he couldn't stand hit!"

Of far more immediate and positive value to us were the explicit directions Jake gave for locating the Big Falls. Following his directions, we found them without much trouble (save that of making our way up the creek) on the second prong above Chigger Branch. This little prong is very rough and steep. A few hundred yards along it brought us to the very foot of the falls, dropping down a great cliff on the side of the ridge.

Our guess as to their height was around three hundred feet, with the greatest sheer drop something less than a hundred. It was impossible to make anything like an accurate estimate, as there was no place from which we could look upon the whole thing. Even had we climbed around to the top and tried dropping a string over, the broken face of the rocks would have defeated us. Nor was it possible to get a picture worthwhile. We were much too close. Possibly we might have climbed high up on the opposite side of the canyon and looked squarely on them, but a single glance at that steep slope took the notion right out of our minds.

The weather had been dry for weeks, the main creek was very low, and only a bare trickle of water was coming over the falls. There were evidences about of high water, but that must have been after a storm. Even in damp weather there wasn't sufficient drainage area above to sustain more than a very modest volume of water over the falls. But the cliffs and all the other surrounding would justify the classical remark of Hodge Mathes: "All needed to make this one of the grandest cascades in America is water."

For anyone interested in visiting them, these are the directions: the Big Falls are some five or six miles above Devil Fork, on the second stream on the left above Chigger Branch. Both these branches are small and care must be taken not to over run them, particularly in times of low water. The Falls Branch drops over a four foot ledge as it enters the main stream.

Almost back to camp on our way down stream we are discussing one of the *essential* things that simply *must* happen if a trip up the Creek is to be perfect—someone must fall in while rock-hopping. No one had, and the trip seemed doomed to failure, even if we had found the falls. Then in the grand tradition, Henry saved us, with a magnificent splash. Essaying to walk alongside a smooth rock chute carrying the whole stream flow, his foot slipped and

At the foot of the Falls of Doubt

he landed in the chute in a sitting position. Down it he shot, propelled by the full force of the current, to drop up to his neck in the pool below. He had at last found the big falls of Clark's Creek.

Another big feed with more birch applesauce and another long bull-fest concluded a successful day.

September 7, 1919

Nothing to do this day but to go home, and we lay in our blankets late, having breakfast about midmorning. Jake Phillips came by again and stayed an hour, moving back down the creek as we went, heightening our suspicion that he was keeping an eye on us. At the Sally Hole, Walter and Henry took a dip, but the chilly water made a very hasty one.

On our way up the river we purchased an enormous watermelon, the biggest one we could find in the patch, and at a shady spot on the river bank went to work on it. One would never have thought it possible, but we left nothing of that melon but the thin green rind. Then we were too full to do more than lie on the sand for an hour or so. With the load of melon on board, how we did welcome a lift by a passing car to Taylor's Bridge, where Henry's father met us and brought us home.

DATE: JUNE 15-24, 1920

DESTINATION: BLACK MOUNTAINS.

OBJECT: EXPLORATION.

WEATHER: FAIR, RAIN, CLOUDY.

PARTY: WALTER S. DIEHL, PAUL M. FINK.

For several years past Walter and I had tramped and camped in the Great Smokies and visited Big Bald, Unaka, the Roan and others of the high mountains along the Tennessee-North Carolina state line. From many of these peaks we had looked to the eastward to the Black Mountains, with Mt. Mitchell, highest peak of the Mississippi, in their center. Neither of us had ever been closer to that lofty range, and now the urge was on us to see if the Blacks were as ruggedly beautiful, close up, as were the Smokies. Certain it was that they were far more widely known, more accessible and much more visited. Logging operations had been going on in full force on their slopes for many years.

Confident in our ignorance that we would find easy going, with many plain trails to follow, we planned an ambitious jaunt. Starting at Mt. Celo, northern most peak of the Blacks, we would traverse the whole length of that range to its junction with the Blue Ridge, and then along those mountains and the Great Craggies to Asheville. Normally it would not have been too strenuous a trip, but unforeseen trail conditions and unfavorable weather changed our plans en route.

June 15, 1920

The beginning, by rail from Johnson City, was spectacular, through the wild gorge above Erwin, cut deep in the Unaka Mountains by the Nolichucky River. The road bed of the CC&O Railway following the river—there was no other way for it to go—is blasted out of the rocky flank of the mountain, whose sides drop precipitously hundreds of feet to the water, tumbling and foaming along the boulders choking the river bed.

At the little station of Kona we left the CC&O, the rest of the rail trip to

The "Stemwinding" Locomotive of the Black Mountain R.R.

Murchison, at the foot of Mt. Mitchell, to be by the mixed train of the Black Mountain Railroad.

You never can tell what you will find at a country store. Driven by hunger pains, we walked over to see what this one had to offer in the way of canned food for a lunch. To our great surprise, at one end was an oilcloth-covered lunch counter, neat and clean. The sole items on the menu were chicken pot pie, apple pie and coffee. Either that or go hungry, so with considerable misgivings we ordered the lot.

Such a surprise we had! That chicken pot pie was as savory as any we had ever tasted, the portions large, and the apple pie delicious. Filled to the gills, we loafed on the station platform awaiting our train. Originally built to serve the Brown Brothers' lumbering operations, the Black Mountain Railway had not many miles of track, all in the Cane River gallery, with its other terminus at Eskota, a short distance beyond our destination, Murchison.

The motive power of the road was Shea type logging locomotives, with three steam cylinders mounted vertically on the right side of the boiler, instead of one horizontal cylinder on each side, as in ordinary locomotives. These drove a long shaft, lengthwise of the engine that in turn transmitted power to the drive wheels through gears. The arrangement was powerful enough to climb any kind of grade, but couldn't produce anything remotely resembling speed.

The charming little hotel at Murchison was operated by A. G. "Dolph" Wilson, whose father, "Big Tom" Wilson, in 1857 found the body of Prof. Elisha

Mitchell, after that explorer had fallen to his death on the side of the mountain that bears his name. Dolph, a small, soft-voiced man, was no mean bear hunter in his own right. Thus far he had bagged only 103 bears, but had high hopes of beating his father's score.

The food of the hotel, served country style, was plentiful and well prepared. Our appetites—and capacities—did full justice to it. So gorged we could hardly move, we lounged on the porch after supper, listening, entranced, to Dolph's stories of bear and deer hunting in the Black Mountains.

June 16, 1920

Dolph Wilson had told us of a beautiful spot, Ogles Meadow Knob, atop the high ridge on the western side of the Cane River Valley. From there we could get a fine broadside view of the whole Black Mountain, which we hoped to traverse in a few days. As a bit of hardening for the hard going ahead, we started afoot up a wagon road crossing the ridge close to the Knob.

On the way up we met a native, Byrd Wheeler by name, balsam peddler, herb doctor and quaint character in general, and sat down on a log by the side of the road for a chat.

Balsam gathering, one of his main sources of livelihood, is a time honored occupation in the mountains. Under the outer bark of the balsam fir are many small blisters, each containing from a few drops to a small teaspoonful of viscous, aromatic liquid. The equipment of the balsam gatherer is very simple—a small glass vial, a turkey quill open at both ends, and the keen point of his knife blade. A tiny hole is pricked in the bottom of a promising blister. The upper end of the quill, its open point in the neck of the bottle, is held close to this hole, and then the thumb of the operator bears down on the blister. A crystal clear fluid oozes out, to trickle down the quill into the bottle. It takes many a blister to yield an ounce of balsam, but the woodsman isn't pressed for time, and what he gathers is clear profit.

This woods product really does have some medicinal value, but to the mountain folk it is the universal panacea, prescribed for every ailment from cuts and bruises to kidney trouble, as well as for a general invigorator.

Wheeler had some unique ideas as to anatomy and physiology. By his account, the body had two pulses, "one of the heart and one of the stummick." People who died suddenly were frequently victims of "paralysis of the heart,"

Ogles Meadow Knob

Ogles Meadow Inn

etc. We would have listened to him long, but the top of the mountain was calling us.

A steep road, too rugged for cars, turned north at the gap, and led to the summit. All along the way was bordered with a dense growth of flame azalea, just at the height of its season, with masses of glowing blossoms in all hues from lemon yellow to deep scarlet. On top of the mountain were scattered clumps of purple rhododendron at the peak of its blooming season. Never before had we seen the two growing and blooming so close together.

The summit of Ogles Meadow Knob is a rolling, grassy bald, some hundred acres in extent, mostly open, the few scattered trees giving the aspect of a beautiful park. As often in the southern mountains, a free-flowing spring of icy water breaks out not far from the top.

Nestling in a small hollow on the northeast side of the bald was the Ogles Meadow Inn, a charming little chalet of nearly a dozen rooms. Its season was not yet open and no one was there, but the porch with its quaint rustic furniture, was so inviting we must go in and rest a few minutes. By the side of the front door was a neatly lettered, home-made sign—"No one allowed in the kitchen without permission. No sitting or wallowing on the beds in the daytime." Rather a peculiar legend, to say the least, and we speculated a while as to just what it really meant—and why.

Rested, we wandered across the grassy top to the "Well," where the side of the mountain dropped sharply a thousand feet from beneath our feet, like the half of a gigantic bowl. Precipitous though the sides of the abyss were, they were completely forest-clad, and there were few bare cliffs showing.

Here, perched on the rim of the Well, was an admirable spot to look over all the peaks of the Black Mountains, the Craggies and other high points, and we tried to familiarize ourselves with the contours of the mountains we were to visit. The atmosphere was far too hazy for photography, though with the glass we could pick up the tower on Mt. Mitchell.

Back to the hotel in Murchison in time for a romp on the lawn before supper with the three bright children of Dr. Justice of Marion, N.C. Gorged again, we sat on the front steps until a late hour listening to the soft voice of Dolph Wilson, with more of his inexhaustible store of bear stories.

June 17, 1920

A trail-tramper in those days needs be either an incurable optimist, or heedless of what hardships might be in store for him. Had we known what was ahead of us in the next two or three days we wouldn't have been so light-hearted as we shouldered our heavy packs and started for Mt. Celo. Dolph had told us we probably would find some pretty rough travelling, but at that he didn't know just how rough it really would be. He hadn't been along that route for a year or two.

We hadn't inquired the hotel rates and, thinking of the fine food and the quantities of it we had put away, were astonished when Dolph, in response to a request for our bill, said

"Well-I-I, I don't know. Would a dollar a day a piece be too much?"

We'd eaten more than that every meal.

Our way led first down Cane River to Pensacola, next up along the logging railway a mile up Cattail Creek, and then to the left toward a deep gap in the ridge running west from Grassy Knob. At first there were traces of a trail, but soon we lost it, no difficult matter at all when one recalls the dense brush choking the way. Striking for the top of the ridge by the shortest route, we followed for a time a steep, rocky ravine, full of bushes and down timber, a heart-breaking climb strongly reminiscent of the pull up from the West Prong of the Little Pigeon River to Newfound Gap, in the Smokies. The top of the ridge finally gained, it was easy going along a clear trail, through open woods and on an easy slope. Grassy Knob offered a tempting spot to camp, with plenty of good water close by, but it was too early in the day for us to think of stopping.

A short way beyond Grassy Knob we ran full tilt into the kind of travelling that was to be our portion the next two days, all the way to Deep Gap. Fortunately for our peace of mind, we were ignorant of that fact, and hoped it would last but a short while. A worse tangle to push through one could hardly imagine. Even a laurel slick could hardly surpass it in general cussedness.

Several years before, the northern part of the Black Mountains had been logged over. Fire was allowed to get out into the slash, and the tree laps were partially burned. In some places the flames had consumed even the balsam needles and duff of the forest floor from between the tree roots, to a depth of two or three feet. Drifted leaves now carpeted the ground and one, walking on seemingly safe footing, would without warning drop into a hole to his knees or deeper. Burdened with a pack, a sprained joint or a broken leg was a constant peril.

Following the conflagration, a dense growth of firecherry had sprung up everywhere, from pencil size to big as one's wrist. Mixed in were blackberry briars in generous amounts, all laced together with bamboo briars.

On this first day we were not yet hardened to our heavy packs, weighing, with full outfit and supplies for ten days, over fifty pounds apiece. We were already fatigued by the tough pull up the ravine as we plunged into this tangled, trailless wilderness, to fairly swim through it for a little distance. At the first breather-halt we were almost exhausted, and broached one of our packs in search of nourishment to help us on our way. Dried apples were the first thing we found and dried apples we immediately ate, too desperately in need of food to dig further into the packs. No authority on camping has ever recommended dried apples as an emergency ration, but on this occasion they did the job and gave the necessary energy to keep us going.

The hellish jungle continued until we were just under the top of Mt. Celo. It was just giving way to unburned balsam and spruce when threatening clouds started us looking anxiously for shelter. First a brisk thunder shower passed to the north of us, then one to the south. We were congratulating ourselves that we had escaped when a smart shower came down the middle and caught us.

Hastily we holed up between the spreading roots of leaning balsam trees, pulled a thatched roof of ferns over us, and for the moment escaped a wetting. Then, as we started on, the bushes did that little job even more efficiently than the shower would have. Nothing other than falling in the river will wet one more thoroughly than wading through waist high bushes after a rain. Experience has taught us that it is better to take it in the first place and save trouble. There's no escape.

It was now late in the afternoon and we began a hunt for firewood, water and a campsite. All were found at the head of a little ravine close up on the northeast side of the top of Mt. Celo. Following the rain, every crevice among the rocks was running full of water. Fuel is always damp in a spruce forest and the rain had made matter worse, but finally some wood was found, more or less dry. A fire was eventually coaxed to burn, and supper was under way.

As usual when we were getting our supplies together, Walter's father had cut one of his incomparable hams and given us a generous supply. The menu for the first night's meal was naturally to be centered about a pan of savory fried ham. Walter, in charge of the frying pan, decided some red ham and gravy was indicated, but he overlooked the fact that cooking over a stove and over an open fire called for different techniques. When he poured a cupfull of water into the pan, a sheet of lurid flame leaped twenty feet into the air. Startled, he threw the pan away, scattering the blazing grease and, but for the rain, almost set the top of the mountain on fire. After a second trial with the same result, he decided something was lacking in his method, and gave up experimenting. The ham alone, without the gravy, was delicious.

June 18, 1920

The climb up through the balsam forest to the top of Mt. Celo was just a little steep and rough, but in no wise difficult. As we neared the summit, the gloom under the trees grew deeper and wisps of cloud began to drift about us, a portent of the conditions that were to be our portion for the next few days.

Had the atmosphere been clear there was a great opportunity for a magnificent view out over the Toe River Valley and the eastern side of the Blacks, for a jutting ledge afforded an unobstructed outlook to the southward. But thick clouds of mist were all around us and we could see but a few yards in any direction. True, at one time they did seem to be rifting. Far beneath we could see dim outlines of open fields and woodland come into view, like the developing images on a photographic plate, but soon they faded out and the clouds closed around us again.

A fine open trail led to the south, and we patted ourselves on the back for the easy going ahead, after the rugged work of the previous day. It wasn't to last. In a few hundred yards we were back in burn and firecherry once more, not to win clear of it the rest of the day. All the way the clouds hung close around, blowing over from a solid bank of mist to the west and eddying in great wreaths of vapor on the eastern slope. Visibility was seldom more than a hundred yards. We had no chance to take compass sights on other peaks and travelled by dead reckoning, ignorant of our position save that we were on the main divide somewhere between Celo and Deep Gap.

Even if the cloud had not been around us there would have been little opportunity to see out. The firecherry grew far above our heads and the foliage so dense that even only twenty-five feet apart we would lose sight of one another. The holes where the forest duff had burned from between the roots of the spruce stumps were more and deeper than we had seen the day before. Several times each of us fell through this leafy covering up to his waist, suspended by his pack, caught on a root.

All day we pushed on as best we might, making a very slow time. Toward evening a deeper sag than usual on the ridge made us believe that we had reached Deep Gap. Our canteens were long since dry and we were beginning to "spit cotton." In search of water and a spot level enough to make camp we began dropping down through the tangle on the western side. Some four hundred feet below the crest we emerged from the cherry brush into a railroad grade. From its eroded condition it must have been abandoned several years.

A tiny stream tumbled down the bank, trickled across the roadbed and disappeared again down the slope. It was a poor enough spot, as campsites go, but we weren't choosy, too nearly exhausted from the strenuous going of the day. A quick, rather sketchy supper, and we bedded down on a tiny, sloping patch of grass. It was no Ostermoor, but tired as we were, we needed no rocking to put us to sleep. We didn't even trouble to put up the little Compac tent. When a drizzle began falling on our faces in the night we wakened just enough to crawl into it as a sort of glorified double sleeping bag, and went right back to sleep.

The total mileage for the day had been between three and four miles, a distance we could cover in an hour on a good trail, but we were in agreement that it was one of the hardest, most arduous day's travel we had ever done. There was not too much climbing along the route, and before the country was logged it should have been easy to have walked from Celo to Mt. Mitchell in a short day. Now our advice would have been to keep away from that section.

Beating one's way through was a terrific struggle, with nothing to see to reward one for the hard labor.

June 19, 1920

A succession of showers blew over during the night, and just before dawn we slid deeper into the protection of the Compac, and even then didn't entirely escape a little wetting. Our packs had been snugly tucked away under a stump and were not even damp.

The arduous travelling of the day before brought a decision to look around a bit before pushing on. The packs were safely cached under a ledge and we started along the railroad grade, searching for an easier way back up to the divide and to avoid the firecherry in so doing. Rounding the point of a ridge we saw ahead of us the real Deep Gap, much lower than the one we had mistaken for it the night before. Sure now that we knew just where we were, we regained the packs and started on our way.

The railway had run very nearly into the gap, and a short climb of a hundred

Cane River Valley

and fifty feet put us there. The trail south from it was often steep and rough and in some places overgrown with bushes, but in no place was the traveling anything like as strenuous as on the day before.

The clouds persisted, right down on us, and twice brisk showers made us hole up in the shelter of overhanging rocks. The mist still made compass bearings impossible and for most of the day, until we reached the boundary of the Mt. Mitchell State Park, we remained ignorant of our exact position. From this point on there was an excellent, well kept trail all the way to Mt. Mitchell. We felt as if we were riding a gravy train.

On the northern side of the Black Brothers was an excellent outlook over the valley of the Cane River. For the first time in a couple of days the clouds lifted for a brief few minutes. Wanting some pictures, I set my Kodak up on its tripod. The light proved too poor for very successful photography, and I turned my back on the scene long enough to slip the camera back in its case. Facing about, I was startled and almost frightened. Before me was not the view across deep valleys to high mountains, but simply nothing.

In those few seconds the clouds had closed in again and everything had disappeared in a moment, just as though a curtain had been dropped between. Many times had I seen the clouds gather and hide a scene from view, but never before had it happened so abruptly, with so little warning.

We had been expecting to find the forest ranger at his cabin on Mt. Mitchell and were disappointed to learn that he was away for a day or so. We did find J. M. Carpenter, a school teacher from Booneville, Miss., spending his summer

The ranger's cabin

vacation in a tent on the mountain. He showed us the spring where we were allowed to cut firewood, and best of all, told us that travelers were allowed to sleep on the hay in one room of the cabin.

This pole cabin, with breezeway between, had been built close in front of the shelving cliff that had sheltered generations of visitors to and campers on the mountain. The face of the rock was blackened by the smoke of a thousand campfires.

Scattered about on the ground was evidence that some misguided camper had attempted to cook a "mess" of soupbeans, unaware that high altitude so lowers the boiling point of water that it is impossible to cook dried beans at this altitude, 6,700 feet above the sea. If he didn't know it before he learned soon, for the half-cooked beans, still hard as bullets, were lying all about.

Our evening fire was started close to the same rock used by so many before us. Supper preparations were well under way when a driving rain blew up, to make culinary operations anything but pleasant. In a trice we were wet through and shivering, for the temperature was in the forties. We had other troubles, too. As each dash of rain struck the hot grease in the frying pan, a blaze flared up, and we very nearly set this mountain on fire too, just as we had done at Celo.

Fortunately there was a partial change of dry clothing in our pack, and we weren't forced to sleep in wet garments. Our single blankets, even with the tent spread over us, weren't enough to keep us warm. We burrowed deep into the loose hay on the floor, and shivered and shook the greater part of the night,

The tower on top

listening to the rain pattering on the roof and the feet of patrolling woodmice pattering on the floor.

June 20, 1920

When we awoke our old friend the dense cloud was close wrapped around the mountain top and the rain was still falling, conditions that were to persist the whole day long, and keep us housed up in the cabin. We did not leave its shelter at all except for firewood and water and for one futile trip to the lookout tower on top, a couple of hundred yards away. We thanked our lucky stars the rain had not begun two days before, when we were entangled in the briars and firecherry near Mt. Celo, with no place for refuge by day and only the little tent to shelter us at night.

In pity, Mr. Carpenter unlocked the ranger's side of the cabin. Now we had the use of the stove for cooking, for warmth and, much more needed, a thorough drying-out of our clothes and bedding. He joined us in a hearty meal at noon. Afterwards we drew up chairs around the cheery stove and proceeded to get acquainted.

Toward night the ranger, D. L. Moser, and his sons, Dave and "Slim," came up from their home at Swannanoa and seemed both surprised and pleased to find visitors enjoying his hospitality in his absence. An excellent example of the highest type of native mountaineer, he proved a most interesting and entertaining host, devoted to his task of caring for the Mt. Mitchell State Park.

At nightfall the rain, after dripping intermittently all day, began falling harder than ever. We crawled back into our nests in the hay, now dry and warm, with forebodings that the weather on the morrow would be little changed from what we had been having.

June 21, 1920

To our great surprise and greater delight, the sun was brilliant and the clouds had vanished. There was all the promise of a glorious day. Such an opportunity was not to be lost, and we hastened to hang our blankets, spare clothing and the tent out in the sun. So damp had our entire outfit gotten in the heavy showers and high humidity that not even the heat of the stove was sufficient to drive out all the moisture.

Several years before, the Perley & Crockett Lumber Co., logging the slopes of Mt. Mitchell, had built a wooden tower on the very summit of the mountain, just beside the mound of rough stones marking the grave of Dr. Elisha Mitchell, who in 1843 proved this the highest peak in the East, and who came to a tragic death on its slopes.

Our first view from the tower was somewhat of a disappointment. Though the sun was bright, there was enough haze in the atmosphere to soften the outlines and partially obscure the form of the far mountains. At that, we could see plainly enough to get an idea of how grand a view it would be on a clear day, when every ridge and valley would be in full detail. One could gaze in every direction, unobstructed, to the far horizon.

The night before we had discussed our plans with Mr. Moser. He advised that we not attempt to follow the top of the divide all the way to Balsam Gap, for the travelling would be long and rough, and not in any way rewarding. Instead, he suggested that we go to the next gap to the south, and from thence

Walter takes the sun

follow the railroad to Balsam Gap, a somewhat shorter and much easier route. We finally decided to leave our packs at the cabin and travel light to Clingmans Peak and Potato Knob. Then the next day we would go on toward our original destination, following for quite a distance the highest level of the railroad.

Though the summit of Clingmans Peak was only a few feet lower than Mt. Mitchell, there was no good lookout point, the haze was thickening and there was little of interest to repay us for the trip. Tendrils of mist were beginning to drift among the trees, and we hurriedly returned to our base. Well enough for us that we did, for we reached the cabin barely in time to gather in our blankets and tent before one of the daily rains wet them down once more.

During our absence a young man from West Virginia had climbed to the top, via the logging railroad and the half mile of trail up from the camp. How he managed to stay safely on the trail that long was a mystery; he was about the greenest tenderfoot we had ever encountered. He sat around the cabin only half an hour before starting back, but his ignorance of the mountains and the

The northern end of the range

Toward the Blue Ridge

outdoors in general gave us much amusement. He voiced a wish to see Prof. Mitchell's grave, at the very top of the mountain and marked by a big cairn of rocks, with breast-high head and foot stones at the ends. We gave him directions, but back he came, unable to locate it until one of us led him up again. As Slim Moser remarked,

"The blamed fool climbed all over that pile of rocks looking for the grave."

As we all sat talking in the cabin, the youngster stared fixedly out the window a few moments, then jumped excitedly to his feet, shouting

"There's a bear out there!"

"Where," asked Moser, reaching for his rifle, standing in the corner.

"Right there! See, in the trail! At the edge of the trees!"

"Oh, heck, that's no bear. It's a groundhog." Moser, disgusted, set his gun back in its place.

"A groundhog? So that's a groundhog? Well, I declare. It's the biggest one I ever saw."

Privately we came to the conclusion that it was also the only one he had ever seen.

Shortly after the visitor departed the rain started again, continuing most of the afternoon, while we all lounged around the stove and swapped yarns.

One of the interesting things Moser told us was the important role firecherry played in Nature's reforestation program. The seeds, in their hard, woody shells can remain dormant but viable for a very long period, even more than fifty years, not germinating until exposed to the sun's heat. Carried by the birds, they lie embedded in the forest floor under the cool, moist shade of the spruce and balsam, waiting patiently a change in conditions.

After the area has been denuded of its timber by the logger or by fire, the sunlight reaches the earth. Under its heat the firecherry springs into life at once, growing thickly, giving a dense shade during the summer months.

Spruce seeds, on the contrary, will not germinate except in a moist, shaded situation. Blown from seed trees left standing, they find the conditions under the close-growing, sheltering cherry to their liking, and a seedling soon appears. By the time the conifers are old and sturdy enough to stand on their own and do not need protective cover, the cherry, a short-lived tree, dies. The spruce forest is once more in complete possession of the area. All this may take more than one man's lifetime, but that is a very short period in a forest cycle.

During a short interim between showers I strolled up to the tower for a look at the weather. The cloud had the whole mountain fogged in, but to my surprise it extended not fifty feet above my head. Through an occasional rift I could see the bright blue sky, with big cumulus clouds drifting high above.

Me

June 22, 1920

Talking things over before we had gone to sleep, our plans had undergone a drastic change. The days spent rain-bound had consumed so much time that there was little left. It would now be virtually impossible for us to complete the trip as originally planned, even if trail conditions from here on should prove ideal. All indications were to the contrary—that we would have continued bad weather, with some rough terrain along the way, particularly in the vicinity of the Great Craggies. Pondering over all this, we decided to loaf another day where we were, then descend by the Blue Sea Falls to Eskota and Murchison, and go back home by rail.

To our great surprise and joy, the morning dawned with a clear sky. Very early the mists began to rise out of the valleys below, presaging by far the clearest day of the trip. A few hours later this proved correct.

During the morning Mr. Carpenter and I strolled down the trail to the commissary of the Perley & Crockett Lumber Co., half a mile below on the west side of the mountain, where he had been securing his supplies. On our way back we passed the cookhouse, where Mrs. Brink, the lady in charge, took pity on us and most kindly gave us a couple of luscious blackberry pies, a gift accepted with alacrity. How good those pies did taste, and how much they added to our dinner.

The ranger and his boys were off in the vicinity of the Black Brothers, taking advantage of the general dampness to burn some brush in safety. Using his stove, Walter and I cooked up a real man-sized meal, and invited Carpenter to join us. He proved no mean trencherman and played his part nobly, but was by no means capable of competing with two such appetites and capacities as ours. Outclassed, he stopped early, to sit at one side and watch us eat, with a look of mingled envy and admiration on his face. I'll admit that our performance should have been enough to fill any stranger with a sense of awe.

The vista from the tower that afternoon was glorious, fully repaying us for staying on the mountain top another day. In every direction we could see on and on into the distance, until some far away range of mountains blocked the vision or else the lowlands merged into the horizon. Every peak of the Black and Great Craggy Mountains was clear and seemed close at hand. Table Rock and Hawksbill, rimming the gorge of Linville River, were prominent landmarks on the eastern skyline. Plain to view were Grandfather, Beech, Roan, Unaka, Big Bald, Flattop, Big Butte, Ogles Meadow Knob and a thousand

Sunset on the peak

lesser known peaks. Dimly on the horizon to the northeast was Whitetop, close to the point where Virginia, North Carolina and Tennessee meet.

To the southeast and seeming at our feet lay the town of Marion and the Catawba River, its winding course showing like a chain of blue lakes. Away to the west a band of dense haze cut the Great Smokies from our vision, though at times we fancied we could detect the faint outlines of Guyot and Le Conte.

The air was cold and the wind so cutting that for most of the hours spent in the tower we crouched in the shelter of the railing to protect us from the penetrating chill. The sunsets on the peak are famous for their gorgeous beauty. We had high hopes of seeing one worthwhile, but this treat was not for us that day. As the sun dropped low there were no clouds other than the haze bank on the horizon, and the sky showed little vivid coloring. From our high perch we did have the experience of watching the shadows of the mountains creep slowly across the ridges and valleys to the east, marking the end of day there, while we were yet in the full light of the sun.

That night the sky was cloudless and the air cold and clear as glass. Every star was out and a small crescent moon hung low in the west. Mr. Carpenter had a small astronomical telescope and, well wrapped in our blankets against the chill, sometime was spent in star gazing and speculating on the wonders of the night sky. With our binoculars we could pick out the street lights of Marion. Once we even caught a glimpse of the headlight of a CC&O train as it slowly passed between tunnels at the top of the Blue Ridge near Altapass.

Blue Sea Falls

June 23, 1920

After favoring us with one single day of sunshine and clear atmosphere, the weather reverted to type. Soon after daylight we had another smart shower, bringing a fear we would have to spend yet another damp day on the mountain. Fortunately it was of but brief duration. By nine o'clock the sun was shining again. We hurriedly packed and an hour before noon we started down the mountain. At the lumber camp we struck a trail down Wilsons Ridge and then following a little stream joining the Blue Sea Fork just below the falls. Part of the way was through firecherry, part across a section recently burned over—all of it rough going. Clouds again wrapped the high peaks, and a few slight sprinkles of rain caught us.

Before the timber was cut from the slopes of Mt. Mitchell, the Blue Sea Falls must have been beautiful. Now the volume of water in the stream had dwindled away to a large extent, and both the brink of the falls and the deep pool at the foot were choked with refuse washed down from the timber cuttings above. Just another illustration of how ruthless logging mars the natural beauty of a country.

The end of steel was just below the falls, and a loaded log train stood ready to pull out, so we snatched just time enough for a hurried glimpse and to snap a single picture. When the choice lay between getting a good picture, then carrying our loads several miles, or of slighting the picture and riding, there was no delay. We rode.

At Murchison we stopped again with Dolph Wilson and, our appetites heightened by living on our own cooking for a week, we found his table more enticing than before. At "a dollar a day apiece," he lost plenty on us.

June 24, 1920

The Limited Express of the Black Mountain Railway (limited particularly as to speed) took over five hours to make the twenty-one miles between Murchison and Kona. On the steeper grades it barely crawled along the track. More than once we stepped off and leisurely strolled along beside the cars, keeping pace without effort. To amuse ourselves and pass away the time, we gathered small boulders from the roadbed and piled them on the steps of the coach, until the conductor made us unload them. Probably he thought the extra tonnage of free freight would stop the train entirely. At Kona we parked our packs, much lighter than they were before, and started in search of another chicken pot pie like the one we found going in. We found it, equally as good, and we did it justice.

The evening train to Jonesboro had gone when we reached Johnson City, and I had to phone home for my car. While waiting for it, and as a safety measure, we sneaked around the back streets to a barber shop and had a two weeks growth of whiskers removed, lest our families fail to recognize us.

DATE: JUNE 2-12, 1921

DESTINATION: LE CONTE AND VICINITY.

OBJECT: DETERMINING HEIGHT OF LE CONTE.

WEATHER: CLOUDY, WITH SHOWERS.

PARTY: WALTER S. DIEHL, FRANK BAIN, DAVID BAIN, PAUL M. FINK.

When this trip was made, there were no good maps of the Smoky Mountains. All that existed were the U.S. Geological Survey topographic sheets, based on surveys made around 1900. These were admittedly merely reconnaissance maps, fair enough in a general way, but in details so far from accurate that as a guide for exploration on the ground, they were only good enough to get lost by. For *that* they were highly efficient, as we found to our sorrow more than once.

No precise elevations were shown for the peaks of the Smokies. The altitude of Le Conte was merely indicated to be above 6600 feet. We had formed an idea it was more than that. In the summer of 1920 Walter and I had spent a week among the Black Mountains, whose loftiest point, Mt. Mitchell, registered 6711 feet above the sea, considered the highest mountain in the East. We knew Le Conte *appeared* higher than that, and the urge to prove it was upon us. To run a line of levels was out of the question for us. We hadn't the time available, and if we had, Walter was the only one with the engineering skill to do the job. Triangulation offered a great chance for error, for not within many miles was there a known elevation, from which to take a sight on Le Conte. The ever present haze was an obstacle, too.

This left barometric observation the only means available to us. This, too, we knew was susceptible of mistake, for with the changing atmospheric pressure the top of a mountain could at times seem to rise and fall like the waves of a stormy sea. We believed that a series of readings, made over several days and checked against the barograph records at the Knoxville and Asheville weather stations (about equally distant from and on opposite sides of Le Conte) would give an average figure close enough to settle the question. To guard further against error, we decided to use two aneroid barometers, and had them and our thermometer calibrated by the U.S. Bureau of Standards in Washington.

Frank Bain, friend, schoolmate, and trailmate of Walter's shared our belief, and he was invited to be a member of the party.

Walter and I assembled our outfit and supplies at Jonesboro. On the trip we were to make the first real test of our new lightweight tent, as designed by Walter and fabricated by me. The material was a lightweight but very strong balloon silk that Walter had salvaged from the remains of the first experimental balloon to use helium as an inflatant. In its design the tent combined many of the good features of both the Baker and the Forester models. Six feet high at the rope ridge, with a six foot wide front tapering to a four foot rear and a triangular roof, its floor space easily took care of three men and their duffle. A six by six front awning gave ample room to stir about and in case of rain a small cooking fire could be built under its shelter. Complete, with braided linen ridge rope and guy lines, it weighed a little less than five pounds.

June 2, 1921

Walter and I boarded the train at Jonesboro, to meet Frank, coming direct from Washington. En route to Knoxville, the last details of our plans were completed. Arriving there, the observer in charge of the Weather Bureau office was very cooperative, promising to supply us with a copy of his barograph record for the days we were to be in the mountains. Our instruments were checked against his for any possible variation.

Then on to Fountain City, to the hospitable roof of "Doc" S. H. Essary, of the Agriculture Department of the University of Tennessee. It had been our hope that "Doc," a Smoky devotee and a trailmate of both Walter and Frank, could make this trip with us. To our great and mutual disappointment, professional engagements prevented his coming.

Here, to the accompaniment of "Doc's" pithy comments, the loads were apportioned and the packs made up. Frank, who had lost a shoulder blade during the war, and consequently could not use shoulder straps, was allotted the lighter, bulkier articles, the tent, blankets, etc., to be carried with a tumpline. His load weighed about thirty-five pounds. Walter's and mine were about fifty-five pounds each, stowed in navy sea bags and carried by combination shoulder straps and tumplines of our own devising and manufacture. These were quite similar, differing only in a few minor details.

Experience had shown us that loads of more than forty pounds, carried with shoulder straps alone, quickly grew wearisome and the straps painfully cutting. A trumpline lets the weight of the pack rest mainly on the hips, supported by long thongs from the ends of a broad leather band over the top of the head. By it one can carry a surprising load, but the packer must plod along slightly stooped, his head down, seeing little but the trail at his feet. Let him straighten his back and lift his head to look at the scenery, and his pack drops to the ground behind him. We had found that combining the two was far more satisfactory than either alone.

June 3, 1921

The start was not too auspicious, for me at any rate. Unslinging my pack in the railway station, an unguarded corner of my axe, strapped to the back of my pack, gave a nasty cut to my little finger, so deep it had to be closely bandaged the whole trip. Fortunately, no infection or other complication set up.

Elkmont, reached by rail over the K&A Railroad to Walland and the logging road of the Little River Lumber Company via Tuckaleechee Cove, Townsend and the gorge of the Little River, was then the only convenient point of entry on the northeast side of the Smokies. Only a few minutes were spent here. Packs on backs, we started our trek, along the old Forestry trail crossing Sugarland Mountain at the Huskey Gap. Here, as we topped out on the ridge, we caught our first glimpse of the massive mountain whose height we proposed to determine. Its bulk filled all the landscape to the east, and its northern slopes swept so boldly upward from the low valleys at its base that there was small wonder we had come to believe it the highest of all.

For nearly a thousand feet the trail dropped to the old road beside the West Prong of the Little Pigeon River. Road it was in name only. In a few miles it ceased to be negotiable even by a jolt wagon, and degenerated into a rock strewn path along which a horse, with care, might pick his way. Slowly, with many a pause to "blow," we followed it past the Chimney Tops to Fort Harry Ford. Our heavy packs were galling to tender shoulders, and we gladly stopped at the rude pole cabin that hunters had built since Walter and I had passed that way two years before. Its dirt floor wasn't too inviting, so as no rain was threatening we made our beds outside.

One great pest of the mountains is the tiny black gnats, the "punkies or no-seeums" that breed in countless legions by the margins of the streams and in marshy places. Bad enough in daytime, at dusk they swarm out by the millions, covering every exposed inch of skin, hands, wrists, faces, necks and even

Fort Harry Ford

into the short hair of the temples and back of the head. The bite of a single gnat is not noticeable, but the visitation of an army of them will leave one's skin spotted with minute red dots and an intolerable itching.

Here at Fort Harry was the greatest concentration of hungry punkies we had ever seen. No doubt they had been on meager rations for a time, and now all came out to feast on our tender lowland skins. Only by dint of liberal applications of fly dope, pipe smoke and a smudge of damp, rotten wood on the campfire did we drive away enough that we could tolerate the remainder.

Camp in Bear Pen Hollow

June 4, 1921

Climbing Le Conte under heavy pack was going to be a strenuous job, and we thought best to do a little hardening before tackling it. Bear Pen Hollow, where the real climb up the mountain would begin, was only a couple of miles farther on. We planned to set up camp there and spend two or three days fishing and exploring in the vicinity.

As we moved leisurely up the trail, we remarked about how civilization seemed to be encroaching on the wilderness. Two years before, the ranger's cabin at the Grassy Patch had been the only structure above Cole's home, the last permanent habitation, standing a little below the present (1957) Chimneys Camp Ground. Now there were three more cabins, at Fort Harry Ford, Le Conte Crossing and at Bear Pen Hollow. All were too rudely built to have been intended as homes, merely pole cabins with little, if any, chinking between the logs, and probably only shelters for hunters, herders or "possession cabins" for lumber companies. Whatever their reason, their very presence was evidence of more invasion of the back country.

Here in Bear Pen Hollow—so called from a log bear-trap or pen built here years before—our new tent was christened, the first time either Frank or Walter had seen it. They professed themselves well pleased with its appearance. A thick bed of hemlock browse was cut and laid in it, a stone fireplace built just in front of the awning, firewood chopped and piled under shelter, and we set for whatever might come. It might rain as it would, and our woods housekeeping chores could be carried on in the dry.

Speckled trout, not large but fine in the frying pan, were in every pool, and riffle in the stream, and we set out to get a big mess for supper. The fish outsmarted us though. The water, as usual, was clear as glass. Trout could be seen everywhere, but they were having none of what we had to offer-flies, worms, grubs or "stickbait." When we finally called it a day and checked strings, a total of five was all we could show, less than a meal for even one hungry fisherman.

In our absence, Frank's younger brother David had come over from the family cabin at Elkmont, to be with us for the rest of the trip. Our tent had been designed for three only, but by lowering the ridge a little and spreading out the bottoms of the side walls, it easily accommodated one more.

June 5, 1921

On previous trips Walter and I had gotten to know well Davis Bracken, whose home was next to the last house on the river. He had charge of the cabin at the Grassy Patch, where we had stayed in 1919, when en route to the eastern end of the Smoky Range. In the meantime we had been told he had moved away after some trouble with the Newman boys, and so we had stopped to visit with him as we passed his home. Now, as we were straightening up camp after breakfast, he came walking up the trail with a surveyor of the Champion Lumber Company, owners of some forty thousand acres of choice timberland on the northeast slopes of the Smokies. All of us sat down for half an hour's chat.

Walter still had the urge to fish, and went on up the stream with them, heading for the Walker Camp Branch, the right-hand stream at the Grassy Patch, along which the present highway has been built. Frank, David and I followed a little later, bound for the Alum Cave and the Arch Rock, with a little fishing on the side.

Reaching the Alum Cave then was a very different thing from today. No smooth, graded, well-signed trail—no gentle climb. For half a mile or so one rock-hopped up the creek, then turned into a dim trail that clung close to the creek a little while, to plunge abruptly into the laurel and up the side of a steep ridge, where the way to go—no footway—was only vaguely marked, if at all. Up it we went, walking some, clambering and crawling more, hauling ourselves up by friendly bushes and saplings, to reach finally the Cave, some fifteen hundred feet above the bed of the creek.

The Chimney Tops, from Bear Pen Hollow

Properly speaking, this is not a cave, but a great ledge hanging more than a hundred feet above our heads. Beneath its shelter, a hundred yards long and fifty feet deep, where the driven rain could never penetrate, the dust was ankle deep, rising in puffs from beneath our feet. The bare rock is strongly impregnated with the alum that gives its name to the spot. Leached out by ground water along the seams of the rocks were handsful of alum crystals. A little search found the spot where Walter and I had registered on a previous trip in 1916.

Slipping and sliding swiftly back down to the stream, we fished on up toward the Arch Rock, another of the freaks of Nature scattered throughout the Smokies.

Here one of the rocky ribs of the mountain, dipping sharply down to the creek, has a hole completely through it, twenty feet high at its lower end and barely high enough to stand erect at its upper opening. This is very plainly not the result of erosion by running water, for the surfaces are not smooth, but jagged and broken. Probably at some time the strata of the slate rock have been shattered by internal stresses, with ground water and frost completing the job. So deep in the recesses of the mountains was this feature hidden that probably not one person a year visited it, and many of the natives had never so much as heard of it. Frank had been coming into the Smokies for years longer than I, but it was his first visit to either the Arch Rock or the Alum Cave.

At the Grassy Patch we sat down for another chat with the Champion Fiber

Company's surveyor. From him we learned the details of our friend Davis Bracken's troubles with the Newmans.

A still operated by one of the Newmans had been raided by the "revenoo'ers" and the owner accused Bracken of having "Turned him up." Threats were voiced, and on one occasion Newman had lain out in the laurels all night, waiting a chance to bush-whack the old man. Bracken was by nature a peaceable person, inclined to avoid trouble when possible, but amply able to take care of himself if need be.

Finally Newman, intoxicated, stopped in front of Bracken's home, cursing and threatening him. Coming inside the yard, he drew his gun and fired at Bracken, standing on the porch above him, the bullet passing under Bracken's upraised arm, cutting his shirt but not touching the skin. Convinced things had gone far enough Bracken stepped back inside the open door, picked up his own pistol and killed Newman as he was climbing the porch steps.

It was so patently a case of self defense that at the trial Bracken came clear. Fearing the effect on his family of further trouble with the Newmans and their relatives, he rented his home in the Sugarlands and moved to the lowlands near Cleveland. Before many months the longing for the high hills, fresh air and sparkling mountain water was more than he could resist, and he came back to his old home and his old job as timber cruiser.

The surveyor told us further of the plans of the Champion people for logging their vast timber holdings. Surveys had already been made for a railroad over the mountain through Indian Gap, and work on it was scheduled to begin in two or three years.

Walter was waiting at camp with some twenty trout, more than Frank and I together could boast. The day we had arrived Frank had rummaged around the old cabin nearby and unearthed an old dutch oven. With the utensil available, no one had any craving for fried flapjacks. Frank was a superb camp cook, and the bread his culinary skill produced in that dutch oven was as fine as any stove could bake—and better than most. Pone cornbread, fried trout, rice, stewed fruit and coffee made a banquet more tasty than any hotel could have offered. David's conscience wouldn't allow him to eat fish caught on Sunday, but none of the others had any qualms along that line. If we had, normally hearty appetites heightened by the day's exercise overcame them.

The higher Top, edge-on

June 6, 1921

The Chimney Tops, pointing to the sky across the river from our camp, were calling to us. Walter had climbed them before, but the others had not. The previous evening Buford Cole, a teenage lad living at the last house, had chanced by. He told of a new and shorter (and steeper) route to the top of the Chimneys, and agreed to guide us. As soon as he arrived we set out.

Up the old wagon road along the Road Prong we went to the Lower Beech Flats, next following the stream bed and a steep, rocky ravine for a quarter of a mile. *Then* the real climb began. The scramble up the mountain side to the Alum Cave wasn't even a breather for this. Dragging ourselves up by main strength, hanging on by fingernails and eyebrows, clawing for toe-holds in the slippery earth, we painfully struggled upwards for hundreds of feet, to emerge

One Top, from the other

breathless on the crest of the knife-edge ridge connecting the Tops with the main divide of Sugarland Mountain.

Familiar now to millions of tourists as one of the spectacular features along the highway crossing the Smokies, the Chimney Tops, generally spoken of now-a-days as simply the Chimneys, are two acute points on an exceedingly sharp ridge. As one inches his way along the crest, flanked by a sheer drop of a hundred feet on either side, it might be likened to a great ledge sitting on edge, were it not that the bedding planes of the rock, a slate formation, are horizontal. For its last seventy-five feet the average thickness of the first and highest top surely does not exceed thirty feet. Save where the bare rock is sheer, it is mantled with dense laurel and sand myrtle, rooted in every crevice in the rocks. Opening at its highest point is the mouth of a chimney, turning to the outside some twenty feet below. Up it a cool current of air continually blows. Right here the apex of the ridge is broader than its thickness some feet below.

The Chimney Tops are a rare vantage point to get a view of the broad top of Le Conte. Today we were disappointed, for the summit of the mountains was wrapped in mist, a cloud whose trailing tendrils were just above our heads. Haze at the lower levels allowed only dim vistas down the valley. Distant photography was entirely out of the question.

Returning, we chanced upon a clump of ramps, a lily-leaved cousin of the onion, high in favor with the hill folk. Some onions may possess more fire and tear-evoking pungency, but none of the tribe has the potent and permanent aroma of the ramp, that not only flavors the breath, but permeates the whole body for days. They were plentiful, and we dug about a quart of the small bulbs, carried them back to camp and stewed them for supper. Wise judgment prompted the use of a tin can rather than one of the pots of the cook kit, for so redolent with the rank flavor was it that it had to be thrown away in the morning. Frank, Walter and I were more than satisfied with a mere taste. The boys, Buford in particular, cleaned up the rest, to their later sorrow.

The tent stretched out a little more to shelter five reasonably well. The boys, sleeping under the fly kept dry in a smart shower, though a wind-driven rain might have dampened them.

June 7, 1921

Buford's over-indulgence in ramps had made a sick boy of him, the strongest symptom a complete lack of appetite. Normally he would eat more than any two of us. As we broke camp we left him sitting on a log, waiting to get up enough energy to make the three mile walk home.

Time had come for us to get to the top of Le Conte for our barometric observations, the main objective of the trip. It was to be a hard pull to the top, we knew, but by now we were a little more hardened than we were when we left our several office jobs a week before. The packs too, had been lightened some by our appetites.

The trail, such as it was, showed a little more signs of travel than when Walter and I had travelled it five years before. The first five hundred feet was relatively easy, but the next thousand, the headwall of the ravine, was much worse, often greater than thirty degrees. We stopped to blow many times before attaining the top of the ridge.

Previously we had followed this ridge, by way of Sharp Top (now Balsam Point) and on to the top. This time Davis Bracken had given us fool proof instructions on how to find the much easier Tag Tree trail, whose junction with the older route was marked by a six inch balsam tree, with a score of tin tobacco tags stuck into its bark.

Legs were growing weary and packstraps were cutting painfully into our shoulders, and anything offering shorter distance and less climbing had a strong appeal. The rest of the way, by the Tag Tree trail, was through heavy brush and over rocky ledges but on an easy grade, dimly marked but readily

Le Conte's Cliff Top

followed, circling under the Sharp Top. We emerged into an open balsam forest on the north side, a few feet below the Cliff Top.

Trailing wisps of clouds were drifting through the trees, and it seemed the better part of wisdom to rig a snug shelter before going up for a lookout. Walter's well-known faculty for finding water was put to work, while Frank and I set about pitching the tent. As we finished pegging it down he returned, with news of a seep, tiny but sufficient for our needs, at the base of the ledges not far away. He and I rustled firewood and browse for beds, while Frank broke out the groceries and busied himself with the pots and pans. All finished together and sat down to a hearty meal, to discover that the heartbreaking pull up the mountain had in no wise ruined our appetites.

By five o'clock we were out on top, to find the clouds lifted and the atmosphere fairly clear, though the light was too poor for photography. It was over-late for much further exploration, and we contented ourselves with looking about, and with taking our first barometer readings. We were a little puzzled when our instruments that in Knoxville had registered the same, here showed a variation of about .3 inch. That was all cleared up when we checked with our calibration charts at home. Now it worried us, fearing that one instrument or the other had been injured by some fall or jar.

There is no better spot for viewing the central sector of the Smokies than from the Cliff Top of Le Conte, looking across the great gulf of Huggins Hell

Our home on top

and the headwaters of the Little Pigeon River, two thirds of a vertical mile below our perch on the cliffs. It is a land of high, sharp ridges and deep, narrow valleys, and must be seen from some such grandstand seat for its ruggedness to be fully grasped.

We were well tired that night and spent little time in the usual evening sport about the camp fire—spinning yarns. With crisp mountain air—around 50 degrees—tired muscles and a well-filled stomach, a deep, springy bed of aromatic balsam browse beats any Ostermoor mattress. In a matter of minutes we were beyond being bothered by any vagrant bear, hoot owl or other night prowler.

June 8, 1921

Puffs of light cloud were blowing about the Cliff Top when we made the 7:30 A.M. readings, with only occasional glimpses of the valley below. None of us had ever been to the other two tops of the mountain, and it was with a bit of the feeling of explorers entering an unknown wilderness that we stepped into the serried balsams. Scattered blazes and occasional bits of trail for a few yards were all very confusing, though there was little danger of losing the way if one didn't wander from the apex of the ridge.

Le Conte's Far Top

The Main Top boasted a mantle of densest timber, with only a single lookout, a very poor one to the South. Barometer readings indicated it from 75 to 100 feet higher than the open Cliff Top. Nothing was to be gained by staying here, so after taking observations and carving our names and the date on one of the larger trees we pushed on to the eastern end of the mountain. This, for want of any name known to us, we christened Far Top (now Myrtle Point.)

With about the same distance between, the walk to the Far Top was much like that between the Cliff and Main Tops, through trailless, heavy timber and bushes. Toward the end, the ridge narrowed and the footing grew much rougher and broken.

We found the Far Top open, its surface hidden by so tangled a growth of sand myrtle that perforce we walked on rather than through it. The shrub was in full bloom, and gnats, flies and countless other insects rose in swarms about us as we struggled through.

Here the view embraced almost all we could see from the Cliff Top, and more. Through handicapping haze and cloud we could look down into Sevierville and out over the rolling country from northwest to northeast. On anything like a clear night the lights of Knoxville should be plainly in sight. The great gulf at our feet on the north side of Mt. Collins (now Mt. Kephart), was never clear of clouds, and the mists boiling up from this nucleus obscured the high mountains on the eastern end of the Smoky range.

We had long pondered and discussed the possibilities of a traverse of the lead connecting Le Conte with the North Carolina state line. From here it looked possible, though far from inviting, offering only very rugged climbing on a laurel-choked backbone, where the traveler would have to continually push or chop his way through. Cliffs on either side and along the top added little charm to the prospect. A distance of about three miles, we concluded that a man would do well to make the traverse in a day of hard travelling.

Here, in the triangle encompassed by Mts. Le Conte, Collins and Mingus, is the wildest, ruggedest country I'd ever seen. There are no valleys, only ravines and canyons, the ridges between knives and saws, with scores of rocky cliffs. Over it all grows a primeval forest of spruce and balsam on the heights and mingled hardwoods on the lower levels, untouched by axe or saw. One mistaking the few open spaces for grassy slopes would be in sad error, for what at a distance seems smooth as a lawn is in reality a "laurel slick," so choked with kalmia or small rhododendron that even the bears cannot make their way through.

Beyond any doubt there are thousands of spots here where to use an Irishism, the hand of man has never trod. Hand is right, for harsh experience told me one would travel on hands and knees many times before reaching some of the places we could see.

On the way back David twisted his ankle among the rocks and reached camp with difficulty. Mid-afternoon on the Cliff Top we noticed a sharp drop in barometric pressure, coupled with masses of thunderheads boiling up in the west. A storm was brewing, and back to the tent we hastened, to make everything shipshape for anything that might ensue. Frank in particular was keen to get off the top. A few years previously he had been knocked down by a lightning bolt on the western end of the Smokies, and had no craving to repeat the experience. I, too, had ridden out a severe electric storm on top the Bald Mountains, and understood his feeling.

This had been my birthday, by far the most enjoyable I'd ever seen. Ever since we had been out Frank had been promising to bake me a pie for the celebration, but now the threatening weather made him call it off. The dinner menu was thoroughly satisfactory, though—erbswurst soup with rice and onions added, fried country ham, stewed apricots, bannock bread and cocoa. What greater delicacies could hungry men ask?

The orchestral background for the meal was a crescendo rumble of thunder. The dishes were hardly washed when the storm struck. To our great relief, it was not nearly so severe as we had feared. Just a moderate amount of lightning and a couple of dashing showers of rain. We were safe and dry, for the tent shed water like a duck's back, and at the same time displayed an unexpected good point. Rainwater collected on the flat roof of the front fly, and when it finally poured over a low spot at the edge we could catch it in a conveniently placed bucket, a much more convenient and drier process than wading through wet bushes to the spring, and slowly dipping up a bucketfull.

June 9, 1921

The whole mountain top was swathed in cloud when we rose, with little hope of seeing out. The trip to the High Top for readings consumed an hour or so. Afterward, Frank and I spent a good part of the day in clearing pathways on the Cliff Top, and in marking and chopping out a trail toward the High Top.

The bald spot on the Cliff Top was covered with a waisthigh stand of sand myrtle and rhododendron punctatum, so thick and tangled one could hardly push a way through. Scattered among the bushes were a few burned areas, each several yards across. We could account for these in no other way than as the result of lightning strokes in severe electrical storms.

We knew that the summits of higher mountains were frequently struck. On the southern side of the peak are the cliffs giving it the name. A total of several hundred feet high they are not sheer, but formed of ledge on ledge, with bushes growing everywhere a root could find hold. Possible they could be climbed from beneath, but clambering over and through the vegetation might prove a more strenuous undertaking than scaling bare rock.

Rain sent us scurrying back to camp in mid-afternoon for shelter, where David was still nursing the foot that had confined him to camp all day. Shower followed shower, and it looked as though I'd lost my bet that we'd have at least one clear view every day we were on top. About sunset I went to the tiny spring, and what I saw from there made me hasten back to lead the others out on top, to bear witness my record as a weather prophet was intact for one more day.

It was late, with light too poor for photography, though the rain had washed away the haze. The atmosphere was clearer than any day previously, and the eastern and middle sectors of the Smokies were all spread out before us.

The spectacle was a wonderful one. High, precipitous ridges and peaks, with deep canyons between, were everywhere, so that one was awed by the im-

Ledges under the Cliff Top

mensity of it all, was bewildered and lost part of the sense of contrast. Mountain after mountain, range after range, so far as the eye could see, until they merged into the blue of the horizon. Before us were dozens of lofty, unnamed peaks and knobs, that in another setting would be famed for their height and majestic beauty. Here they were only small parts of so vast a scene that their absence would hardly be noted. The spectacular Chimney Tops that had towered so high above our camp in Bear Pen Hollow were here so dwarfed by their lofty neighbors that they could hardly be found in the chasm at our feet.

June 10, 1921

For a great and welcome change, the sun was shining in a clear blue sky on this, our last morning on top. David's foot was still troubling him, so he was left to police camp while the rest of us made our last visit to the several tops of the mountain for final observations. Sorrowfully we returned, for our outing was nearly at its end, and months of office work faced each of us before we could again have the opportunity of camping among the high hills.

As we struck the tent and made up our packs, much lighter now than when we had come in, the sky grew overcast, and soon stray tag ends of mist began drifting about us through the timber. By the time we had reached the upper of the Tag Tree trail a light shower was falling.

Frank had voiced an intention of going to the Sharp Top for some botanical specimens. David chose to go with him, so Walter and I proceeded on down the mountain, slipping and sliding along the muddy trail, to find shelter in the pole cabin in Bear Pen Hollow to await the others.

The rough plank door of the cabin stood ajar. Seeking refuge from rain like ourselves, a junco darted in, flying almost into our faces before either saw the other. Whether he was more startled than we I'll never know, but certainly he threw on his aerial brakes so suddenly we could distinctly hear the hiss of air through his wing feathers as he changed course and sped out through an unchinked crack between the logs.

Frank and David soon came in, soaking wet, driven in by the rain before they could collect specimens. As the downpour slackened, Frank went to the side of the ridge across the stream. In a very few minutes he was back, specimens in hand and a report of very fresh bear sign in the laurel.

At Le Conte Crossing, where we planned to spend the night, we found the river up over a couple of feet, lapping over the footlog as we crossed. Most of the run-off had fallen on the watershed of the Road Prong, for the branch we had come down was hardly milky. We'd been hoping for some dingy water, for a final bit of better fishing, but even now they wouldn't bite.

No one bothers to shave on a trip like this and our ten days' growth of beard gave us a feral, savage look, much too unkempt to go back to civilization. Someone had goofed in making up the list of supplies. There was no shaving cream, only a little bit of toilet soap, no mirror and only a single razor blade, it a trifle rusty from forest dampness. There was no pleasure in the prospect of shaving with such gear, and we drew straws for turns in facing the ordeal. Walter won first place, I second and Frank the last.

There was no warm water to use, only that of the icy river. The soap wouldn't lather in it, to soften our beards and to wash out the accumulated dirt, flydope, twigs and leaves matted in them. Walter got through his job without too much difficulty, but sawing through his wiry beard hadn't helped the edge of the razor blade any. When my turn came about as much was pulled out and scraped off as was cut.

Poor Frank got the raw end of the deal. His crippled shoulder wouldn't let him reach all his face, so we had, to play barber for his benefit. Walter held him, while I, disregarding his shrieks of anguish, literally dug the whiskers off his skin with the dull blade. Finally the job was done, and we turned in with scratched and smarting faces.

June 11, 1921

We took the precaution of first testing the temperature of the water before our morning dip in the creek. Fifty-five degrees. That didn't sound too bad, so we stripped and waded in. Then we realized just how cold fifty-five degree water, in a mountain stream at daylight, really is. If there is any such thing as liquid ice it was running in that creek that morning. We were hardly in before we were hastily climbing out. I slipped on a slick rock and dropped back in up to my neck, and nearly lost my breath from the shock. Cleanliness may be next to godliness in civilization, but that morning we had serious doubts as to its being so desirable a virtue, right there.

Down the river we marched and up over Sugarland Mountain, to reach Elkmont just as the noon train disappeared around the curve. Nothing remained but to explore the village, visit the Bain cottage, etc., until the late train took us to Townsend for the night.

We were hardly settled in our room in the Company hotel (everything in Townsend belonged to the Little River Lumber Company, whose headquarters and big band mill were there) before, without knock or ceremony, the door opened and the town marshal walked in. He questioned us closely as to who we were, whence we came, our business in town, and the like. Then it developed that word had come to him some rum-runners were expected in town that night. So when he heard that three hard-looking characters, with bulging packs had arrived on the evening train, we were suspected. A mutual recognition between the marshal, Walter and Frank came when they called meeting on a trail in the western part of the Smokies a few years before. All suspicion lifted, he stayed for quite a chat, giving us many interesting bits of information about the mountains. He, Andy Gregory by name and a self-trained surveyor often employed by the lumber company, was a grandson of Russell Gregory, an early settler for whom the Gregory Bald was named.

June 12, 1921

The early train took us to Knoxville, then by trolley to Doc Essary's at Fountain City. He was not at home, so we just walked in, took possession, and phoned him at the University of Tennessee. On his arrival we collaborated in preparing and eating an enormous meal. Lying on the grass under the shade trees in his front yard, a bull session was in order until Walter and I had to tear ourselves away reluctantly to catch the train for Jonesboro.

The results of our survey are shown by the following letter from Walter of the U.S. Geological Survey, and excerpt from my letter to Myron H. Avery, October 24th, 1929.

Washington, D.C.
August 15, 1921
The Director,
U.S. Geological Survey,
Washington, D.C.

Dear Sir:
Subject: Mt. Le Conte-Barometric observations on.
Enclosures (herewith):
    (A) Calibration curve for U.S.G.S. Aneroid Barometer No. 603
    (B) Correction curves for readings on U.S.G.S. No. 603 and Tycos Barometers.
    (C) Photostatic copy of meteorological data for Knoxville, Tenn., June 2 to 10, 1921.
    (D) Photostatic copy of meteorological data for Asheville, N.C., June 2 to 10, 1921.
    (E) Observed data and computations (4 sheets)
    (F) U.S.G.S. Topographic map of Mt. Guyot Quandrangle

I take pleasure in transmitting herewith enclosures (A) to (F) inclusive, meteorological data obtained on and near Mt. Le Conte, Sevier County, Tenn., (Mt. Guyot Quandrangle) during the early part of June, 1921, by a party consisting of the following:
H. F. Bain, Dept. of Agriculture, Washington, D. C.
David Bain, Knoxville, Tennessee
Paul M. Fink, Jonesboro, Tennessee
W. S. Diehl, Navy Department, Washington, D. C.

Two aneroids were used; a privately owned Tycos and U.S.G.S. No. 603, which was borrowed for this trip. Temperature readings were taken with a standard chemical thermometer. The aneroids were adjusted at the U.S. Weather Bureau, Knoxville, Tenn., June 2, 1921 and calibrated at the Bureau of Standards upon return. The calibration data is given in enclosures (A) and (B).

The observations and calculations are given in enclosure (E). It is to be noted that the altitudes are for dry air. The humidity for the period covered by the observations will average high—probably in the neighborhood of 75%.

According to the average of the readings given by the two aneroids the height of the main top of Le Conte is 6,558 ft., uncorrected for humidity. According to the Tycos instruments the height is 6,626 ft. In view of the known information concerning Mt. Le Conte and the inconsistencies between the observed field and calibration readings, it is thought that the true height is in the neighborhood of 6,600 ft. plus the humidity correction (which is about 60-80 ft.) i.e., $6,650\pm30$ ft.

Mt. Le Conte consists of three definite tops, the eastern and western tops being approximately the same height and about 50 ft. lower than the main or central top. Each of these three tops has a name of its own according to the natives of the surrounding territory. A feature which is not shown on the map is the depth of the gap between the western and the main top. According to the barometers this gap is about 150 ft. deep.

The location of various observation stations are indicated in blue pencil on enclosure (F). The elevation of prominent peaks on this sheet seem to be fairly accurate but the intermediate topography and nomenclature should be revised.

Respectfully,
(signed)   W. S. Diehl

Excerpt from letter of Paul M. Fink to Myron H. Avery, October 24, 1929

"Here's the reason the Coast and Geodetic Survey (C. & G. S.) made their triangulation. After we made our barometrical survey we thought that there was a chance the Le Conte could prove higher than Mitchell, so we went to work to have a line of levels run to the top. Even with Diehl getting a leave of absence and doing his part of the work gratis, the expense would have been something like $750.00 or more, a sum we were not prepared to pay entirely out of our own pockets, though we figured we two could put up about half of it. I went to the Knoxville Chamber of Commerce with the project, figuring that the advertising Knoxville might get from the project would interest them. They appeared to be very favorably impressed, and asked that we wait with the project until it could be passed on by their Board of Directors. On one pretext and another they put me off for a couple of months, and then, first thing I knew, they had worked through their member of Congress and had the C. & G. S. send down a triangulation party to do the work. Rather underhanded, I called it, inasmuch as they said nothing to us, and had been putting me off all along, and I made a special trip to Knoxville to tell the Secretary of the Chamber of Commerce just what I thought about it all, using words of one syllable, easily understood by anyone. Carlos Campbell was with the C. of C. at that time, and he will tell you they gave us a dirty deal."

The results of the U.S. Coast & Geodetic Survey's triangulation, as reported in the newspapers, was 6,593 ft. As the story came to me later, theodolite observations were made from a hill in Knoxville, with a nearby bench mark to furnish the starting elevation. A local party was sent on the mountain to erect a target, but did not put it in the highest point, and as a result the final figures were too low. Be that true or not, the altitude as shown on the present map is 6,593 feet. Two other peaks of the Smokies, Clingmans Dome, 6,642 feet, and Mt. Guyot, 6,621 feet, exceed this, as do Mt. Mitchell, 6,684 feet, and one of the Black Brothers, in the Black mountains.

Even though their actual elevation above the sea is greater, all these are slightly higher points on lofty ridges. Le Conte, standing out alone and rising from a much lower base, has a far greater scenic height, and is by far a more spectacular mountain than any of the others.

Grub List

Bacon	9 lb.	Cornmeal	4 lb.
Ham	4 lb.	Rice	2 lb. 8 oz.
Dried beef	1 lb. 8 oz.	Oatmeal	2 lb.
Bouillon cubes	4 oz.	Baking powder	8 oz.
Dehydrated soup	1 lb.	Coffee	2 lb.
Erbswurst	8 oz.	Cocoa	1 lb.
Cheese, canned	2 lb.	Sugar	7 lb.
Crisco	1 lb. 8 oz.	Evaporated fruit	3 lb. 8 oz.
Powdered milk	1 lb. 8 oz.	Raisins	3 lb.
Powdered eggs	1 lb. 8 oz.	Sweet chocolate	3 lb.
Flour	12 lb.	Salt, pepper, etc.	1 lb.
		Total	64 lb. 4 oz.

This, with a small additional supply brought by David, was sufficient for four men for ten days. Two pounds more sugar and the same amount less flour would have been of advantage.

DATE: JUNE 10-12, 1922

DESTINATION: ROAN MOUNTAIN.

OBJECT: OUTING.

WEATHER: FAIR, FOGGY.

PARTY: ROBERT H. DULANEY, SID WALMSLEY, PAUL M. FINK.

When Bob and I were planning a short trip to the Roan, someone suggested that we take with us Sid Walmsley, a young Englishman not long in this country. Propositioned, he jumped at the opportunity. Not only was he anxious to see the beauties of the Roan, but more than that, the climb would take him to a greater altitude than any peak in the British Isles.

June 10, 1922

To ride the morning "Narrow Gauge" train from Johnson City called for an early start from Jonesboro. It was not yet a time of paved roads and fast cars. Construction work on the highway between Jonesboro and Johnson City made us take a long, rough detour by Boones Creek, over a clay road. It had rained the day before, the road was slick, and of course the car stuck in a deep mud hole, where it took our best efforts, a fence rail and some time to get the car out and on solid ground once more. Even with all that delay, we were at the station in time for the train. Ever since dawn the clouds had been hanging low, and there was scant promise of good weather for our outing.

The trip through the deep, rocky gorge of the Doe River, with its cliffs and tunnels, was nothing new to Bob and me, but always interesting to see how the stream had cut its way through the quartzite ribs of the Unakas. We were more impressed by the remark of a fellow traveler, that in some ways it compared very favorable with some portions of the Canadian Rockies.

No time was lost at Roan Mountain Station for we wished to reach Cloudland in time for a little exploration before supper. A mile or two on our way we stopped at the shelving rock, where the frontiersmen in 1780 made their first

Site of first night's camp, Kings Mountain

night's camp on the way to their victory over the British forces at the battle of Kings Mountain.

The clouds had all cleared away by now, and we pushed on rapidly, along the rough country road to the little settlement of Burbank. Then for a while the way was steep and rocky, 'til our feet struck the lower end of the old stage road. The grade on this was easy, as it wound up the mountain side in a series of switchbacks. Once a good carriage road, neglect had let it become so washed out that it was impassable for any kind of vehicle.

It was not long before sunset when we finally emerged from under the timber into the open grassy space of Carvers Gap, the first close-up either of the others had ever had of a "bald." The hour was too late to spend more than a moment admiring its serene beauty. As we pushed on toward Cloudland, we promised ourselves we would spend more time in the Gap on the morrow.

As we rounded Roan High Knob and came in sight of old Cloudland Hotel, we heard gunshots and loud shouts from the balsams beyond. It was not at all reassuring to us. We feared some of the valley folks had met on the mountain for a weekend drinking bout, not an uncommon practice.

Our first care was to find those essentials for a night's camp, firewood and water. Just as we located them, near the site of a cabin built some years before by an old friend, Dulaney Maher, a man appeared from out of the timber. After a short chat, we were invited to share his fire and campsite, a few yards away. With some misgivings we accepted.

Our host was Rexter Ledford, living at Buladean, N.C., at the western foot of the mountain, who was combining a trip up the mountain to look after his livestock with an opportunity to spend a night on top. This, I later found, was a little habit frequently indulged in by the natives. Conversation with Ledford during the evening brought out that he frequently brought apples by wagon across the mountains to Jonesboro. In subsequent years he stopped in to see me frequently, and I bought many a bushel of excellent apples from him.

At his invitation I used his fire to cook supper for the boys, while they gathered browse and made our bed on the deep grass at the edge of the timber.

It was the season of the full moon and by its light Ledford and I took the binoculars up to the old hotel site to look at the lights of Johnson City, away to the northward. The atmosphere was almost entirely free from haze, and clearer than usual. As distinctly as though we were only three miles away instead of thirty, we could distinguish the lights of individual cars, moving down Roan Street facing us, then turning off into some side street.

June 11, 1922

What a change from the cloudless sky, when we went to sleep. During the night, mist had moved in and settled down on the mountain, no unusual circumstance for the place. We couldn't see fifty yards. It was no encouraging prospect, for we'd been talking of following the state line eastward, over Grassy Ridge Bald, Big Yellow and the Hump to Elk Park.

There was little to do after breakfast but sit around the fire and talk. Ledford assured us there was a plain trail all the way to the Hump, and that we'd have no trouble at all in following it. Toward noon, when the clouds gave great promise of clearing away, we decided to wait no longer.

Dropping down to Carvers Gap on the old road around the High Knob, the mist had almost entirely disappeared, with a fairly clear outlook to the north and east, the direction we were headed. Everything looked propitious.

It wasn't to be, though. Before we had walked to the top of the Grassy Ridge the cloud blew in again from North Carolina. It was to be with us the rest of the afternoon, punctuated by brief rain squalls. Not a bit of shelter was in sight or reach, so we plodded on, trying to keep on the trail as best we might, by compass and map. These were little better than useless in the thick fog with no landmarks to check on, and a ridge winding in every direction. To complicate matters further, the whole top of the mountain was a veritable maze of sheep and cattle paths. The real trail was soon hopelessly lost among them.

Distances in a fog are most deceptive, and some of the tributary ridges in that region have a very deceiving way of being a little higher than the main divide. As a result, we hadn't gone as far as we thought when we turned to the right along an ascending ridge that seemed to be headed in the proper direction.

For a while all was very encouraging. There were plenty of signs of travel along the crest, and the general trend was eastward, just as the divide should run from Grassy Ridge to the Big Yellow. Then our trail gradually petered out and the ridge grew rough and rocky, particularly on the right side, almost precipitous in spots. How high the cliffs were we never knew. They were still going straight down when they passed from sight in the mists below. Dense patches of kalmia and rhododendron appeared. All together, the ridge had taken unto itself some of the characteristics of the Smoky terrain.

By now I had more than a mere suspicion that we were lost, though I believed that we were near the head of Heaton Creek, emptying into Doe River. It was mid-afternoon with no hope of the cloud lifting. The best bet, as always when lost in the mountains, was to drop down to water and follow the stream on out.

The side of the mountain was rough and steep; the bushes and the trees above dripping wet from the continual drizzle. Down we went, slipping and sliding, sometimes falling, an estimated two thousand feet to the bed of a stream, a tiny one it is true, but water just the same. Our canteens had long been empty, and our first act was to fill up on the cool, clear water. Part of the time in the rocky bed of the stream, part on a very old abandoned tram road, we followed it to a small clearing with a cabin standing in it.

Unwilling to admit we were lost but anxious to find out just where we were, we approached an old lady sitting on the porch and asked

"What is this creek we have been following?"

"You're on Jerry Creek, that runs into Roarin' Creek, down a little ways."

That didn't help a bit, for none of us had ever so much as heard of either stream. I tried another tack.

"How far is it to Burbank?"

"Burbank, at the foot of Roan Mountain? Why, that's 'way over yan in Tennessee!"

We were lost, all right, miles away from where we had hoped, and even in

A tunnel on the "Narrow Gauge"

a different state. Her husband came up and further questions brought out the route to the rocked road, some six miles away at Plumtree, N. C. We were very fortunate to find there a car owner willing to take us ten miles further to Elk Park.

It was dark when we checked in the hotel and the dining room was closed. The only cafe in town was nearly out of everything when we sat down at the counter, and completely out when we were at last satisfied. We needed no rocking to sleep that night.

June 12, 1922

After a hearty breakfast at the hotel, the early train took us back to Johnson City, via the Gorge of Doe River again. Our car was waiting, and we were soon at home, with a new supply of memories of the mountains. And as usual, the difficulties and hardships brought more pleasure in retrospect than the times when everything went smoothly, with nothing to worry us.

DATE: AUGUST 10-16, 1922

DESTINATION: WESTERN END OF THE SMOKIES.

OBJECT: EXPLORATION.

WEATHER: FAIR, SHOWERS.

PARTY: WALTER S. DIEHL, HENRY W. PATTON, PAUL M. FINK.

It was an ambitious trip we planned this year. Leaving the railhead at Elkmont, we would go along Miry Ridge to the state line at Cold Spring Knob. Setting up camp there, we'd take a leisurely day's stroll eastward to Silers Bald, Clingmans Dome and Meigs Post, and return. Then our intention was to travel west, past the Hall Cabin, Briar Knob, Thunderhead, the Spence Cabin, Little Bald, Ekaneetlee Gap, Cold Spring and the Parson Bald, on to Gregory Bald, last of the important peaks on that end of the range. From there we would retrace our steps to the Spence Cabin, to descend along the old wagon road to Townsend and the railway home.

An ambitious program, but not an impossible one. With the open timber, generally easy slopes and good trails so common to that section, and granted reasonably favorable weather, it could easily have been covered in the week at our disposal. Just how painstakingly we were able to adhere to the schedule will develop later.

It was to be the first long trip Henry had made with both Walter and me, though we had camped with him elsewhere and knew him to be a good woodsman and a congenial trailmate. We had had hopes of including Prof. S. H. (Doc) Essary, of the University of Tennessee, to join the party, but conflicting engagements had made it impossible.

August 10, 1922

Henry preceded Walter and me to Knoxville. We travelled on a late train, and went to Doc Essary's home at Fountain City for the night, and a long bullfest.

August 11, 1922

From Elkmont the way to our first mountain objective, Miry Ridge, led past the Appalachian Club summer cottages and along the old wagon road through Jakes Gap. Hardly a mile past the last cottage the jinx that invariably accompanied Henry and me showed itself, with its constant companion, Jupiter Pluvius. The first gentle sprinkle of rain grew to a shower, and long before we had gone a half mile further we were well wet through. Our lunch of canned beans and chile con carne was eaten under the dubious shelter of leaning trunks of trees about a tiny spring by the roadside.

We knew that the trail to the top of Miry Ridge bore to the left up a little ravine, and at the first indication of the trail we left the road. By the time we had gone a few hundred yards we were completely lost in a tangle of laurel, while the bushes completed the job of drenching started by the rain.

Retracing our steps with difficulty, we found that we had left the road one ravine too soon. The real trail was plainly marked and not to be mistaken—there were too many signs of use. Though by no means lasting so long, a part of the trail was very steep, quite like that up the head of Bear Pen Hollow, on the way to the top of Le Conte. Water was oozing everywhere through the blanket of moss covering the ledges on the mountainside, amply justifying the local name, Dripping Spring Mountain.

Near the place Prof. Hill of the University of Tennessee, climbing slowly and laboriously, made the most apt observation that there was no valid reason for any man to get lost climbing Miry Ridge. Here there were only two directions, straight up and straight down.

The name of Miry Ridge is drawn from the peculiar swampy condition of its top. The trail, cut through the laurel, led along the very crest of the ridge. Here the rock strata of the mountain have made a long, narrow basin of the summit. The abundant rainfall is caught and cannot escape, turning the fallen leaves and decayed vegetation into a sloppy, malodorous black muck ankle to calf deep. Through this mess the tramper must splash his way.

The greater part was through laurel and brushy, cut-over timber. We could find but one good observation point, the Ben Parton Lookout. From here we could see across the upper waters of the Fish Camp Prong of Little River, where logging was then in progress, to the main range of the Smokies, with Silers Bald as the most prominent landmark.

By this time it was not long before sunset, and there was little time to spare, even if the chilly breeze hadn't made resting a bit uncomfortable. The first day's climb is always the hardest on soft muscles, and we were well nigh exhausted. For strength to push on we made a hasty late lunch of energy-laden cheese, raisins and sweet chocolate before hurrying on to Cold Spring Knob, at the head of Miry Ridge. Here we had planned to set up a two-day camp.

Darkness was almost at hand when we arrived at the Cold Spring and chose a tent site just across the trail from it. Tired and hungry though we were, the first duty was to get everything under shelter and ready for the night. Henry, the best cook among us, was urged to get about his culinary duties instantly. Walter was detailed to prepare the campsite and gather moss, grass and ferns for bedding, while I was to forage for firewood. In spite of the handicap of damp kindling, Henry, a purist in the craft of firemaking, had a pot of hot tea ready in a few minutes, the most bracing cup I'd ever sipped. Stimulated by it, we put extra steam into our efforts, but at that it was black dark long before all chores were done. Swathed in our blankets against the chilly night breeze, we ate our supper by the light of the carbide lamp.

Our fern bed was far from a Beauty Rest mattress and scarcely wide enough for the three of us, but we were much too weary to notice any such minor discomforts. Soon our snores were echoing among the ridges and peaks.

August 12, 1922

The sun was already far above the horizon when, with a last sleepy yawn; we rolled out of our blankets. From the door, framed in an opening among the trees, was a scene that alone was worth all the exertion of the trip. The air was crystal clear, fairly sparkling in the morning light. Thunderhead and Blockhouse, companion peaks, with a halo of fleecy clouds hovering over their rounded summits, filled the center of the picture.

The dividing ridge of the Smokies lay between us, every ridge and hollow as clearly delineated as in a steel engraving. By the varying tones of green in its foliage, every clump of laurel and conifers could be distinguished amid the main canopy of hardwoods covering the slopes. The whole was a picture whose beauty made it memorable, even in a country where beautiful vistas are on every hand.

The salt could not be found when preparing supper the night before, and we had supposed it mislaid in the darkness. Strict search by day didn't bring it to light and no one remembered putting this essential condiment in any of

Old Thunderhead

the packs. There was a chance of finding some at the Hall Cabin, where hunters or herders might have left a surplus. How to fill its place in the meantime was question. Henry put an extra portion of sugar in his bread, and found it a fair emergency substitute. The soup was flavored by the addition of bouillon cubes, themselves about 90% salt. Ham and dried fruits needed no salt, so we suffered little hardship.

Two natives, Jud Hall and a companion answering to "Pink," herders searching for strayed cattle, dropped by the spring for a drink just as we were getting ready to leave for Silers Bald.

All headed in the same direction, we started along the trail in company.

Both these men, Hall particularly so, were well acquainted with Horace Kephart, famed writer on the Smokies and outdoor life. One of the stories Hall told was of the time he, Kephart, Bob Barnett and one other were engaged by a bear hunting club to build a shack near where the Hall Cabin later stood. The club was to furnish tools, all supplies and a two gallon jug of corn whiskey, while they were to get out the lumber with a whipsaw and build the shack. The first log was duly sawn into boards, the work punctuated by frequent visits to the jug. After one log, all hands agreed that it was hard labor and that while they would eat the food and drink the liquor, if the club wanted a cabin they could build it themselves.

Pink, who had worked in the now abandoned copper mines on Hazel

Silers Bald

Creek, near where Kephart had spent so much of his first years in the Smokies, told us that the formations on Hazel Creek were identical with those at Alum Cave, on the side of Mt. Le Conte, and also the old prospect pits on Silers Bald. All this was news to us.

After a mile or so of pleasant companionship our ways separated. They continued their search for strayed cattle, we kept along the divide eastward Silers Bald and Clingmans Dome, passing on our way the almost obliterated old copper workings.

The outlook from the top of Silers was a great disappointment. After the brilliant early morning we had hoped for a good close-up of the Dome, but the clouds had blown in. Hanging at an altitude of around 6,000 feet, they blotted it out completely, and we were not to see it clearly all day. With no indication the mists would shortly clear away, there was no incentive to travel further, and we spent the time loafing in the open field, in a light too poor for successful photography. The bank of cloud dropped lower and lower, until it was all around us, bringing with it a smart shower that drove us for shelter under jutting ledges of rock.

The return to camp was so timed that we had opportunity to gather in many more armfuls of the fragrant cinnamon fern, to make our bed more roomy and the mattress deeper. Henry was by far the best camp cook of the party, and accordingly that duty was assigned to him for the rest of the trip, while Walter and I divided the other chores of wildwood housekeeping.

The view across the ridges toward Thunderhead, so beautifully clear in the morning, had changed completely and acquired a new beauty, vastly different but equally striking. A heavy pall of cloud covered most of the western sky, save for a band of vivid light at the horizon. Against it all the nearer peaks were silhouetted, while Thunderhead and Blockhouse, on the skyline, were flooded with a golden glow. In all, it was one of the strangest but most striking light effects we had ever seen.

August 13, 1922

On rising we could enjoy the same magnificent view as on the previous morning, but it was of very short duration. Soon the clouds were drifting around us again, but fortunately bearing no rain. Breakfast over, camp broken and packs made, we started leisurely on our way. Everything had gone nearly as planned, and the rest of the trip was to be in easy stages. This day we did not propose going beyond Briar Knob, a short tramp along the top, following a good trail through open timber and with but little climbing before us.

The Hall Cabin seemed totally deserted as we came near it, and we laid down our packs, to enter in search of salt. Two steps from the open door we were startled to hear from inside a feminine voice, inquiring

"Gertrude, where is my powder puff?"

Truly an astonishing thing to hear this deep in the mountains. Instantly we dropped our plans to search for salt, silently picked up our packs and stole away.

Soon we had the explanation. J. W. Fisher, Superintendent of the big band mill of the Ritter Lumber Co., at Ritter, N. C., with two other men and three young ladies, had been camping at the Hall Cabin over the week end.

Close by the spring we built a little fire, to brew a pot of tea for lunch. As we ate, Fisher came down from the cabin for a bucket of water and sat down to chat. The Shrine button on the collar of my shirt caught his eye, and he made himself known as a Royal Arch Mason, headed for the Shrine. Taking the water to the cabin he shortly returned, hands filled with bread, jam and peaches, to finish out our customarily rather scanty noon meal, and with the offer of more bread from their supplies. Their party was returning that afternoon, and did not wish to carry anything back.

To say this addition to our food supply was gladly received goes without comment. We had been using an aluminum mess kit as a dutch oven, and while it served very well for lightweight or emergency duty, our lazy dispositions did not demand that we make bread when it might be given us.

After a couple of hours pleasantly spent at the Hall Cabin everyone left at the same time, they dropping down a steep trail to the railroad grade not far below on the Carolina side, we packing westward along the divide, bound for Briar Knob. We did no amount of strenuous climbing, but before long Henry dubbed it the mountain with the patent receding top. Time after time we were cheered by seeing just ahead what appeared to be the summit, only to find on gaining it that there was yet another little rise to be surmounted. There were a dozen such tantalizing disappointments before we finally stood on the real summit.

It was not too long past noon. Fresh and untired by the easy travel of morning, we decided it best to push on to Thunderhead, where there were better campsites than Briar Knob afforded, with water and firewood in abundance. It would also put us a little ahead of our schedule, with more time for loafing and enjoying the beauties of the bald top of Thunderhead.

To our left hand lay a deep valley or gorge, so forbidding that the mountain folk, with a genius for apt naming, called it Desolation. When one looks down into it from above, with its welter of abrupt ridges and slopes, jagged crags and gloomy depths, all choked with a well-nigh impenetrable tangle of laurel and rhododendron, he does not wonder at the appropriateness of the name.

Cattle trails were everywhere under the open timber. Intermittent waves of thick mist were blowing about us. Without lookouts from which to check our route, it was no simple task to find our way to the Laurel Top—highest point of Thunderhead. At one time we began to fear that we had followed the wrong path too far to the right and had gotten out on Defeat Ridge, a long, high lead running northward into Tennessee. A timely rifting of the cloud, disclosing

The topmost tops of Thunderhead

Rocky Top, where the stony ledges have been literally blasted to bits by the lightning strokes that so often smite the mountain, set us right. Now we were on a downhill slope. A dashing shower caught us before we could reach the shelter of the Spence Cabin.

Here in the Old Field we set up our tent in one of the most charming campsites I have ever seen. The grass grew rank and long beneath scattered oak and chestnut trees, a hundred yards above the cabin and an equal walk from the cold, free-running spring.

Before the evening chores were well underway, John T. Sparks, of Cades Cove, a herder staying at the cabin, strolled up and with typical mountain hospitality invited us to stay with him. The fresh air and the beauty of our camp setting was too attractive and we declined his offer with thanks, completing our camp-making and preparation for supper just as darkness fell. Night on the mountain tops, as in the tropics, comes on swiftly with hardly an appreciable interval of twilight between sunset and dark.

We were still well wet from the afternoon shower. Sleeping in damp clothes was nothing new to us, but never from choice when better conditions were to be had. So we shed as many wet garments as we could and hung them on rustic racks about the fire to dry, while we, swathed in our blankets like Indian warriors, lounged about the camp. My clothes were first to dry and, fully clad once more, in the dim light I picked my way to the top of the ridge a couple

Won't that pot ever boil?

of hundred yards from camp to see if the lights of Maryville and Knoxville were visible.

Shouts came from the direction of the tent and in a few moments I was joined by the others. Walter, clad in hardly enough clothing to mention and with his blanket for a swirling cape, gave a magnificent exhibition of his version of aesthetic dancing in the moonlight, a truly thrilling spectacle. Henry and I attempted to emulate his example, but could not even approach the heights of artistry he attained.

August 14, 1922

Our plans, made before starting for either time, place, direction, etc., were all tentative and subject to change on the instant for real cause or some mere whim. Both reasons went into effect this day.

The original schedule had called for an easy trek down to Ekaneetlee Gap or thereabouts for the night, then on to Gregory Bald the following day. At sunrise the weather appeared propitious, but only for a brief time. Before breakfast could be cooked and eaten, low-flying clouds put in their appearance, with spitting showers. The prospect of splashing along a slick, muddy trail in soaking clothes, no shelter along the way and the certainty of a wet camp at evening didn't sound at all enticing that morning. Then, too, an overpowering

The clouds move in

feeling of laziness, the *dolce far piente* often spoken of by old Nessmuck, was catching up on us.

Which of the two, good judgment or simply whim, was the most potent I'll not attempt to say, but the result was the same. We settled right down where we were and didn't stray more than a few hundred yards from the tent all day. The greater part of our energy was consumed in cooking and eating a single meal, beginning about 7:00 A.M. and lasting approximately twelve hours. We'd cook awhile, devour the product, loaf a little, cook something else, eat that, loaf some more, then repeat all over again. It's astonishing the amount of food it takes to satisfy an outdoor-heightened appetite.

During the afternoon Walter Gregory, brother of the City Marshal of Townsend whom Walter, Frank Bain and I had met under peculiar circumstances the year before, came by and stopped for a chat. Among the interesting things he told us were stories of Quill Rose, a famous mountain character formerly living down on Hazel Creek. Rose, a famous moonshiner, was the patriarch of the clan. To use Gregory's words,

"Quill made and drunk more licker than ary other man that ever lived in these mountains. When he got too old an' broke-down to make his own licker, he hired himself two men to keep him supplied."

The moon was shining brightly when we rolled up in our blankets. My position was at the edge of the bed, close to the sidewall of the tent that had been pitched on a slight slope. During the night I slid down a bit, to wake with my nose almost against the cloth. To my sleep-filled eyes the glow of the moonlight through the fabric had all the appearance of gazing into a dense mist. I waked the others to see this extraordinary heavy fog, and was given the raspberry for my error.

August 15, 1922

A bright morning sun partially received our ambition to go further west, and for a little while we toyed with the idea of leaving camp as it was, travelling light down to Ekaneetlee Gap and returning that afternoon. It was a very feasible plan but after we had surrounded a very hearty breakfast we began to lose interest in walking any distance. Soon a unanimous decision was reached that the Laurel Top of Thunderhead was as far as we had any desire to travel that day.

Thunderhead, the name generally bestowed to all of the two mile long groups of natural bald peaks, is among the most beautiful of all the southern mountains. Its hundreds of acres of grassy fields, kept cropped short by herds of cattle and sheep driven up from the lowlands for summer pasture, with open forest of wind-gnarled chestnuts and oaks, makes one think of the park lands of a vast country estate.

Walter and I wandered around for some time with our Kodaks, getting a number of pictures characteristic of this most photogenic portion of the western end of the Smokies. It was well up in the morning before a start was made for Laurel Top, but we were to get only as far as the Rocky Top, where a keen shower drove us to hole up under leaning trees or shelving ledges. These proved token shelter only, not enough to save us from another complete wetting.

Dense, wind-driven clouds followed close behind the rain, and we abandoned the idea of going on higher. Leisurely we strolled back toward camp just in time to meet a herd of over a hundred cattle driven over from North Carolina. One of the drovers, Jud Hall, our friend of a few days before, hailed us with the question,

"Is there any liquor over at the cabin?"

We couldn't give him a definite answer, though we did have some ideas on the subject, and kept our eyes open. A few minutes after the herders gathered at the cabin, one man sauntered off along the trail going down the mountain, returning in a few minutes with a half-gallon glass jar in his hands. Before long Jud came up to our camp, stood around for a few minutes, then asked if we had

Stunted timber borders the Old Field

an empty bottle. The only container we could supply was an empty friction top tin. It must have answered the need, for we never saw it again.

During the morning we had spent a pleasant hour chatting with John Sparks, the herder stopping at the cabin while looking after his cattle grazing on the mountain. His colorful description of the many incidents of a herder's life was most interesting. In particular, one adventure of his father's intrigued us, throwing first-hand light on the theory that the American members of the cat tribe never attack man unless first wounded or cornered.

Late one autumn, just before the cattle were driven down to the lowlands of the Cove for the winter, the elder Sparks had been staying at the Spence cabin. For several weeks strange tracks much larger than those of a wildcat, had been seen in the neighborhood of Thunderhead. No one knew just what kind of animal might have made them unless it be a "painter," a beast supposedly exterminated in the Smokies for years. Occasionally some timid person reported hearing one scream at night but this was generally attributed to a great horned owl whose wild, unearthly yell is one of the most blood curdling sounds in the night woods.

That night there was a light "skift" of snow on the mountain top. The old man, out looking for some strayed stock, had been delayed and darkness overtook him a mile from shelter. Through the dusk and by the faint light of the stars reflected from the snow, he caught glimpses of a shadowy form seeming to him about the size of a shepherd dog slinking through the sparse timber and laurel, first on one side, then the other, keeping pace with him.

Not expecting to be out after dark nor to encounter any predatory beast, his gun had been left at the cabin and he was totally unarmed except for his big pocket knife. This he opened and carried in his right hand ready for instant use if necessary.

As it became darker the animal grew bolder coming closer and closer, two or three times giving voice to a sort of yowling squall somewhat like an enormous cat.

Suddenly, the beast sprang from behind, landing on Spark's back and left shoulder almost knocking him flat on his face, and began ripping his clothing with its claws. Fortunately, his right hand was free. As best he could, he stabbed at his assailant cutting back under his left arm with some little success. Spitting like an angry tomcat, the marauder dropped to the ground and vanished in the bushes. Wanting no further encounter, he ran the rest of the way to the cabin, fearing each moment he might feel its claws and fangs in his back again.

In proof of his story, he exhibited to the others gathered about the fire his overall jumper with the left sleeve, shoulder, and side slit to ribbons by the keen claws. His arm, side, and hip were crisscrossed with long scratches, fortunately, none very deep. Evidence of his valiant self-defense, his knife blade was bloody, with tufts of tawny hair sticking to it.

At daylight next morning, some of the men with their hounds went to the spot. There they found tracks with blood spots on the snow. The trail was plain for a little distance, then it entered a patch of laurel too dense for the men to push through. The dogs were reluctant to follow further but after a bit of urging entered the thicket. Soon they returned and no amount of persuasion would get them to pick up the trail again.

No one could say with certainty just what the beast might be. One man suggested it might be a "link" (Canada Lynx). Considering all evidence this

Storm-twisted timber

appeared plausible, as a stray specimen had very occasionally been known to wander south along the higher mountain ranges.

Some years later I recounted this to Horace Kephart, living at Bryson City, North Carolina. He attested its verity, for a year or two after its happening he had heard of it from Sparks himself, who then removed his shirt and showed the scars of the claw marks on his arms and back.

Another of Sparks' stories was of the four months he had spent in the Maryville jail after conviction on a charge of illicit distilling locally known as "blockading." A posse under U.S. Marshal Burkett Ivens made a successful raid into Cades Cove, taking back several stills and their operators, Sparks among them.

At the trial the officers testified that a plain, open path led directly from Sparks' house to the still. On this circumstantial evidence the jury found him guilty for though he admitted knowing of the still he wouldn't name the operator. In concluding his yarn he laughed and said,

"I guess it was all right, though, even if it wasn't my still they found. *Mine* was just a little further up the trail."

During part of the afternoon we idled about the camp, watching a succession of showers chase one another across the ridges south of us. So engrossed were we that we failed to notice one coming up behind us until a burst of raindrops in the treetops drove us to shelter under the tent. The sturdy little balloon-silk woods-home did its duty nobly, and though the shower was a

The Spence Cabin

heavy one, not a single drop came through. We were not so fortunate with surface water. Our camp had been made on a gentle slope, and we had neglected to dig a ditch around the tent. A trickle of moisture soon began to invade our residence, and make it unpleasantly muddy under foot.

When the rain has passed on, Mr. Sparks came up again, with a renewed invitation to move into the cabin. This time we accepted gladly, and soon had our outfit snug under his hospitable roof. That night the 12 x 20 foot cabin, two rooms and a loft, was to give lodging to eight; we three, Sparks, Lee Harrington, his two teenage sons and another herder whose name we did not catch.

Our contribution to the evening meal was a big pail of stewed fruit and a pot of "speckled pup" (rice with raisins). The pone of corn bread Sparks baked in the old dutch oven in the fireplace had a flavor no other method of cooking can compare but we couldn't hand him much on his method of frying "side meat". His idea seemed to be that as soon as the thick slices of "middling" were warmed through and the fat portion translucent it was done and ready for eating. After a meal of such fat meat, corn bread, and sorghum molasses, one ceases to wonder at the strength and endurance of the natives. It takes real men to handle that kind of rations as a steady diet, and the weaklings die young.

The rain brought a chill to the air and the warmth of the wood fire in the big stone fireplace was welcome. The conversation as we sat about after supper was largely confined to two topics—livestock, and the making (and makers) of the blockade liquor.

One of the characters discussed was Hol Rose, a Federal prohibition agent, whose killing while attempting an arrest had been discussed in one of Horace Kephart's magazine articles. From the point of view of these men, Rose had brought his fate upon himself by his nosiness and by the misuse of the powers of his office, raiding and destroying the stills of others while permitting his relatives and friends to operate undisturbed.

Our sleeping quarters were up in the loft reached by a ladder nailed to the side of the house. The others occupied bunks on the lower floor. Before we climbed to our beds, our host warned us we would probably find a few fleas. His advice was,

"Don't scratch 'em or aggrevate 'em none. Pretty soon they'll get their bellies full and go off and leave ye alone."

Personally, he didn't mind them crawling on him, "jest so long as they don't drag their feet."

He had said we would probably find some fleas. How right he was—SOME FLEAS! Never did I imagine there were so many of those creatures in the world. There must have been millions, and every single one of them joined in a parade up and down my frame with frequent pauses for refreshments. The other fellows had them too. In the darkness I could hear them writhe, scratch, and softly swear. During the night I smelled fly-dope, but if citronella was any help at all it was negligible.

Fleas were not the only visitors we had. Occasionally we could hear the faint patter of woods mice feet running along the logs of the cabin walls. As the glow of the fire below grew faint, a bat or two fluttered in through the open ends of the gable.

August 16, 1922

A typical high Smoky morning, a heavy cloud down over everything, met us as we looked out the door on this, our last day on top. Breakfast was quite similar to supper the night before, save that we substituted our bacon for Sparks' fat side meat, also superintended its cooking. How the natives liked the change we never knew, but for us it added several hundred percent to the enjoyment of the meal.

All the other herders were gone by the time our packs were made. As we

Bote Mountain

bade Sparks goodbye he gave us a cordial, hospitable invitation to return when we could and stay as long as we liked. There was no comment from the fleas who had feasted so royally on us the night before.

In the 1850's Dr. Isaac Anderson, the President of Maryville College, promoted the building of a wagon road from Cades Cove to the Spence Cabin, with either the promise or the expectation that a similar road to be constructed on the Carolina side to give shorter communication between the East Tennessee Valley and the interior settlements on the Little Tennessee and Tuckasegee Rivers. The Carolina portion of the road was never completed, but that leading northward along the side of the great buttressing ridge known as Bote Mountain was still in good shape. In no place was the grade excessive, and with a small amount of labor would have been passible by cars in dry weather. Down this old road we started, a twelve mile tramp to Townsend, in Tuckaleechee Cove, where we would catch a train on the Little River Railroad to Knoxville.

From the top down to Laurel Creek we made good time. Then we began to lag for the way up to the Gap was long, a hard pull, and a hot one, for we had grown accustomed to the thinner, cooler atmosphere of the higher elevations. Now the denser, heated air of the lower valleys was most oppressive. The trail was not particularly steep in any place but like the climb up Briar Knob, seemingly with no end. A dozen times we thought we had reached the gap only to find it still ahead of us just around the next bend in the road. A shortcut descent on the other side was so steep our packs nearly rode us to death. By now we should have learned that a shortcut usually had some concealed drawback, but we never seemed to learn.

The concentrated, waterfree, lightweight rations so necessary on a long backpacking trip will furnish every dietary need and when properly prepared are very palatable, but they don't include everything one might want. After several days a fellow's appetite begins to call for some of those luxuries and delicacies that a packsack can't carry. For some time now we had been estimating just what amounts of ice cream and watermelon we could put away in a given length of time. Here at Townsend, in the couple of hours we had to wait on the train, was the opportunity for a test, and right well did we prove it.

First, an uncounted succession of cold drinks and ice cream cones was sent down to prepare the way. Then a deal was made for the largest melon at the commissary, and it was carefully carried down to the river bank. When we finally laboriously climbed back up, to lie torpid on the shady side of the station all that remained of that melon was the rind, eaten down to the white. Not a trace of the red meat was left.

Henry left the party in Knoxville. Walter and I found that due to delays caused by labor troubles, train No. 42 was running so late we could get home by midnight, no doubt the first time the trip from the top of Thunderhead to Jonesboro had been made in a single day.

At the station in Knoxville we chatted for a while with "Doc" Essary, who reported a grand trip to Le Conte the previous Sunday making the ascent from the north, via the Scratch-britches Trail. Since the publicity given the U.S. Coast & Geodetic instrumental survey early in 1922 (the result of our barometric survey the year before) had attracted so much attention to Le Conte, such a number of persons had climbed it that a good part of the charm of the mountain had been ruined for those of us who prefer our wilderness wild and uncontaminated by civilization.

This trip, for several reasons, was one of the most enjoyable we had ever made. The work of packing had been relatively easy, not the back-breaking labor we had undergone on some other expeditions. On only three days did we cover much mileage and on but one of them, the tramp from Elkmont up Miry Ridge to Cold Spring Knob, did we do any amount of steep climbing. The remainder of the time was spent in short side trips without packs, in loafing, and in eating, mainly the latter two.

A more congenial party could hardly have been found. Walter and I had made many trips into the Smokies together and, Henry, an old friend, good woodsman, and camp mate, was a welcome addition to the group. All along the way we formed interesting new acquaintances, mainly with natives who were self-confessed "blockaders." We were not in any manner customers for their products, yet something must have made them confident we were not "revenu'ers." They had no hesitancy in telling us of various incidents in "stillin' licker" and in offering to procure a supply for us.

The weather was not exactly what we might have ordered, had the weatherman been inclined to listen. Not a single day without at least one shower and the clouds almost continually hung about the higher peaks. This, and the haze that replaced the clouds, made for poor visibility. The times we could look out to the distant ranges were not often. Yet with it all, only once was the rainfall so heavy that it inconvenienced us more than a short time. This was on the last evening out, when a downpour sent water running under the tent, and forced us to take refuge in the cabin.

Grub List – three men, six days

Bacon	3 lb. 4 oz.	Rice	1 lb. 8 oz.
Ham	2 lb.	Oatmeal	1 lb. 8 oz.
Bouillon cubes	4 oz.	Navy beans	2 lb. (8 oz. not used)
Dehydrated soups	1 lb.	Baking powder	8 oz.
Cheese, canned	1 lb. 8 oz.	Coffee	1 lb. 8 oz.
Powdered milk	1 lb.	Tea	4 oz.
Powdered eggs	1 lb.	Cocoa	4 oz.
Flour	8 lb.	Sugar	5 lb.
Corn meal	3 lb.	Raisins	2 lb.
Rockihominy	8 oz.	Salt, pepper, etc.	1 lb.
Evaporated fruits	2 lb.		
Sweet chocolate	2 lb.		
		Total	41 lb.

DATE: NOVEMBER 4, 1922

DESTINATION: GREAT SMOKY MOUNTAINS.

OBJECT: FIRST AERIAL OBSERVATION OF THE SMOKIES.

WEATHER: FAIR, HAZY.

PILOT: JAMES G. RAY.

OBSERVER: PAUL M. FINK.

By the autumn of 1922 I had been visiting the Smokies for several years, and had covered afoot a goodly portion of the main divide along the state line, as well as other outlying points. From the higher mountains I had often looked out to the distant ranges and down onto the lesser ridges close at hand, and had wondered how the whole would appear, view from far above. Walter Diehl, my trailmate on many trips who had been trained as a Navy pilot during the war, told me I'd looked out from so many high tops that a view from a plane wouldn't be too great a novelty. Just the same, I wanted to see those mountains from a much higher elevation completely out of touch with the old Earth.

Flying then was nothing like it is today (1958). There was no network of airlines covering the country, no palatial jet liners and no cabin planes. Most flying was being done by former military pilots operating out of small local fields, the most of them using the open cockpit, two seated Curtiss "Jenny" biplanes used as trainers during the war.

When my craving for an eagle's-eye view of the Smokies reached the point of action, it was with just such a pilot and in just such a plane. The pilot was James G. Ray, a competent flyer using the Knoxville flying field as a base. Ray, incidentally, was later vice-president of the Pitcairn Autogyro Co., (the autogyro was predecessor of the helicopter) and the first man to land an autogyro on the grounds of the White House in Washington.

Nearly five years after this first flight, I wrote a feature article on it for the *Knoxville News-Sentinel*, appearing in the February 27, 1927 issue.

As this was the first flight over the Smokies the pictures taken were the first aerial views of these mountains. They were made with no special equipment, just the same Kodak ordinarily carried on my mountain trips.

The account on the following pages is the article which was carried by the *Knoxville News-Sentinel*.

THE GREAT SMOKIES FROM THE AIR

Man who made first flight over future National Park tells what he saw.

(Editor's note: Paul M. Fink was one of the earliest advocates of the establishment of a national park in the Great Smokies. According to Carlos Campbell, secretary of the Knoxville Chamber of Commerce, Mr. Fink wrote letters urging that steps be taken in this direction years before the beginning of last year's successful drive. Mr. Fink lives in Jonesboro. He has been a haunter of the Smokies for years but even Mr. Campbell did not know of the fact that he had made the first flight across them.)

"Contact!"

At the voice of the pilot the mechanician gave a deft swing to the big propeller, the motor sputtered brokenly for a few seconds and then caught with a roar. A few minutes of warming up and then the pilot turned to me, already strapped in the observer's seat. Faintly I could hear his words through the roar of the engine.

"All ready?"

"Yes."

"Let's go."

The drumming roar of the engine grew louder, the retaining blocks were knocked from in front of the wheels, and we were in motion. A short run down the field and we left the earth without a jar, bound for the first flight along the Great Smoky Mountains, that massive range whose unbroken divide forms for sixty miles the boundary between Tennessee and North Carolina.

For several years all my vacations had been devoted to camping and tramping in these mountains, the eastern end of which is conceded to be the wildest and roughest portion of the country east of the Mississippi. Probably no area of equal size in all the East is so little known and for good reason, for the untold thousands of acres of forest where the timberman's axe has not yet been heard cover a terrain so rugged that only the most hardened traveler can win his way through. West of Clingmans Dome the tops are more open and travel is easier, but eastward from this point there is no trail, not even of animals along the crest, and the traveler is forced to depend for his existence solely on the contents of his pack.

For a distance of thirty miles the altitude is seldom less than 6,000 feet and the way, sometimes shown by blazes, more often unmarked, is through a forest of balsam so dense that even at noon the light is subdued, with frequent patches of rhododendron, and all on a ridge whose characteristics vary all the way from the comb of a steep roof to the edge of a saw.

Such is Smoky. Weeks of wandering along the ridges and through the valleys had made me long for an opportunity to see the whole from some vantage point so that I could properly grasp the idea of the immensity of it all, for I had always been, so to speak, too close to the trees to see the forest. From the air was the only way and I had determined that the first opportunity to see Smoky from that angle would be immediately embraced.

The experienced and capable pilot of the Knoxville Aero Corporation, James G. Ray, was consulted. He expressed the opinion that it would not be very difficult or dangerous—in fact, just such a flight as he would like to make. Arrangements were soon completed and one fine morning in November we took to the air.

Indian summer intensifies the haze that occasionally hangs over the southern mountains, giving the name to the Great Smokies. On this particular morning when we left the earth the mountains thirty miles away were hidden from us. At a thousand feet, as we were bound due south above the winding course of the Tennessee River, the mist was hanging like a great curtain around the whole horizon, and my heart sank for I feared that if the mist were so heavy in the lowland it would be more and more so on the heights, and our trip would be a failure.

Fifteen minutes later we were passing four thousand feet above Maryville and only faintly could we see the bulk of Chilhowee Mountain five or six miles away and directly ahead of us. More and more gloom descended upon us, and just a little more discouragement would have caused us to come back to the starting point to await more propitious weather.

But better things were in store for us. As we crossed Chilhowee at an altitude of 5,400 feet, the haze bank began to show some signs of possessing a definite limit in its height with a cloudless sky above. Away to the east, seemingly suspended in the heavens with no connection with the earth below, was a blue peak, its familiar three-fanged top proclaiming it to be Mt. Le Conte, on whose summit I had spent a week the year before in an effort to prove its altitude superior to that of Mt. Mitchell. Another and another peak swam into view—Clingmans Dome, Thunderhead, Guyot—and as we climbed higher and higher and drew nearer the main range the mist dissolved and left the whole scene before our eyes.

Scattered along the top of the western end of the Smokies are a number of those peculiar clearings or "balds" so often found in the Appalachians. To the most westerly of these, the Parson Bald, we set our course before turning eastward to follow the main divide, passing en route over Cades Cove, a beautiful valley some three miles long by half as wide, level as a floor and ringed in by mountains rising hundreds of feet above it. Such coves, too, are frequently met within the mountains.

Close to the Parson Bald is the Gregory Bald, another open space where cattle were grazing, lifting their heads as the roar of our plane reached them, perhaps wondering whence came the great bird that dwarfed the native eagles. Over these peaks we circled, casting an interested eye as the great roll of white smoke boiling up from a forest fire in the dust-dry timber of the southern slopes. Afraid to risk too close an investigation, Pilot Ray turned the nose of our machine eastward toward that higher and wilder part of the Smokies to see which way we had come.

Late in the fall as it was, all the foliage had not fallen from the dense hardwood forests covering the mountains and the great patches of rhododendron, known to the natives as "laurel slicks," showed plainly on the ridges their evergreen leaves contrasting strongly with the brown of the deciduous trees.

Flying at a fairly low altitude, for we were in easy gliding range of Cades Cove should the motor cut out, we drew near to old Thunderhead, one of the best known as well as most beautiful of the southern mountains. Beneath us was the "Old Field," many acres in extent, and so smooth that we could have landed on the very mountain top had we so desired. By the spring at the edge of the timber stood the Spence

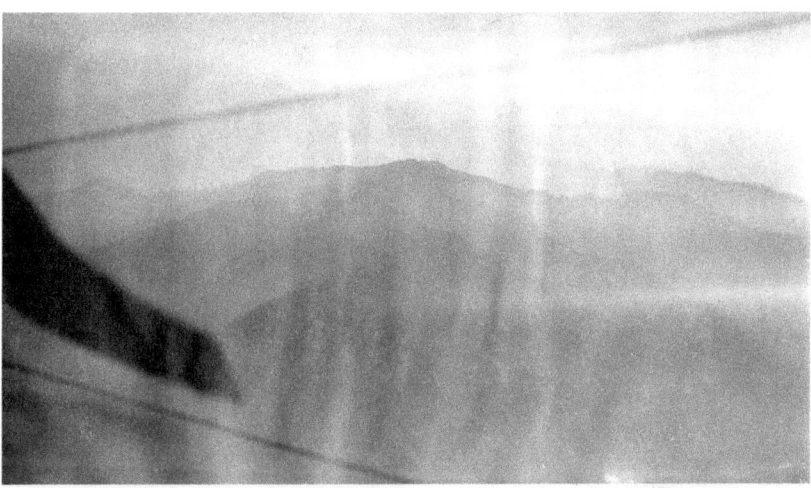

Approaching Le Conte

Cabin, one of the three cabins to be found on the top of Smoky along its whole length, and close by I could distinguish the very trees under which my tent had been pitched a few months before. As we passed over the cabin the herder of the sheep grazing in the Old Field came out and we could see him waving to us from his doorstep.

Leaving Cades Cove and Thunderhead behind us we began climbing to higher altitudes, for the peaks grew more lofty toward the east and we must have plenty of leeway in case they should cause any contrary air currents. Passing the Hall Cabin, the last of the three, we were 6,800 feet up and leaving the main divide, we directed our flight across Miry Ridge, the logging camp and summer resort of Elkmont and the long ridge of Sugarland Mountain, toward the three tops of Le Conte, the monarch of the Smokies. Sitting some miles north of the state line and cut off from the main chain of Smoky by canyons thousands of feet deep, Le Conte gives to the beholder an impression of immense bulk and sheer height that is unrivaled in the Appalachians.

Here was another place I had frequently pitched my tent, on the summit of Le Conte and its foot, and all the ridges had a familiar look for I'd often seen them from the Cliff Top. The Chimney Tops, themselves no small peaks, were almost lost in the tangled confusion of ridges in the Alum Cave Creek ravine and when finally located appeared as mere knobs of a steep divide for we were now nearly 4,500

Le Conte (center)

feet above them, our altimeter reading a little better than nine thousand feet above the sea. Here we were 2,500 feet above the highest point on Le Conte and all its slopes and peaks were plainly shown, densely covered with a virgin forest of spruce, to which the axe had never yet been laid. The Cliff Top clearing, carpeted with the same sand myrtle of the pine barrens of New Jersey, seemed like a closely clipped lawn and just off it stood the clump of balsams in which our camp was pitched a year or so previously when two friends and I spent a week there engaged in making a barometric survey of the mountain.

Circling to gain additional altitude, we were now to attempt the most ticklish part of the flight, that over the wildest part of the range where there was no house or clearing for miles and where a forced landing might prove a serious matter should our motor cut out. We passed high over the impenetrable vastness of Huggins Hell and pointed back toward the state line and that section of which Horace Kephart speaks in "Our Southern Highlanders," when he says, "The most rugged and difficult part of the Smokies (and of the United States east of Colorado) is in the sawtooth mountains between Collins and Guyot."

Passing just north of Mr. Collins we flew over the great gulf or bowl on the headwaters of Greenbrier Creek, one of the tributaries of the East Prong of the Little Pigeon. Hardly shown on the maps, this enormous chasm is hundreds of feet deep, its precipitous sides forest-clad,

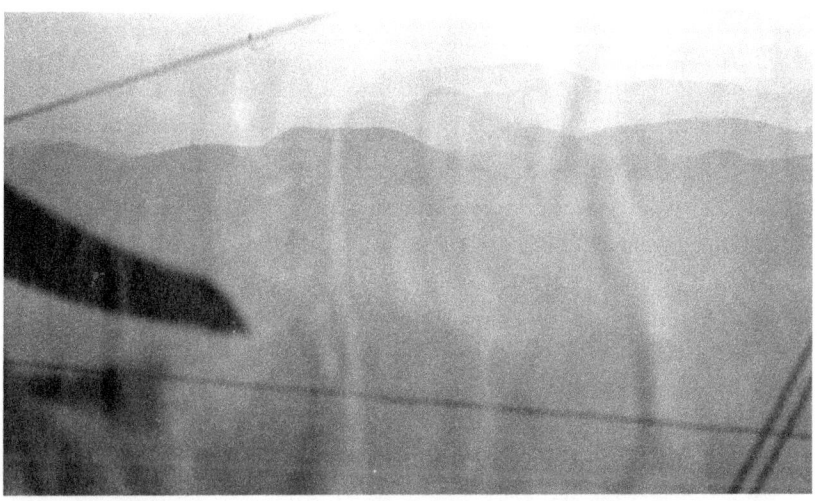

Guyot and its neighbors

though seemingly too perpendicular for vegetation to take root. Of all the ravines of Smoky, I consider this second only to the Alum Cave Creek Canyon.

As we sailed above it we could very distinctly tell why the few miles of divide just east of Collins had been given the name of "Sawteeth," for it resembles nothing on earth so much as the edge of a titanic saw. The ridge is extremely narrow, only a foot or so wide at the top with a precipitous descent for hundreds of feet into Tennessee and a slope almost as steep into Carolina. Perched on this narrow ridge are a series of sharp, jagged peaks a hundred or more feet above the general level of the crest, forming the teeth of the saw and completing the resemblance. Every inch is covered with dense bushes and stunted balsams and not a vestige of a trail along the top could we see. Two or three years before I had tramped along this part of Smoky with a companion and at that time had been impressed with its roughness and wild grandeur, but not until this opportunity of taking in the whole from above did I fully realize just how rugged and tumbled the mountain mass really was.

The bulk of Mt. Guyot began to loom up greater and greater before us as we winged steadily eastward following the divide, passing over Laurel Top, Hughes Ridge, and other peaks that as yet have been given no name, though their altitude of more than six thousand feet in another setting would make them widely known. Here all the recognition they are accorded is something like "the first sharp knob east of Hughes," etc.

From our lofty perch we were plainly shown why the foot traveler along Smoky is so often led astray from his true course. Naturally he would consider the state line, following the watershed, to be the higher but these mountains have a bewildering habit of often permitting the tributary ridges to be more conspicuous and lofty, tempting the explorer to follow them, only to be disillusioned when they finally drop away toward the valleys, leaving him to retrace his weary steps and try another lead. His compass cannot always save him from error for the true divide winds in every direction.

Logging has been in progress for several years on the Big Creek side of Guyot and as we circled over its top we could plainly tell the extent of the operations, the uncut spruce standing black on the top and on the Tennessee slopes in sharp contrast with the bare, eroded mountainside after the lumbermen had removed the timber.

Beyond Guyot, Smoky extends some miles to the Pigeon River, but this last big mountain was the goal we had set for ourselves. After we had sailed several times over its peak at an altitude of nearly ten thousand feet the nose of our plane was pointed back toward the point where Knoxville lay hidden by the haze masking the horizon. Compass navigation brought us safely to our destination where a long glide and a three-point landing ended the first flight over the length of the Great Smokies.

DATE: JUNE 14-18, 1923

DESTINATION: RICH MOUNTAIN, BIG BUTTE AND WESTWARD.

OBJECT: EXPLORATION ALONG THE STATE LINE.

WEATHER: FAIR, HOT AND HAZY.

PARTY: ROBERT H. DULANEY, PAUL M. FINK.

In plain sight from our residence was a stretch of mountains along the state line from Rich Mountain across Big Butte, or Cold Spring Mountain, and on to Camp Creek Bald, that neither of us had ever visited and that seemed to offer possibilities. It had been there all the time but we hadn't worried about if due, no doubt, to the method of reasoning which tells that the things far away are most desirable and that those close at hand are not of much interest. Whatever the cause, we'd never been further into these mountains than Copeland's plantation on top of Rich Mountain. This summer, when the call of the Red Gods became too insistent, Bob and I decided to see what was there.

June 14, 1923

So hazy was the atmosphere that when we topped the hill at the Conklin schoolhouse we could hardly see the outlines of the mountains two or three miles away across the river, a poor prospect for seeing the beauties of the country we planned to traverse. It was past mid-afternoon when we left the car at the Sally Hole, the old swimming hole on Clarks Creek and the end of wheeled transportation, slung our packs and started. Knowing only that we were started westward, we in no wise were certain where we would come out.

Only a mile or so did we pack that afternoon; to the mouth of Sill Branch where each of us had camped previously. As we laid our loads down, an enthusiastic reception committee of "punkies" or black gnats, rushed or flew out to meet us. From the way they went to work on our tender skins, they hadn't seen fresh meat from birth.

These pests of the woods are most in evidence close to streams or muddy spots where they breed in millions. Hardly half as big as the head of a pin, their bite leaves a tiny red spot and a lasting itch. Tobacco smoke or a smudge of

Bob plays chef

rotten wood helps drive them away as do most of the commercial fly-dopes. Smear it on lavishly not overlooking the wrists and the short hair at the back of the neck. Dusk and dawn are their favorite hours to attack.

Supper was over and the dishes washed up, a thick hemlock browse bed laid, and we were sitting by the fire smoking a last pipe before turning in. With no warning, from a small tree just across the road came the most awesome, bloodcurdling scream I've ever heard in the woods. Startled out of our skins and, I'll admit, not a little frightened we jumped to our feet. One grabbed the axe and the other a club, and backed up against trees, ready to do our best to fight off the panther or whatever ferocious wild beast might have given out that terrifying screech. A few seconds silence, and from the tree swooped on noiseless wings, a great horned owl.

We had heard before that the scream of an owl was often attributed to one of the big cats but never before had we heard one. The usual hooting and calling of the owls was familiar to us.

Fortunately for our peace of mind, the scream was not repeated nor did any other of the forest folk disturb us during the night.

June 15, 1923

Not so frequently as bad luck, good luck sometimes comes our way on the trail. Just as we shouldered our packs dreading the long, hard pull as we would climb from the valley of Clark Creek to the ridge of Rich Mountain, a man and a boy leading a horse hove into sight from down the creek bound for the cultivated fields on top of the mountain. The man, a Mr. Ratliff, we already knew. After a few minutes chat we all started together along the well-beaten track up Sill Branch. The boy was greatly interested in our packs, the kind of outfit we carried, how much it all weighed, etc. Knowing the steepness of the climb ahead of us he took pity on us as human beasts of burden and suggested that we tie our packs on the horse's back. We waited for no second invitation and in a few moments were stepping out free and unburdened.

Ratliff had much of interest to tell us concerning the country and the things in it. From him we learned that the falls on Sill Branch are on a fork entering the main stream at the Blockade, a line of cliffs to the right; that on Chigger Branch are the finest poplar trees in the whole country; that the tops of the maiden-hair fern, made into tea, would cure Bright's disease; and that this was to be a "snake year." There had been but a few seen the season before and to his way of thinking this invariably indicates a large number in the succeeding year.

The folks living on Clark Creek call it two miles from our camp to the top. At the Blockade, a quarter of a mile along the trail, we began to wonder just how much climbing there was to be in those miles and consulted our aneroid barometer. At the last water where the trail leaves the stream and starts up the long, steep ridge leading to the summit, we had ascended 650 feet and the point where we left the Ratliff's was 950 feet above this. Estimating the climb from camp to the Blockade as 200 feet, in no wise an excessive figure, this would give an ascent of 1,800 feet in the two miles.

Mr. Ratliff gave us parting instructions to follow a plain trail for about a mile, then take the right-hand and a little later the left-hand fork. That was fortunate for us for the big timber and the brush were so dense that we got only an occasional glimpse out. Then the haze was so dense we could raise no prominent landmark to orient us. Maps and compass are of little value on a ridge that never seems to make up its mind just where it wants to go but wanders in every direction.

The high point marked on the map as Wilson Knob, locally known as Grassy Knob or the "Big Stomp," was strongly reminiscent of Briar Knob in

Resting on Wilson Knob

the Smokies, a mountain that seemingly has no top. After climbing a while you see daylight ahead at the top of a steep little pull and you know you will be out on top in a few more steps. When those steps are behind you, you realize there is some little mistake, for there is yet another little rise to surmount. At the top of this, too, there is disappointment for there is still another just ahead. A dozen times did we think the long pull was over before we finally came out into the clearing that has given the name to the Grassy Knob.

This, under ordinary circumstances our first opportunity to take a look out across the country where we had been and where we hoped to go, was disappointing. The haze was still hanging so heavily we could see but a short distance, not enough to decide which lead we should follow to reach Big Butte, (also known as Cold Spring Mountain), our destination for the night.

We knew our direction was in general westerly. A plain path started that way first by a spring where we refilled our canteens, long since emptied in the stiff climb to the top. Past an old "gant-lot," where cattle grazing in the clearing were gathered and held preparatory to taking them off the mountain, we followed the crest of a ridge toward the west. For a time all went well but it was too good to last. The trail grew dimmer and dimmer, the bushes and briars thicker, and to our right, across a ravine in whose depths we could faintly hear the rushing waters of a stream that shouldn't have been there, loomed a ridge higher than the one we were on. Into our minds crept the idea we had followed the wrong lead and were lost. We wouldn't admit it to ourselves until after a few minutes the ridge we were on began dropping off smartly toward the stream.

Late as it was and with no certainty just where we were heading, there was no choice but to retrace our steps to the spring and make camp for the night.

The old gant lot, with its level surface, short grass, and old rails for firewood, was all we could ask for a campsite. So slight was the chance for rain we didn't bother to put up the tent. Bob took over the duties of cook but our appetites, sharpened to a keen edge by the day's exertions, wouldn't allow him to do the job in any orderly fashion. As soon as each item was done, it was immediately devoured without waiting for any other.

Either our fly dope had lost its efficiency or else the punkies on the high tops have a fondness for the flavor of citronella. They swarmed all over us—hands, arms, necks, faces, everywhere. No matter how thickly we plastered on the dope, it didn't seem to drive off a single one. Tobacco smoke was the only thing that helped and that not too much.

June 16, 1923

Luck was with us this morning. The air had cleared somewhat during the night and now we could see the top of Big Butte and trace the greater part of the route we should have to follow to reach it. No wonder we were misled the evening before. The true route started northward rather than west along a ridge bearing only the faintest of trails. This ridge, the divide between the streams flowing into South Indian Creek and those running north into Nolichucky River, lies across the head of Clark Creek and connects Rich Mountain with the range fronting the Nolichucky River.

Unfortunately, we could not find a spot from which we could get a clear look down into the canyon of Clark Creek, unquestionably one of the wildest spots in this part of the mountains.

A very deep, narrow gorge, its steep, almost precipitous walls rising hun-

Hunter's lean-to at Fort Davy

dreds of feet above the rocky bed of the stream, choked with rhododendron, Clark Creek offers an outstanding example of an untouched bit of the southern mountains, where conditions can be found rugged enough to satisfy the hardiest soul.

A trail coming up from Painters Creek joined the one we were following at Fort Davy, a well-known campsite used by hunters, herders, and forest rangers for years unnumbered. Here stood a solitary, gnarled old apple tree planted a generation ago by no one knows who. Whether it still bears fruit we could not tell. Certainly there was none on it as we passed. We searched, for our appetites would have welcomed fried apples for supper.

The way on to Big Butte was plain with no hard going until the last climb up the Butte itself. For a short distance this was as steep as the one up the side of Rich Mountain and this time we had no horse to carry our packs. Packing was not so arduous now, though, for we were getting hardened to it and the loads had been lightened by the inroads our appetites had made.

At the top of the steep pull we emerged from the timber into a tract of huckleberry bushes growing thick where a fire two or three years before had destroyed a heavy stand of kalmia. In the grassy clearing yet some distance before us, hundreds of acres in extent, we could see cattle and horses grazing and hear the shouts of the herders calling the stock to the salt log.

A frame cabin used by herders and forest rangers stood not far above the spring. At one time people lived here the year round. To save the exertion of carrying water up the steep slope from the spring someone had rigged up an ingenious device called a "telegraph" by the natives. From the house down to the spring ran a wire supported by posts. On this wire travelled a pulley from which a bucket was suspended. Gravity pulled the empty bucket down and dropped it in the spring. Filled, it was pulled back up to the house by a long cord attached to it. In addition to climbing the steep bank, we couldn't blame anyone for not wanting to visit the spring. Millions of punkies filled the air above it.

Clearing the top of the mountain had been the work of human hands and not that of Nature but it was so long ago—about 1885—that all the stumps had decayed and the raw scars obliterated. To all appearances, Big Butte could join the ranks of the natural balds in our mountains. Like the others, it is a spot of great beauty, where one could rest and enjoy sweet idleness for days. The great open spaces carpeted with long soft grass, the scattered trees, on every hand a wide view across mountains, valleys and lowlands to the far horizon, and over all a silence broken only by the rustle of the breeze and the tinkling of the bells on the cattle—it brings to me a sense of peace and contentment nothing else can give. Other places may be rugged and majestic and more beautiful in a wild sort of way but nothing in all the mountains possess the charm hanging over the balds.

From the top of the Butte a spur equally as high ran southward toward Green Ridge. Blithely we struck out along this, heading straight into North Carolina, until a glance at our compass convinced us that we were in error. Set right once more, we headed west along the state line with an anxious eye kept on a thunderstorm hanging over a range off to the left. Fortunately, the wind was blowing from us and we were saved a wetting. There was no place for shelter had the rain veered in our direction.

Of all the trails we have followed few have surpassed that one leading west from the Butte. Plainly marked in short grass on an easy grade through open timber, it was a joy to pack along it. But such things never last very long in the wilds. This was no exception to the general rule; its very excellence made what was to follow seem worse by contrast.

We were patting ourselves on the back and thinking what an easy day's travel we had had when our dream ended abruptly—likewise our trail. A broad path from the north crossed through a little gap. The one we were following ran into it and stopped. We were in a quandary. Should we push on along the trailless ridge toward our objective, or should we see if the new trail led around the knob ahead, and then on toward where we wanted to go? Loathe to hit the brush when there was a path in sight, we tried each direction for some little distance, until it became plain this was simply a trail crossing the mountain and would only take us to lower levels. To reach Camp Creek Bald there appeared no other course than following the divide. This we essayed to do, and right there Lady Luck deserted us.

There was no sign of a trail so we started climbing directly out of the gap. Brush and weeds were thick and near the top the ridge was strewn with great rocks. Higher than these and growing among them was rhododendron. Into the midst of it we pushed determined to get through. Almost at the beginning we might have had to admit defeat and turn back had we not found in the laurel a strip evidently chopped out during a state line survey some years before. It was already nearly obliterated by new growth and difficult enough to shove through but we persevered for a few hundred yards until we finally came to a good lookout.

Had I not known where we were, I would have sworn we were in the Eastern Smokies, for every feature of the terrain was similar. To the north the side of the mountain was nearly precipitous, hundreds of feet to the ravine below. On the south, the slope while not so abrupt, was steep indeed. The ridge on which we stood was of rough quartzite ledges. A few weathered patches of paint proved we were still on the state line.

When we looked at what was before us our hearts fell. For a couple of miles the divide was fully as rough and wild as the little bit over which we had just fought our way. We knew we could not hope to traverse it that evening at the pace the ruggedness dictated. It lacked but a little time until sunset and we must have light enough to find water and make camp before night. To be caught on that ridge in the dark was something to fear.

There were some indications we could soon find water on the Carolina side and in the morning regain the top by a ridge that would let us bypass all the rough going we could see before us. At any rate, we decided to drop down for the night and in doing so found the going almost as strenuous as along the divide. Loose boulders on a steep slope overgrown by laurel and other brush with plenty of bamboo briars made it more interesting. In struggling through all this mess I lost the heels from both shoes. From then on the lack of them threw me down every few yards with my pack on top of me.

Water was not so close to the top as we had hoped and even when found was in such a narrow, steep-sided ravine that we had to tramp splashing down the stream bed some little way before we could find a spot large and level enough to make a rude camp. At that, it wasn't sufficiently level or open enough to pitch the tent or even sleep side by side.

Experience has taught that the best "pick-me-up" when weary from hard packing is a cup of hot tea with plenty of sugar. Now, just as soon as a twig fire could be gotten going the pot was put on to boil, for both of us were almost exhausted by the strenuous afternoon. The tea down, a good meal followed to refresh us and we were soon asleep surrounded by swarms of fireflies.

Inquiry of natives the next day told us that the rough spot where we left the ridge was locally known as "The Stacks." (Stacks and Chimneys are native names used for high, rocky cliffs.) The stream to which we had come down was Chimney Creek, one of the headwaters of Shelton Laurel.

June 17, 1923

Remembering that there was a long climb back to the top and that my missing shoe heels with their hobnails would make travelling difficult, we decided to keep going down the stream on our way out to civilization.

Chimney Creek for some little distance bore all the earmarks of a stream absolutely untouched by man. Not a single stump or axe-mark on a tree or any other visible evidence showed that anyone had ever been there before us. So far as all indications pointed, we might have been a hundred miles from any settlement. The stream wound and tumbled through almost impenetrable rhododendron between the steep banks of a deep ravine. All travel was perforce in the bed of the creek itself over and around boulders ranging in size

An unnamed cascade

from that of a nail keg to half the dimensions of an ordinary room. Going was slow indeed for a mile or so until at last we came to a man-made clearing at the lower end of which the stream disappeared in a cleft in the rocks.

This evidence of logging, later found to be the upper limit of operations of the Laurel River Lumber Company on this tributary, presaged easier travelling for the rest of the journey. Nor were we to be disappointed for just below the cliffs at the lower end of the clearing over which the creek tumbled in a beautiful waterfall, were the rotting remains of an old tramway. Swept away in places by high water, 'tis true, yet easily followed, a veritable boulevard compared to our pathway down from the headwaters of the stream.

This tramway and road led down the valley close by the creek past its confluence with branches draining other hollows until it grew to quite a respect-

Upper Shelton Laurel

able stream. Tilled fields in the valleys and wheel tracks in the old road prepared us for a sight of human habitation but we were astonished to find, sitting beside the very first house, the ubiquitous Model T Ford car.

The remainder of our trip to the French Broad River at Hot Springs, N.C. was without event. To save time and perspiration, a car was secured a few miles further on and we arrived at the railroad in state, but too late for the evening train home. A hurried "director's meeting," a change in plans and our faces were turned toward Asheville arriving by train late at night.

June 18, 1923

Looking over the list of points of interest available in the few hours at our

The summit of Chimney Rock

disposal, Chimney Rock offered the best prospect. Early in the morning we were on our way travelling deluxe in a Cadillac by way of Biltmore and Hickory Nut Gap and down the gorge of the Rocky Broad River, advertised as the Grand Canyon of the East.

Beautiful though it may be, so extravagant a claim brought a smile, for in comparison to such chasms as the gorges of Doe, the Linville, and the Nolichucky River, the valley of the Rocky Broad had little to offer. It could be utterly lost in the Alum Cave Creek-Huggins Hell country of the Smokies.

Chimney Rock on the side of Sugarloaf Mountain some twenty-five miles south of Asheville across the Rocky Broad from the Old Rumbling Bald, is a formation of a kind seldom seen in the southern mountains where the slopes are generally covered with trees and undergrowth and where bare rock cliffs

Devil's Head

of any size are somewhat of a rarity. From the bed of the river the side of the mountain rises smartly up to the base of the great cliffs six or seven hundred feet in height, whose sheer walls form the face of the mountain. With a smooth, unscalable front, the cliffs are bare of all vegetation save for a ledge midway up. Here a few stunted trees and bushes have found footing. Along this ledge a path, dubbed the Appian Way, leads from Chimney Rock to Hickory Nut Falls.

At the eastern end of the mighty rampart is the Chimney Rock itself, a great column of stone rising a sheer two hundred feet from base to crest separated from the side of the mountain by a deep cleft like the gigantic thumb of a colossal fist.

From the highway to the base of the Rock an excellent road has been built with parking space at its upper end, with a tea-room, cafeteria, and other provisions for the comfort of the tourist. From here starts a series of flights of wooden stairs to all the points of interest—the Moonshiner's Cave, a fissure descending deep into the heart of the rocks; the Needle's Eye where a fat person could come to grief; and to the top of the Chimney Rock itself.

Here is a roughly circular platform thirty feet in diameter with a guard rail fixed to iron posts firmly set in the rock. From the platform one may look up the valley of the Rocky Broad rimmed in by mountains to its source in Hickory Nut Gap. Fifteen hundred feet below, alongside the bed of the river, the road to the lowlands winds like a yellow ribbon stretching into the distance until it is swallowed up in the haze over the foothills.

Close at hand, across the narrow crevice between, are the towering cliffs of the mountain rising yet some hundreds of feet higher. These, too, are reached by wooden stairs making ascent easy for the explorer. Here is the Blockader's Lookout just across from the Rock, and Devil's Head, a large boulder precariously perched on an inaccessible ledge, that, seen from the proper angle, bears a fancied resemblance to His Satanic Majesty. Along the top of the cliffs an open trail leads to Hickory Nut Falls half a mile away.

Our time at the Rock was all too short and we did not have the opportunity to explore all the trails and visit all the interesting spots close at hand for it was necessary that we return to Asheville in time for the afternoon train. We made it home that night.

DATE: JULY 13-21, 1924

DESTINATION: BALSAM MOUNTAINS AND THE GREAT SMOKIES.

OBJECT: EXPLORATION.

WEATHER: VARIED.

PARTY: WALTER S. DIEHL, PAUL M. FINK.

The old proverb, "Pride goeth before a fall," is full of truth. A high opinion of one's capabilities is a wonderful asset. Yet unless balanced by a thorough knowledge of what is to be encountered it can lead one on to great error with consequences unpleasant if not serious. Give ear to the sad tale of two who accounted themselves hardened mountain trampers, able to meet the high and rugged hills more than half way, to push on regardless of obstacles, and to laugh at the trials of the trail.

Looking over all available maps in search of very mild country we had not hitherto seen, the Balsam Range, coming from the south to join the Smokies just west of Mt. Guyot, seemed to offer the greatest possibilities. The mountains seemed to be rugged and very high with a number of peaks above six thousand feet. In addition, I wanted another close-up look at the Eastern Smokies in preparation for the coming visit of the Southern Appalachian National Park Commission.

Laying out a tentative route by map, we decided to hop off at Waynesville, North Carolina, going first to the widely known summer hotel at Eagles Nest. Thence we would follow the high divide of the Plott Balsam westward to Waterrock Knob where the Plott and the Richland Balsam ridges join. There we would turn north and follow the main chain of the Balsams to the junction with the Smokies at Tricorner Knob. Turning westward again along the Smoky divide, we would continue to Indian Gap and out via Elkmont.

Any way one looked at it, it was an ambitious trip, one that given favorable weather and trail conditions, would require a minimum of twelve to fourteen days. We had no pre-knowledge of what impediments to travel were hidden among those ranges. If things had continued all the way as they did on the start it would have taken two months to have made the trip as planned.

July 13, 1924

At Asheville we were misinformed as to the departure time of the early train and missed it by an eyelash. A bus—a big Hudson car—ran to Waynesville, starting from Pack Square, and by taxi we made that with five minutes to spare.

With a long wilderness trip ahead, our food supplies were larger than usual and our packs weighed in the neighborhood of seventy pounds apiece, but packed snugly in our sea-bags they had no outward appearance of being so heavy.

They were leaned against the building waiting for the car. As it pulled up we picked them up, or rather started to, to load them, but the porter forestalled us. Rushing up officiously, he grabbed one in each hand to lift them together, and was astonished to find himself anchored. He looked at them a moment, then without a word picked each one up by itself and put it on the car shaking his head in wonder as to what the packs might contain and the kind of individuals who might carry such a load.

The trip to Waynesville was almost as speedy as it would have been by train and much more pleasant than riding in stuffy coaches. It gave us a better idea of the country too.

There had been a time when we prided ourselves on making a whole trip on our feet and scorned either to ride or to have our packs hauled. We'd gotten over that by now. At Waynesville we chartered the only available vehicle, a one horse surrey, to take us to Eagles Nest. At that, the road was so steep and rough in spots that Walter and I would get out and walk to ease the load on the horse; the packs rode though.

There was no need to wonder why the resort at Eagles Nest had been so popular. Mountain range after mountain range filled almost the entire scope of vision. At one's feet lay the valley with the beautiful town of Waynesville nestling at the base of the mountain. To the southeast, through a low gap in one of the ridges, could be seen Mt. Pisgah, one of the widely advertised scenic attractions of the Land of the Sky.

Now there was no hotel at the very summit of Eagles Nest, only the ruins where a fire of a few years before had completely destroyed it. Another less pretentious one had been built about a quarter of a mile from the top not far from the spring that had furnished water for the former hostelry.

Ahead of us the Plott Balsam loomed black and forbidding against the western sky, its steep sides seeming to reach the very heavens, its top crowned with mist. Our way led across the summit after first surmounting Pine Rock and one or two lesser tops. Some way or another our enthusiasms began to wane as we looked up toward it for we well knew from former bitter experience the effect of a heavy pack on a physique softened by months of office work.

The longer we delayed, dreading it, the worse it would seem, so we gathered our courage and energy, slung packs and started hunting the trail. What there was left of it wasn't hard to find and the grade proved easier than we had dared anticipate. At one time it had been excellent, as woods trails go, but from disuse was now overgrown with bushes. Good resting spots were seldom passed unused and before long it was very evident that we would never reach the top of Plott Balsam that evening. Just before starting the last long pull up to the peak we began keeping an eye out for signs of water. Finding a trickle, small but ample for our needs, camp was made without delay.

On the trail the noon lunch is the lightest meal of the day, just sufficient to delay starvation for a few hours. Our appetites were fully ready for supper just as soon as it could be prepared with a little objection raised to scorched bacon or under-done bread. A thick mattress of hemlock browse made a luxurious bed and so tired were we that not even the hooting of the owls disturbed our rest. During the night we heard some sort of wild animal prowling and snuffling around the camp but didn't trouble to get up to investigate.

July 14, 1924

Experience has often demonstrated that one cannot simply measure off a set distance on the map and say, "I'll camp here tonight." Distance in miles is only one, and often a minor one, of the things to be considered in laying out the day's march. But optimistic as ever, before we broke camp we studied the maps and decided that we'd not be satisfied with anything short of Soco Gap for our next camping place. Thinking now in retrospect, it is certain that had we known what we were to encounter before Soco Gap could be reached, we would have changed our plans right then and there and left that section of the Balsams untouched by our feet.

To the peak of the Plott Balsam was a climb of some 1200 feet in elevation on a rough, steep trail. Easily enough found, like all others we were to encounter it was neglected and overgrown and in places washed out by the heavy rainfall. The last two-hundred and fifty feet was up a broken, rocky ridge. On one occasion I had to boost Walter up to the top of a small cliff and pass the packs up to him. Then, lying on his stomach on the brink, he reached down to assist me to reach his level.

The view from Eagles Nest had been truly great but this one from the summit of Plott Balsam was superb, much more beautiful and vastly wider in scope. The heavy, low-lying clouds and light showers of the previous day had cleared the atmosphere and the visibility was reasonably high.

Along the northern horizon was spread the whole panorama of the Smokies—the junction with the Balsams just west of Mt. Guyot, Old Black, the serrated outline of the Sawteeth, Le Conte's triple fanged top, the rounded dome of Clingmans, and Thunderhead and Gregory Bald at the far western end. The zigzag course of the Balsams and a hundred lesser mountains were at our very feet. The western skyline was the Blue Ridge, with Whitesides an outstanding landmark. The visible arc of the horizon was greater than one usually sees, and the magnificence of the scene was ample compensation for the ruggedness of the climb.

Refreshed by the rest and heartened by the fairly easy going we had encountered thus far and the excellent trail we saw leading away, we were in high spirits as we hoisted our packs onto our backs and started on confident we could see Soco Gap that night. The grade was all one could ask and the way wound through light timber. Wild strawberries were ripening in the tall grass and we stopped to regale ourselves with the tasty fruit. Thrusting aside a handful of leaves I was startled by—and recovered soon enough to catch—a baby rabbit just old enough to run about. After a few moments of captivity he was released to rejoin his companions further away in the bushes. This was the first rabbit we had ever seen above 6,000 feet.

One of the axioms of wilderness travel is that every "gravy train" soon suffers a wreck. This one was no exception for it let us down with a thud, one of the kind commonly spoken of as dull and sickening. The latter adjective is particularly appropriate for what we soon encountered and what was to be our portion for a day or two was enough to make anyone sick.

Leaving the Plott Balsam, we passed through an area whose sparse timber caused it to be overlooked when this section of the Balsam range had been logged a few years previously. Now we were to enter a tract from which the spruce had been stripped then swept by forest fires and finally overgrown by blackberry briars, ranging in size from breast high to giant canes, big as one's wrist, towering six feet above our heads. For a short distance the trail, or rather where the trail had once been, was visible only to disappear completely under the tangle in a few hundred yards.

Somewhere we had read that the blackberries of the high altitudes were thornless. Maybe so, but if any are completely without thorns they grow at more lofty levels than any I have ever reached. To be sure, those we saw this day had only a few thorns, compared to the lowland briars, but when one is forced to fairly swim through them for miles, even infrequent thorns will leave frequent scratches. Our hands, continually in use beating down and thrusting aside the briars, were soon bleeding and raw as pieces of beefsteak.

Travelling through such a tangle would be arduous enough under any circumstances. Now our heavy packs and the effect of the thin atmosphere made it double severe. So thick was the jungle that often, not fifteen feet apart, we could not see one another. The labor of breaking the trail was so exhausting that it was necessary for us to alternate on the task every few minutes. There was no sign of the briars having been disturbed for several years and when at rare intervals we did encounter the remains of the old trail it could only be distinguished by the slightly better footing. Following it was impossible and the attempt was soon abandoned, for there was no danger of losing the way so long as we stayed on the divide leading to Jones Knob just ahead of us.

From Jones Knob, where there was yet a small patch of spruce yet uncut, there was no lookout worthy of the name unless it be to the northeast. Before us, through the timber, was visible the great bulk of Waterrock Knob where the "Ledge," coming from the north, divided into the Richland Balsam and the Plott Balsam spurs, the Plott Balsam turning southwest to the Tuckaseegee River and the Richland Balsam bearing away to the southeast, until it meets the Pisgah range. The maps showed Waterrock as a single top, but in reality it is double, the peaks of equal height separated by half a mile.

While we were lying under the trees resting, a raven questing over the mountains winged so closely over our heads that we distinctly heard the hiss of air through his wings as he hurriedly changed course on sighting us. Up to that time it was the closest contact I had ever had to one of these great birds often seen on the higher peaks in the southern mountains.

Beyond the little fringe of timber at the top of Jones Knob was a continuation of the same kind of rough going that had been impeding our progress before, fully as difficult if not worse, for the top of the ridge grew rougher and more rocky. An hour or so of *swimming* through the tangled mess thoroughly exhausted us. Before long we began thinking of the night camp, an overcast sky and threatening clouds blowing over Waterrock Knob influencing our decision somewhat. To be caught by a rain in the midst of that jungle would have been decidedly unpleasant—even worse than wading waist deep in a mountain stream.

A small clump of birch and moosewood saplings offered a passable location for pitching the tent. Swiftly a space was cleared big enough to set up our camp Walter's infallible nose for water detected a tiny seep only a few yards away. While he developed this trace of dampness into a tiny running spring I was beating out a pathway to a few dead but still standing saplings to supply the night's firewood. Some young balsams gave browse for our bed, fortunately gotten under cover just as a shower came over.

The six-foot awning projecting from the front of our tent surely proved its worth and justified its construction this night. Safe and dry under its shelter, we performed all the evening chores, stripping browse, splitting firewood and cooking the evening meal over a small fire.

It had another use too. In addition to protecting us, the water falling on it was drained off through a hastily devised gutter into our bucket for cooking and drinking. True, it did have a faint but not unpleasant flavor of smoke but at that was far preferable to wading through wet bushes to the spring.

At the cost of exhausting labor, we had covered less than three miles this day, about as rugged a day's travel as we had ever done.

July 15, 1924

There was little pleasant anticipation of the so-called joys of the trail this morning. We knew full well just what we would have to combat before we could reach the summit of Waterrock Knob. The "briar-swimmin" of the previous day was already enough to last us for a full lifetime. Like being lost in the midst of the clouds, it was all right for an experience, but it didn't take long to become wearisome.

There was no alternative. Reluctantly we slung packs and started, sure there was nothing more wicked in the way of impediments to travel than we had already seen. We had something yet to learn. The footing grew more rough and rocky. Among the briars, fully as dense as those we had battled through the day before, were bushes and undergrowth too heavy to be shoved out of the way as we had the briars, necessitating more labor and many more steps to go around.

Heartened in the belief that at Waterrock Knob the trail would change for the better, for we had seen standing timber on the ridge leading north, we pressed on, wading and struggling through the brush, all but hung up, until at long last, exhausted and out of breath, we reached the summit. Here was a cruel disappointment. We had been consulting the map all along, relying on its accuracy, and had forgotten that the day before we had seen two peaks instead of the single one shown on the map. Unable to turn north where we were, there was yet a hard pull ahead, for the second top was yet over half a mile away. Between us and it lay a deep gap.

In the low point of the gap we conceived a great, labor-saving idea. Instead of climbing all the way to the summit of the next peak, we would turn to the right and "circumnavigate" it, reaching the north ridge without the hard climb up and then back down. Brilliant though the idea was, it never would have occurred to us had there been a trail visible. In the absence of any such, we thought that travelling around the mountain side at the same level could be no worse than climbing. In either case there would be the briars to contend with.

Sometimes one may have hard luck for a long time, then comes a change and it gets worse. So it was now. The grade grew steeper, the briars thinned out a trifle and were replaced by bushes, laurel, small timber and everything else that cruel Nature could throw in our way. A few hundred yards progress, at the cost of many minutes time and much perspiration, and we realized our idea wasn't so good after all, and that we'd never get through on that line. Back toward the top we turned our faces once more, up the steepest slope we had yet encountered.

For some reason never known to us, it seemed that the spruce loggers often leave a small crown of uncut timber on the highest points. This one was no exception. So dense was the stand of balsam there was no opportunity for a good look at the surrounding country. The only mountain in plain sight was Black Rock, in the Plott Balsams.

Resting, sitting propped against our packs, trying to get our breath back after the exhausting pull, we held a few minutes consultation on the advisability of going on. It didn't take long to decide to give up the remainder of the trip as first planned, for we could see with half an eye that it would be impossible to complete it in twice the time at our disposal. Even under the best of circumstances the original route had been a very ambitious one, permitting no loafing on the way. The new plan was to continue northward on the top of the Balsams to either Soco Gap or Black Camp Gap, then descend into the Indian country at Cherokee. From there we would go up the Lufty River to Indian Gap on the Smoky divide, then down to the Grassy Patch on Alum Cave Creek for a little trout fishing.

Our spirits rose when we found a faint old trail leading in the direction we wanted to go, promising easier travelling for a while. Blithely we stepped out along it, anticipating a pleasant afternoon's tramp and a good camp in Soco Gap that night. Alas for our high hopes. Hardly was the top of the mountain behind us before the old trail "petered out," leaving us with only the divide to follow. Infrequently the trail popped into view for a few yards, just to tantalize us.

Lying between this and a long ridge running southwest from the other peak of Waterrock Knob is a deep ravine whose near side dropped away from beneath our feet for nearly fifteen hundred feet to the bed of a little stream, with sheer rock cliffs and bare spots, results of landslides, dotting the slope. Logging in this immediate part of the mountains must have stopped only a year or so before. The tree laps were comparatively fresh, and Nature had not had sufficient time to cover over the raw scars of the skidways. Fortunately for us, fire had not ravaged this particular area.

About two o'clock we began to realize that our progress was so slow that this night, too, we would not sleep in Soco Gap. Serious thought was given to where we could find a spot big and level enough to make camp. Patches of dense laurel began to appear along the top of the ridge, and the disheartening difficulty of beating our way through them whetted our desire to get to lower levels and more open country. At the first low point in the ridge we turned left straight down the western slope, overgrown with dense bushy scrub, and so steep and rocky our progress was equally as slow as along the top. Down and down we went, first pushing, then sliding, a thousand feet or more, lured on by the faint murmur of running water, before we reached the topmost trickle of a tiny stream, that we afterward learned was Laurel Branch. The mountain side was yet far too steep for us to make camp, or even bed down, and we clung to the bed of the stream for some little way further. Old rotten stumps showed that the slope had been logged many years before, but there was little other sign man had ever been there before. Finally a few bits of sawn planks, rotting by the brookside, raised hopes that soon we would strike some old logging trail, and bring our troubles to an end.

In the lead for the time—the bed of the stream was far too narrow for us to travel abreast—I glimpsed through the trees what I first took to be the plank side of a tumbledown shack. A few yards further another appeared. Closer inspection showed them to be parts of the inner face of an old dam, long disused and now rotting away, through whose open splashway the little stream ran. The side of the ravine was too steep, rocky and brushcovered to go around, if any other route were feasible. I, not yet fully realizing what the structure really was, as I'd never encountered a splash dam before, walked through the splashway to its further end, hoping for a way to pass through and continue on downstream.

Looking over, I recoiled from the edge and my breath fairly left me, for to my startled eyes it seemed not less than a mile to the rocks below. In reality it was only some sixty feet, the gloom of the deep constricted ravine enhancing the apparent depth. I'm afraid my retreat from the splashway was somewhat more rapid than my approach, for the sudden glimpse of the seemingly bottomless abyss was just a little unnerving.

Scaling the crumbling, decayed inner face of the dam, carefully inspecting every plank before entrusting our weight upon it, we reached the platform at its top and gave the whole structure a thorough lookover, hoping for a way to get down the other side. Nothing even remotely indicating a trail appeared on the precipitous side of the ravine, nor was there a vestige of a stairway or ladder on the dam. A climb down the face, over the damp, slick logs and cumbered as we were with heavy packs, looked so dangerous that we decided that, particularly as it lacked little of being sunset, to make camp just above the dam, where sediment deposited in the basin had formed a tiny level spot. We could wait until morning to discover a feasible way of getting around the obstacle.

The planking of the dam supplied an abundance of firewood, and a clump of wild sunflowers and horse mint furnished our bed. The hard day's work had made us sufficiently weary to fully enjoy the evening meal and the night's sleep.

July 16, 1924

Camp broken and packs made, the first task before us was to find some way past the dam, with a minimum of labor as well as danger. Assuredly, it was not impossible to scale the side of the ravine and then pass around, but the slopes were so steep, rocky and brush-covered it would have proven an awful task. We had already passed through enough of that kind of going in the preceding days to make us exhaust all other means before taking to the bushes again.

Without a doubt a trail had existed at the time the dam was in use, but that had been so many years before that we could discover no traces of it now. No ladder was up the perpendicular face of the dam. Had there been one, we would have been afraid to trust ourselves on the rotten timbers. Next, we thought of lowering our packs by the straps, then attempting to climb down the log cribbing. But their combined length was far too short, and the great size of the tree trunks, three feet and more in diameter, coupled with the fact that the continual spray from above rendered them exceedingly slippery, made the rest of the scheme impracticable. Next plan was to chop a hole through the upper face and go down inside. That, too, was discarded, and for the same reason.

One idea and another was suggested, only to be rejected as not feasible. Finally, after close scrutiny, Walter thought he saw a possible route of descent on the right side. Slipping and sliding, at times lowering ourselves by clinging to stout bushes, we finally reached the rocky bed of the stream in safety. Not until then did we fully realize the enormous size of the structure. Its construction in this rugged, remote location had been no mean feat of logging engineering.

Higher above the bed of the little stream than its own width across the top, the dam towered more than sixty feet above our heads, and the narrowness of the dark ravine it blocked made its height seem even greater. In our minds we tried to envision the spectacular waterfall, when in the days of its use the gates above were opened, to suddenly release the impounded water, to "splash" the logs, cut on the steep slopes and rolled down to the stream, down to the larger river below and on to the log ponds of the sawmills. It was too great a strain on our imaginations, and we could only wish we had been privileged to have seen it then.

The front of the dam was an open cribwork of logs; none less than three feet in diameter. The only sawn timber used in its construction was in the spillway, the inner face, and the platform at the top. A vast amount of labor must have gone into its erection. Even the transportation of the sawn lumber, where there was no wagon road, would have been a prodigious task. The placing of the great logs of the cribbing, with no power crane to assist, would call for the combined efforts of scores of brawny men.

There was nothing to indicate that the spot had been visited for a long time. From the state of decay of the timber we judged that it must have been some twenty-five to thirty years since the dam was in use. Later we found this estimate to be very nearly correct.

There was no way out save to follow the bed of the little stream—rough, rocky and in places overgrown with laurel and choked with drift. Many mountain brooks have I followed, but never before or since have I seen one that for rockiness and rapidity of fall could surpass this Laurel Branch. Seldom could we travel a hundred yards without finding a waterfall from five to twenty-five feet high. There would be no trail around them and we had to descend the best way we could, clambering over and clinging to slick rocks continually wet with spray, often lowering ourselves by holding to the stems of the rhododendron growing beside. In the rough travel of the day before the heel of one of my shoes had been lost. Jumping from rock to rock, one is accustomed to rely on his boot heels, and the hob nails in them, for a sure footing. Now its lack made me slip innumerable times on the slick boulders, throwing me down, pack on top of me, or letting me tumble knee-deep into some pool.

Down, down, down we went, until it seemed we surely must be reaching the valley, and still the stream continued its descent. Toward the middle of the afternoon we found an old tote-road crossing the creek, and not far below this the site of an old, abandoned logging camp. Here we stopped and pitched our tent at once, for chafed by wet clothing and "stove-up" as I was from many falls, travelling had become rather painful and decidedly uncomfortable.

Walter captured a handful of grasshoppers and started fishing, for there had been trouty-looking holes all along the stream. I doctored myself up and then puttered about the work of making camp, cutting weeds for bedding, gathering firewood and all the other chores incident to a shifting camp. When supper was cooked we were forced to content ourselves with bacon, for the expected trout did not materialize, save for a few below legal size. Evidently the creek had been thoroughly fished out.

July 17, 1924

Far from recuperating, in the morning I was far more sore than the evening before, and properly thankful that the prospect for the day was for a good trail under foot and on any easy grade. Packing was uncomfortable at first, and grew more painful as the hours and miles passed.

Our camp had been near the junction of Laurel Branch and Hornbuckle Creek. In a short distance this latter stream emptied into Soco Creek. There we struck the dirt road from the town of Cherokee, in the Qualla Reservation, to Soco Gap—smooth and on an excellent grade, where the miles were the only things to worry us. Ten or twelve of these, with little shade and under a blazing sun, was trouble enough. More than once we longed for a Ford car to ride or a woodland trail to follow.

As the road wound through a part of the "Qualla Boundary" I took advantage of the opportunity, on this and the succeeding days, to observe as best I could the members of the Eastern Band of the Cherokee Indians living here, descendants of that portion of a once powerful nation who had taken refuge in the recesses of the Smokies when the greater part of the tribe was removed West in 1838.

We saw or met only a very few Indians as we slowly plodded along the road. Insofar as we could tell, these, both in garb and manner of living, differed very little, save in color of skin, from the white mountaineers. The few to whom we spoke were neither friendly or otherwise, answering our questions civilly, but with little display of interest. Most spoke good English, though occasionally having difficulty with the sound of R. Some of the older men professed not to understand us, though we had our own ideas about that.

All roads must lead somewhere. This one we were following finally brought us to Cherokee, the main settlement of the Reservation, a little before sunset, a shower catching us just outside the town. Really, it hardly justified the name "town," for it was but a small village, with four or five little stores and a couple of dozen dwellings scattered about. The fine school and hospital maintained by the U. S. Government alone distinguished it from a thousand similar hamlets among the mountains.

The long hours of packing under the hot sun had augmented my "stove up" condition, and I was about all in when we finally reached the settlement. Making a regular camp and getting supper called for more labor than I felt like putting out. Finally we decided to buy our supper at one of the stores, and to sleep that night on the floor of the little railway station. A watermelon topped off our meal, and after a few minutes chat with a white store keeper and some of the passing natives, we turned in at dusk.

July 18, 1924

This morning I was in far worse shape than on the evening before; my body from hips to chest aching and sore as a boil. I was totally unable to carry a pack, and for a while considered hunting a doctor.

When we planned to stay over for the day, Walter decided to spend his time fishing and loafing gloriously. I caught the morning logging train down to Bryson City, to see a doctor if my pain didn't lessen, and to visit awhile with Horace Kephart noted writer on the Smokies, camping and outdoor life. I had never met him in person, but had correspondence with him and a cordial invitation to come to see him any time I chanced to be in the vicinity.

Though there was great difference in our ages, we found many points of mutual interest, and the time spent with him was most pleasant. While in his office I was permitted to read the opening chapters of a novel he was writing, with scenes laid in and around Bryson City, and in the depths of the Smokies.

Returning on the afternoon train, feeling much better, I found that Walter had done his best to procure fish for supper, without success. So as usual—as long as it lasted—the main course for the evening meal was ham. The tent was pitched on the bank of the Lufty River, just below and almost in the shadow of the highway bridge. Interested spectators of our operations were five Indian children, aged from 4 to 8. Two of the little girls were typical little squaws, with round brown faces, and a touch of high color on the prominent cheekbones. The others showed plainly the tinge of mixed blood.

The gift of some raisins from our packs cinched their interest, and they hung close around. Under foot a part of the time, they showed evidence of good training, not offering to touch or meddle with any part of our equipment, no matter how intrigued they might become. After supper we purchased a watermelon at the store and gave each child a piece, offering an additional slice to the one who finished first. Immediately the air was filled with rinds, seeds, and squirting juice, mingled with squeals and grunts. Strict attention to business won, and the successful contestant was a little girl who "said nothing and sawed wood."

The evening before we had chatted quite a bit with J.F. (Jack) Gloyne, employed at Taquette's general store. Further conversation this afternoon brought out the fact that he was of English birth. On the West Coast at the end of World War I he had met and married Lula Owl, a full-blood—with Cherokee father and Catawba mother—graduate nurse serving with the Red Cross, and, following the war, returned with her to Cherokee.

Gloyne proved to be a Scottish Rite Mason and a Shriner, with membership at Tacoma, Washington. Walter and I were both Shriners. This gave a new point of contact, and we enjoyed thoroughly all the time spent with him. Before we left each of us purchased some native bead work, and also arranged for him to send me some Indian weapons and other craft specimens.

Incidentally, these proved to be in part museum pieces. One was the oldest bow yet left on the reservation, and the only one with its original bear gut string. This bow, of locust, was made before the Civil War by Jim Tail, who had killed a bear with it. Tail had served in Thomas's Legion in the Confederate army.

Another choice piece was a ten foot blowgun, with the patina of age on the cane. Then there were large cane baskets, of a size seldom seen today; pottery, some signed by Maude Welch, best pottery worker in the Nation; a couple of wooden dancing masks; ball, sticks, etc., all articles the casual visitor would find very difficult to obtain.

During the time spent in Cherokee and around the store we talked with quite a few of the Indians, and found them very courteous and interesting. Of the nearly 2000 then living in the Qualla Boundary, the majority were of mixed blood, the pure Cherokee strain almost entirely confined to the older fold. Practically all around the town spoke good English, and those who did not speak the language could readily understand what was said to them. In the more remote coves, however, there were yet living some of the older members of the Nation, (properly speaking, it is Cherokee Nation and not Cherokee tribe), who used no other language than their own. These latter were still using the bow and blowgun to some degree in hunting small game. Their cabins and houses are similar to those found elsewhere in the remote mountain districts. This is not necessarily due to the influence of white civilization, for the Cherokee were never a roving people. When the country was first visited by the whites, the Indians were living in towns of log and bark houses and were cultivating the soil.

The Qualla Boundary is owned by the Cherokee Nation as a body corporate and not by the individual Indians and is not an Indian reservation in the same sense as the reservations in the western states. The federal government maintains a hospital and a fine school at Cherokee. Any of the young men and women who wish are eligible to enter college at Carlisle, Pennsylvania, and many have availed themselves of the privilege. The good results of the school at Cherokee are easily to be seen among the younger Indians.

July 19, 1924

A day's rest had relieved my soreness, and I felt fully able to carry a pack once more. It had been our hope to catch the early jitney to Ravenford, where there was a large saw mill, and there beg a ride on the morning logging train that ran almost to Lufty Gap. Some way or other we missed it, so to save time and the labor of packing up the long trail to the top of the Smokies we chartered a Ford car with an Indian boy as driver to convey us some miles up the way. A few years before, the old wagon road up Mingus Mill Creek to Lufty Gap was sufficiently good that a car had been driven all the way to the Gap. In the building of the logging road up the valley, the railroad grade had crossed the old road, in a number of places and rendered it impassable for wheeled vehicles.

Lowering clouds and threatening showers made us dismiss our driver about half way to the gap, for a rain on parts of that road would have made it dangerously slick for a car. Well enough it was that we did, for we had scarcely packed a mile before a shower caught us. Not a smart, driving, invigorating rain, but one of the typical slow Smoky drizzles, when moisture is not only precipitated from the clouds above, but seems to drip from the very atmosphere as well, wetting one to the skin and chilling to the bone, and thoroughly dispiriting the tramper. We tried such shelter as a railroad trestle afforded, but that had more value in its moral effect than for the real protection it gave.

Fortunately the shower was of but short duration, and we were only damp when the cloud finally lifted and we were on our way again. On every ridge were the marks of the logger, cutting everything usable and leaving only enough scrub timber, culls and undergrowth to show that once the slopes bore a magnificent forest.

On this, the North Carolina side of the mountain, the slope is long and easy. The work of packing to the top is not very arduous, though it is very true that a long, gradual climb makes one think he is going on and on and up and up forever, and that the top will never be reached. Quite a distance below the gap we passed out of the area of logging operations and the road, good once more, mounted through a forest of giant hemlocks and mixed hardwoods. Here another rain, a harder one, caught us and though we holed up as best we might, wet us through and through. About this time our plans changed again and we decided to go around Mt. Mingus to Newfound Gap and from there drop down to the Walker Camp Branch for a day of fishing before going in. Getting across to Newfound Gap was easy, for an excellent trail led to it from the road, but the descent into Tennessee was something else again.

In the first place, it was like dropping down the side of a wall. The trail was very infrequently used, and neither the footway nor the marking very plain. The day's rain had softened the soil and made it slippery, and to cap it all, my shoe heel was still off. Anyone who has descended many mountains under pack knows how much one depends on his shoe heels for a firm footing. The absence of mine now slowed me up considerably and every few minutes it would let me down with a heavy thump. No one could have welcomed the sight of the rocky bed of the stream more than did I.

Close to where the trail to the top left the Branch and only a few feet from the margin of the stream is the Cold Spring, well known to the natives and fishermen for the temperature of its water, many degrees colder than that of the usual mountain spring, so cold that it hurts the teeth of the drinker.

Tired as we were, we dropped packs and made camp at the first opportunity, passing successfully that rigid test of woodsmanship, building a fire in the wet woods with only a single match, and no other kindling than the twigs and sticks in hand. Our bed was of hemlock browse and ferns. No Ostermoor mattress could have been more comfortable or more conducive to deep and sound slumber.

July 20, 1924

Walter decided he would see if the trout in these waters bite as voraciously as they one time did, and started up the stream, promising a big mess of fish for dinner. Well aware of his prowess as a disciple of Isaak Walton, I thought it hardly necessary for me to follow his example, but rather than have him do all the work (and be due all the credit) I broke out my tackle and went down the Branch. An hour or so of desultory effort, with not a fin or even a strike to show for it, and I gave up. Returning to camp I put in a hard morning's loafing before time to get dinner. This chore was just getting well under way when Walter returned, empty handed, with only a few barren strikes for his whole morning's fishing. Either the fish were simply not biting for some unexplained reason, or else in the three years since we had last been here, the stream had been completely fished out. We were inclined to the latter belief, for there were abundant evidences of the passage of many men, even beyond the point where the trail to Newfound Gap left the stream. We could think of no other reason for this influx of visitors than the former excellent fishing. In former years the trout had been so numerous, so voracious and so unsophisticated that even so poor an angler as myself had no trouble in catching as many as we could eat.

Now that the fish were gone, there was little excuse for lingering. It would have been a long, hard pull from this camp to Elkmont to catch the afternoon train, so we very leisurely followed the trail downstream, past the cabin at the Grassy Patch, where we had stayed before; our old campsite at Bearpen Hollow; with the Chimney Tops towering above; Le Conte Crossing, where we entered the old road to Lufty Gap from the Tennessee side; and down to Fort Harry Ford.

Here we observed in full degree the time-honored custom of the last night out—cooking and eating every bit we could possibly hold of the choicest foodstuffs remaining in our packs. Supper over, gorged and torpid, we rolled up in our blankets under the stars, not bothering to pitch the tent over our bed of hemlock browse.

July 21, 1924

All this was familiar ground, for both of us had tramped along this way a number of times before. Not hurriedly, but with due regard for the fact that the train left Elkmont shortly after noon and would not wait for our convenience, we moved on down the road beside the river, from the deep, primeval forest of the Smokies to the first house and then the straggling settlement. The road was left where the trail turned sharply westward, to climb the eastern face of Sugarland Mountain, 800 feet of the most wearisome climb in the whole country. Steep and mainly through open scrub pines where the sun beats down so fiercely it saps the strength; coming at the very end of the trip, this crossing of Sugarland is one of the minor ordeals of the trip.

But every mountain must have a top and finally we passed over this one, through the Huskey Gap, stopping for lunch at the little spring just beyond the crest. Now all our troubles were over, for the remaining mile and a half was all down grade, first along an old forestry trail, and then a road down the creek valley to Elkmont. From thence the train carried us to Knoxville, and the next morning home.

So ended the trip, a most enjoyable one, but with some hardships surpassing any other we had ever made. We had before battled through the laurel and brush along the Sawteeth, and considered it about as bad as one could ever find. When we had followed the divide of the Black Mountains from Mt. Celo to Deep Gap we thought we had encountered the very worst trail conditions possible, save for a laurel "slick" alone. Now we had found that a five year stand of blackberry briars, big as one's wrist and twelve feet high, easily surpassed firecherry growing in spruce brulé.

Wearisome, heart breaking labor though it may have been to force our way through the tangled growth and up the steep slopes, yet when it was over—yes, and while we were in the midst of it—there was a sense of exhilaration in the thought of surmounting all Nature's obstacles that made the joy of following the trail worthwhile. Though while in the midst of the jungle we would wrathfully call down curses on our own heads should we ever knowingly get into such a place again, we were hardly out in the open country again before we had forgotten the cruel hardships and would joyfully have tackled once more anything the mountains had to offer.

Grub List – 2 men, ten days

Bacon	5 lb.	Baking powder	4 oz.
Ham	3 lb.	Desiccated potatoes	8 oz.
Egg powder	8 oz.	Dehydrated vegetables	1 lb.
Powdered soups	2 lb.	Navy beans	8 oz.
Cheese, canned	2 lb.	Sweet chocolate	2 lb. 8 oz.
Powdered milk	1 lb.	Sugar	6 lb.
Crisco	8 oz.	Coffee	1 lb.
Flour	7 lb.	Tea	4 oz.
Corn meal	3 lb.	Evaporated apples	1 lb. 8 oz.
Rice	2 lb. 8 oz.	Evaporated apricots	1 lb.
Oatmeal	2 lb.	Evaporated peaches	1 lb.
Dried beef	1 lb.	Raisins	1 lb. 8 oz.
Bouillon cubes	4 oz.	Salt, pepper, etc.	8 oz.
		Total	47 lb. 8 oz.

These supplies, about 2 pounds 6 ounces per man per day, were just a little heavy. There was left a surplus of sugar and flour, and only a little of the dehydrated vegetables was consumed.

THE SOUTHERN APPALACHIAN NATIONAL PARK COMMITTEE SEES LECONTE 1924

Just when and where sentiment for a National Park in the Southern Appalachians first began to take form would be impossible to tell. Traces of it are found in too many places. About the turn of the century the Appalachian National Park Association, an organization to work toward that end, was formed in Asheville. Legislation creating the National Forests seemed to satisfy their wishes and their activities ceased.

The idea did not die but kept cropping up here and there. Sensing the popular demand and at the suggestion of Stephen T. Mather, Director of the National Park Service, Secretary of the Interior Hubert Work appointed, early in 1924, the Southern Appalachian National Park Committee charging it with the duty of visiting and investigating the Southern mountains to see if a suitable site or sites of National Park caliber might be found. The group was composed of Major Wm. A. Welch, general manager of the Palisades Interstate Park, New York; Hon. Henry W. Temple, member of Congress from Pennsylvania; Col. Glenn S. Smith, U.S. Geological Survey; William G. Gregg, retired manufacturer, Hackensack, N. J.; and Harlan P. Kelsey, horticulturist and former president of the Appalachian Mountain Club, Boston.

Pursuing its duties the committee came south and arrived in Asheville the latter part of July, 1924. In the meantime, interested persons in Knoxville had formed the Great Smoky Mountains Conservation Association with W. P. Davis as president and Col. D. C. Chapman as moving spirit. Hearing that the committee was in Asheville, these men and a few others drove over to meet them and to present the claims of the Smokies for their consideration. I chanced to be in Knoxville that day and to have called on Col. Chapman to offer such aid as I might be able to give. When I told him that I had known Mr. Kelsey some years and also that I was familiar with the virtually unknown interior of the Smokies, I was asked to join the party.

Our invitation was accepted. All the committee was not able to come at the time and Messrs. Kelsey and Gregg were sent to take the first look at the area. They arrived in Knoxville August 4, 1924, and were immediately taken by car to Gatlinburg.

The first point of interest to be shown them was the spectacular summit of Le Conte. A trail of sorts had been laid out and partially cleared up the mountain and a rude lookout tower of poles set up on top. To go up and back the same day would be too much of a trip with little time for observation so shelter of a very primitive nature was set up for an overnight stay. A rude shack with tarpaper roof and burlap sides, fitted with a few cots and army blankets, a table and seats of poles and shakes roughly thrown together and a brush lean-to or two comprised all the accommodations on the mountain.

During the latter part of the night before we planned to start, a torrential rain fell. At dawn it ceased and by nine o'clock the clouds cleared away enough to justify the climb.

It was an incongruous cavalcade that gathered at the Mountain View Hotel to start the ascent. The plan had been to hold the group to about fifteen men but everybody wanted to get in on the party and about twenty-five made the trip. In addition to Messrs. Gregg, Kelsey, Davis and Chapman, there were Gens. Frank Maloney and Cary Spence; R.S. Maddox, State Forester; Russell Hanlon, Secy., Knoxville Automobile Club; Loye W. Miller, reporter, *Knoxville News*; Dean Newman, feature writer, and E.E. Burtt, cartoonist, *Knoxville Journal*; A.J. Fisher, Maryville; Dr. Arthur Kendall, President, Washington University, St. Louis; Dr. H. C. Longwell, Princeton University; Dr. R. N. Kesterson, Knoxville; and others whose names I have forgotten. Wiley Oakley and half a dozen other local men acted as guides and did the heavy work of camp making. Certainly not the least in importance was John Morrell, who did such an excellent job of keeping the party fed.

The outing garb of the party was in as wide variety as was the personnel. Riding breeches and leggings predominated, at least among the trailwise. Some of the others had never been in the big mountains before, had only the haziest of notions of what they would encounter, and had dressed as if for a stroll in a city park. There were golf knickers and stockings, business suits, white shirts, high linen collars, low-cut street shoes, straw hats and the like. One shudders to think what a disheveled lot it would have been if we had met a real Smoky Mountain rain enroute. Dr. Kesterson must have feared one, for he carried his umbrella the whole way.

We were to go as far as the Cherokee Orchard on horseback but the supply of saddle horses in Gatlinburg wasn't large enough for the enlarged party and Dr. Kesterson and one or two others were forced to ride mules. I elected to walk rather than ride either and was at the Orchard as soon as any one.

For a mile or so above the Orchard the trail followed Le Conte Creek, now swollen from the night's rain and roaring and rumbling over the rocks in its bed. The trail was wet and muddy and very soon the wearers of street shoes began to see the error of their ways.

Lunch was spread on the great gray boulders at the foot of the Rainbow Falls, now running full spate and showing itself at its best. The rush of the stream carried the falling water so far out from the foot of the cliff that we all walked beneath the falls as we resumed the march onward toward the top.

Before long the strenuous exertion of climbing up the steep, slippery trail began to tell on the older members of the party and those unused to such hard physical exercise. As we gained altitude the rarity of the air also got in its work. Someone was continually dropping out of line to sit, panting, on a convenient log or rock beside the trail, to rest and catch his breath again. By twos and threes the party strung out at great length along the trail, the hardier souls far in the lead. To one of the packers and me was assigned the position of file closers, lest some overfatigued member be unable to make it alone, need help, and unwittingly be left far behind. By rare good fortune no one failed to complete the climb, but the slow-moving rear guard was a full hour later than the leaders in reaching the top.

By that time a thick cloud was sitting atop the mountain and while a few of us went on the short distance to the Cliff Top, there was nothing we could see and the prospect for a successful display of Smoky's greatest attraction was dim indeed. The remainder of the afternoon was spent hovering around the big log fires drying out soaking feet and seeking protection from the dampness of the mist and the penetrating chill of the mountain air. The atmosphere in Knoxville had been hot and humid but here, more than a mile above the sea, the temperature was in the low 50's. That was a feature that many had not anticipated and dressed properly for. Before long the correct costume for the evening was a blanket draped gracefully about the shoulders.

The shelter had been planned to accommodate not more than sixteen men but the party had grown to twenty-five. The guides hurriedly threw up a couple more primitive lean-tos, thatched with balsam fans and furnished with deep beds of the same fragrant material. They were not at all unpleasant sleeping quarters though the roofs were not completely watertight. Now and, then a big drop of moisture would fall full in the face of some sleeper, bringing him to wakefulness with a start.

There wasn't too much sleeping done, though, I'm afraid, at least not in the lean-tos. The fear of the unknown and of all the beasts that prowl in the darkness was upon some of the tenderfeet and the more woodswise did little to dispel it. On the contrary, they did everything possible to augment those fears.

When the bloodcurdling scream of a horned owl came from the spruce trees further out along the mountain, it would be laid at the door (throat, rather) of a hungry panther, prowling in search of a human victim. The theme of conversation immediately changed to hunting adventures and hairsbreadth escapes. A bush rustling in the night breeze was without doubt a lurking bear. So realistic and lurid did the stories grow that two or three of the party lost all desire for sleep and spent the rest of the night sitting swathed in blankets around the fire glancing fearfully over their shoulders at every new and strange sound of the night.

Just as though they sensed the importance of the occasion, Nature and the mountain outdid themselves to put on a real show for the visitors the next morning.

It was barely light enough to see when we rolled out and picked our way along the dim trail under the balsam trees to the Cliff Top to see the sunrise.

As we stood there, on one of the highest points of the Smokies, only a few other distant peaks were to be seen raising their heads above the clouds like tiny blue islets scattered over a fleecy sea. All the depths below were choked with tumbling white mist that occasionally rifted here and there to give us a fleeting glimpse of steep ridges and deep ravines then closed to hide them once more.

Away to the east the sun peeped over the horizon to touch the billows of the white sea with a delicate pink then a deeper rose. As it climbed higher, the clouds began to break away in places, with more and more mountain ranges coming into view. Breakfast time came but not a man wanted to tear himself away from the beautiful, ever-changing scene.

By eight o'clock all the morning mist had been burned away and the air was freer of haze than was ordinarily the case. From our grandstand seat on Le Conte, all the peaks of the Smokies were spread out for the committee to see. Starting far to the west with the great, rounded bald top of Thunderhead, our eyes came on past Silers Bald, Clingmans Dome, Mt. Collins and the Sawteeth, to Hughes Ridge and the immense bulk of Mt. Guyot to the east. At our feet were the bottomless chasms of Alum Cave Creek and Huggins Hell. To the horizon in every direction, ridge was piled on ridge, mountain on mountain, as far as our eyes could reach.

Not a one of us but could have stayed for hours gazing over the matchless scene, but there were other things to be looked at and we had to start down off the mountain to meet the horses sent to the Grassy Patch for us.

A trail, much ruder, steeper, and more rugged than the one up which we had climbed the day before had been marked down the southern side of the mountain by way of Alum Cave to the West Prong of the Little Pigeon River. Most of the party gathered together their possessions and started down, leaving the others to pack the rest of the gear and return by the easier route.

Now the tyros in mountaineering found out the hard way that it is even worse going down a steep slope than climbing up one. This one was steep, no doubt about it, almost precipitous in spots. At times we had to lower ourselves by treeroots and bushes, even slide a few feet when the soaked footing gave way beneath our boots. The last couple of hundred feet above Alum Cave, when we came down a bush-dotted cliff set at an angle of 60 degrees, was even worse. Sitting down, we inched our way along on the seats of our breeches hanging on by whatever chance holds we could grasp.

As usual, the immensity of the overhang of Alum Cave awed those now seeing it for the first time. The committee called a halt to inspect it and for a needed rest. From here on down to the stream below the slope was steep enough but not so rugged or bushy as above.

The labors of the trip the unusual physical exertion of the climb up, and now the telling strain of the descent, was wearing down the older members of the party. Mr. Davis in particular, leaning heavily on his stick, kept plodding gamely on, slower and slower, welcoming a helping hand over the rougher spots.

We found no horses waiting when we all finally gathered at the Grassy Patch at the junction of Alum Cave Creek and the Walker Camp Branch, though Andy Huff of the Mountain View Hotel had promised faithfully to have them there for all the party. We threw ourselves on the ground for a welcome rest but when the time passed mid-afternoon and no horses we began to worry. Finally we decided to move on down the stream hoping to see them any minute. They never came and only next day did we know the reason.

It all came about through a misunderstanding over names and places, not at all surprising when one remembers how little even the natives knew of the interior of the Smokies in those days. The present Indian Gap was called by a variety of names—Indian Gap, Road Gap, Lufty Gap, Wears Gap, Smoky Gap, Grassy Gap and others. When the horse wranglers were directed to take our mounts to the Grassy Patch they probably had never even heard of the place and thought what they had heard called Grassy Gap was the spot intended. So there they went, far from any place we expected to reach. Faithfully they waited for us in the Gap until dark, then, unable to safely pick their way back down the rocky, abandoned roadway, spent the night there.

From the Grassy Patch on down the trail was far easier than anything else encountered that day. The party strung out along it, the younger, hardier members soon gaining a long lead, the leg-weary older ones dropping far behind. Another young man and I stayed with the last group to help them along in case of need. At both Le Conte Crossing and Fort Harry Ford, Mr. Davis and Dr. Kesterson found themselves too exhausted to leap from boulder to boulder in crossing the stream. We had to wade through water hip deep, carrying them piggyback.

It was sundown when we reached Cole's cabin just below the Chimney Tops, and the furthest house up the stream. Mr. Davis's legs had now given out entirely and it was impossible for him to go further. The Cole's, in keeping with mountain hospitality, offered such shelter as they had and prepared supper for the four of us. Dr. Kesterson was in almost as bad condition as Mr. Davis and elected to stay with him. We two younger ones set out for Gatlinburg, seven miles away, after dark. The road was rocky and rutted and we stumbled and fell in the darkness and it was almost midnight before we reached the Mountain View. Nothing would do big hearted Andy Huff but that he raid the kitchen for a late meal. Well fed, we were too tired to worry much about the rest of the party, and tumbled into bed.

Next day we heard that as the others tramped down the road they stopped at every house and hired every horse they could find, saddle or otherwise, 'til Gregg and Kelsey and some of the other more exhausted men were mounted. Most of them proceeded on to Elkmont where it had been planned to spend the night.

The inspection trip continued for several days based on Elkmont but my time was limited and I was forced to leave for home after the visit to Le Conte.

The trip was a very successful one and the two committee members were most favorably impressed. Before long they sent down the others that they too might see at first hand what the Smokies were really like. Their report, as made to Secretary Work after eight months sent investigating and visiting many suggested sites in eight states, said,

"Of these several possible sites, the Great Smoky Mountains easily stand first, because of the height of the mountains, depth of valleys, ruggedness of the area, and the unexampled variety of trees, shrubs and plants."

Dr. H. C. Longwell, one of our party, told of his memories of the trip to the top of Le Conte:

> "My experience on Le Conte will linger in memory as standing out unique, without parallel or duplication. The harmony of colors I saw blended with the peculiar haze reminding me of a spiritual veil is absolutely indescribable. We can receive sensations of pleasure by the symphony of colors through the eye just as the tones and melodies of music please us through the ear.
>
> "I was born in the Rocky Mountains and was reared to contemplate the glorious colors of its scenery. I have stood on the snow crowned mountains of northern Greece and watched the rivers glide at their base, and can well understand how the ancient Greeks were the greatest lovers of beauty of all times.
>
> "I have seen the Bay of Naples from Vesuvius and reveled in the glory of the sunset which bathed the ships in the bay in gold, silver and brass. I have looked upon the beauties of the Alps of Japan, and was entranced with the natural beauty of the Hawaiian Islands.
>
> "The grandeur of the Grand Canyon, as it winds through Arizona into Mexico overwhelmed me. Still not satisfied in craving for natural beauty, I went south a hundred and twenty-five miles into Mexico and gazed upon the lake, forty by five to fifteen miles in width, nestled in the mountains.
>
> "After all these experiences I looked from the top of Mt. Le Conte. It was wholly unique. In its blending of color, its multiplicity of outline, enveloped in its fairy, ghostlike veil of haze, there is nothing else on the face of the earth like it."

DATE: AUGUST 6-12, 1925

DESTINATION: GREAT SMOKIES.

OBJECT: EXPLORATION.

WEATHER: GENERALLY FAIR, SHOWERS.

PARTY: MILTON AILES, JR., MORGAN GILBERT, WALTER S. DIEHL, PAUL M. FINK.

As had been our custom for some ten years, Walter and I had been planning for a week of backpacking somewhere in the big mountains. The Smokies had been our choice again this year, for we had the craving to visit that country once more, before the spruce logger had cut it over and forever spoiled the wonderful primeval forest of the upper levels. Or else it might be purchased for inclusion in the hoped-for National Park. That would permanently preserve the forest, but by building roads and trails to make it easily accessible to the public, it would become so much a public property that the swarm of visitors would take away that solitude that added so much charm for us. We knew that time was rapidly passing and one or the other of these fates would soon befall the Smokies. We grasped the opportunity this year to retrace the trail along the eastern half of the range, out to Mt. Guyot.

Before we had decided just where and when we would go, a request came from Mr. Milton E. Ailes, President of the Riggs National Bank of Washington, D.C., asking that we take his son, Milton, Jr., and a friend into the Smokies with us, that they might gain some personal knowledge of the real ruggedness of the southern mountains.

There is no means of predicting just how a person will react to strenuous camping activities under primitive wilderness conditions. Hence, for safety's sake, we had a firm resolution that we would never take any person deep into the wilds of the Smokies before one or the other of us had tried him out thoroughly under less rigorous conditions. Ailes, Sr. was in a position of exerting great influence favoring the proposed National Park. To spread the gospel of just what wonderful country the Smokies really are and to gain his support, we shelved our resolution and agreed to take the boys with us.

Both of them had been to Boy Scout camps and to dude ranches in the west, and fancied themselves as competent woodsmen. We promised ourselves that if they wanted to see some rough country, we'd see that they got a taste of rough camping also.

A few days before we were to shove off they passed through Jonesboro by car. It was planned that we pick them up in Elkmont.

August 6, 1925

Walter and I went by early bus to Knoxville. There we learned that, contrary to what we had been told, the afternoon train of the Little River Lumber Co., did not go all the way to Elkmont, but spent the night at Townsend. That threatened to wreck our schedule, but we kept on hoping some break of good luck would get us to Elkmont that night.

The break came at Townsend when we learned that George Galyon, Victor Hacker, and his wife, all of Knoxville, were also bound for Elkmont and had chartered the gasoline car used by the officials of the Little River Lumber Co. Explaining our mission, we thrust ourselves upon them and were very graciously permitted to join the party. More than that, we were very graciously not permitted to pay our part of the fare.

At Elkmont, we soon located Ailes and Gilbert and found that quarters had already been arranged for us at the Appalachian Club, through the courtesy of Col. D. C. Chapman. Our gear and supplies were thoroughly checked and packs apportioned, all ready for an early start in the morning.

August 7, 1925

Early hours were in no wise fashionable in the summer resort colony of Elkmont, and it was only by special dispensation that we had eaten our breakfast and were on our way by 8:30, along the trail Walter and I had often used before, crossing Sugarland Mountain at the Huskey Gap and down to the valley of the Little Pigeon River. Up the stream we turned, bound for the crest of the Smokies at the low point variously known as Indian, Wears, Lufty, Grassy, Smoky or Road Gap.

The original schedule had been to make the first night's camp at this gap, no great feat for a trail-hardened tramper with an early start and under a moderate pack. We had failed to take into consideration our physical condition, soft after months of office work and with no preliminary hardening. Our pace

Our first view of Le Conte

grew slower and slower, and the rest stops more frequent and longer. When in midafternoon we came to Fort Harry and caught a glimpse of trout in the pools we decided, without a single dissenting vote, to make camp then and there, and try to add some of those trout to the menu for the evening meal. A fine plan, from our standpoint, but the trout had no mind to cooperate, and with one accord refused to offer themselves as a sacrifice to our appetites.

The boys were put to work gathering firewood, while we busied ourselves with the other chores of woods housekeeping. When the wood pile had grown to some size, Walter walked over, looked at it a moment and in an assumed ferocious voice, demanded

"Who in heck brought this junk in?"

"We did, sir," came the astonished answer. "Our scoutmaster always told us to pick up fallen wood, and never cut down anything standing."

A few hearty kicks from Walter sent the pile of rotten limbs flying back into the brush.

"Don't *ever* bring in anything like that again! You couldn't burn it in a bonfire. Here—give me the axe! I'll show you what real firewood is like."

And so the first lesson in wilderness woodsmanship was given.

The same rock fireplace and crotched sticks Walter and I had used the year before served in preparing supper. Substitution of fried ham for fish didn't keep our trail-sharpened appetites from doing full justice to the meal. Afterward, a few pipes and a few yarns, and we all settled down into a luxurious bed of ferns and hemlock browse.

The river at Fort Henry

Many times and many places I have heard the voices in the rushing waters of a mountain stream, swirling and tumbling over the boulders in its bed, but never so plainly as that night. At times I could almost make out the very words. Once I seemed to hear a wagon coming far down the road jolting and bouncing over the rocks and the voice of the driver as he shouted to his horses.

August 8, 1925

Travel along the top of the Smokies had always been dependent on water, and how close to the divide it may be found. Having to drop down the mountainside a thousand or two feet each evening in search of enough water to make camp, then climb back up the steep slope in the morning, added much to the always strenuous job of packing. In routing this trip we had counted on finding water in the same places as in former trips, and planned each day's journey accordingly. Already we had made one unscheduled stop and now, in order not to disorganize the schedule completely, thought it the better plan to make only a very easy trip to Indian Gap this day. We would then start from there on the morrow, to pursue our itinerary as originally laid out. This would throw us but a single day late, with the advantage of hardening us gradually in the meantime.

We had just finished packing our gear when Mr. McCarter, the new ranger for the Champion Lumber Company, came along the trail and stopped for a

Falls on the Road Prong

chat. He had recently been placed over the same territory formerly patrolled by our old friend, Davis Bracken.

Among the things of interest he told us was of the abundance of game then in the mountains. Bear were plentiful and an occasional deer strayed up from the open woods further west. One had been killed along the Little Pigeon River that spring.

A timber wolf was also reported to be ranging in the neighborhood of Le Conte and across toward Clingmans Dome.

The climb up to the gap, some 2,200 feet higher than Fort Harry, is a long, steady pull on an easy grade along an old road built during the Civil War; but now impassable except by horse or foot. All the way is through a dense virgin forest, save for the little clearing at the Upper Beech Flats. From here one has an excellent view back to Le Conte and Bullhead.

We have found that a cup of strong, hot tea at the lunch halt is a good pick-me-up. Today we asked the boys if they liked hot tea. When they assented, we asked again if they liked it strong. Blissfully ignorant of what strong might mean in our vocabulary, they agreed to that also.

Brewed in our canteen cups over a hasty twig fire, it was scalding hot, black as sin, and potent enough to tan an alligator's hide. Ailes didn't understand that we intended to dilute it a bit with branch water, and took a good sized nip, neat. His eyelids flew up and down like a roller curtain. When he finally caught his breath, he commented politely but very weakly,

"You do make it strong, don't you?"

Indian Gap was reached shortly after noon. Here we fell in with a native cattle herder named Messer, and sat down for a long chat.

Walter and I had known for a long time that the different peaks of Le Conte had local names, but had never been able to determine definitely just what they were. Messer seemed thoroughly familiar with the country. From him we learned that what we knew as Myrtle Point was formerly Mt. Safford; the Cliff Top was called the High Chimneys; and that the central or higher peak alone was named Le Conte. He also told us that the knob just east of Laurel Top was Mt. Sterling, and that big mountain just west of Mt. Guyot at the junction of the Smoky divide and the Balsam range was called Horseshoe Ridge. The Balsams, or at least the northern end, was locally known as the Ledge.

Messer was also familiar with the details of Davis Bracken's latest trouble, he being kin to both the Bracken and the Newman families. In this second killing it seems that Davis and some of the Newmans were drinking together, peaceably enough. Alcohol brought latent resentment for the first affair to the surface, and Davis was forced to defend himself; very efficiently done. Conviction of murder came as a result of perjured evidence.

Wild turkeys are often found in the vicinity of Indian Gap, but evidently there were none this year, for as we walked through the thick grass of the clearing grasshoppers rose in swarms from under our feet. A favorite morsel for the turkeys, they would all have been cleared out if the fowls were ranging there.

A good spring was some two hundred and fifty feet down on the Tennessee side. Hunting a supply closer to the top where we planned to spend the night, we found a likely-looking marshy spot just inside the timber and below the road in North Carolina. Several test "wells" were scooped out of the mud, but filled and cleared too slowly to be encouraging. When a shower threatened we stopped the search and holed up as best we could. It didn't save us from a good wetting though. After the shower passed on, the tent was pitched right in the gap, supper prepared, and the boys fed. They may have been city reared, but their appetites responded wonderfully to wildwood's fare.

Shortly before dusk another party showed up, a couple of boys from Charleston, South Carolina. They were totally unused to wilderness camping and should never have ventured into the Smoky country without a guide. After we had given them explicit directions where water was to be found, the one

Le Conte from Newfound Gap

sent to the spring went more than a quarter of a mile beyond without locating it. Alarmed by his long absence and fearing he would be hopelessly lost in the gathering darkness, Walter and I warned all the others not to leave the gap while we went in search; finally finding him waterless, far down the trail.

Before slipping into our blankets, we two changed our wet clothing for such dry replacements as we carried. The process was punctuated by examples of our ideas of interpretative dancing to the accompaniment of raucous shouts and very off-key singing—our idea of a musical accompaniment—must have been very entertaining if not edifying to our lowland friends. We caught glimpses of them, shyly peeping around the corners of their tent. The boys in our party were already past being astonished by anything we might do.

August 9, 1925

From Indian Gap to Newfound Gap was an easy two miles on a clear trail under a wonderful hemlock forest. There were hundreds of the giant trees, four feet and more in diameter. The tall shafts of their trunks rising full sixty feet to the first limb. In some recent storm lightning had found a target in one of them, the explosive power of the bolt rending the whole upper half into bits. Fragments the size of fence rails were thrown a hundred feet away from the shattered, still standing trunk.

The trail did not follow the state line over Mt. Mingus, but skirted its southern slope, to reach the divide again at Newfound Gap, not to wander far from it again for thirty miles, at the crossing of the Pigeon River. To the top of Mt. Collins was a long, gradual climb on a generally well-marked, open trail, save in a few places where recent logging operations had left tree laps piled to the top of the ridge necessitating a detour. Part of the way was delightful going, like strolling through a vast park. The top of the mountain was fairly broad and the timber open, with little underbrush, and with deep grass underfoot.

Bears must truly have been very plentiful, as Ranger McCarter had told us. We saw scores of proof of their presence. The black bear has a way of advertising his presence by rearing on his hind feet beside a balsam tree, then, reaching back over his shoulder, biting into and tearing off a strip of bark. He may then turn and strike the trunk with his front paws, leaving claw marks in the bark. Not infrequently a larger bear will chance by and register on the same tree, his fang and claw marks higher than the first set, a clear warning to the smaller bear to walk softly and give due respect to his betters. Most of the valleys below us in North Carolina had been recently logged, the cuttings frequently extending to the state line. This was also the property line between the holding of different companies, but we noticed that the timber cutters were in no wise scrupulous in observing actual boundaries if a few choice trees stood just beyond. We did not pass through any areas of actual cutting, but at intervals could hear faintly the shrill whistles of the locomotives and steam skidders far below.

If there is a single puff of cloud to be found anywhere in all the Smokies it will be in the deep chasm lying at the northeastern extremity of Mt. Collins, between it and the beginning of the Sawteeth. When all the rest of the atmosphere is clear, an observer perched on the Myrtle Point of Le Conte may often look out over clouds swirling and tumbling above this, like steam rising from a mighty cauldron. The spot might well be called "The Birthplace of the Mists."

All morning there had been no hint of rain, but here, as usual, the fog was thick. As we stood on the rocky rim of the Jump-off we could see but a few feet below us. Flat rocks sailed out into space would vanish with an eerie whistling, long seconds before we could hear the faint whisper of their crashing into the trees, many hundreds of feet below. Here on the edge of the gulf we ate our lunch, hoping that before we pushed on we would be granted at least a single peep into the depths, but no indication came that the clouds would ever be lifting.

Formerly an old tree with a large H blaze marked the spot where the trail turned sharply to the right as it left the top of Mt. Collins, to continue eastward toward Mt. Guyot, but this had fallen since our last visit. There was no danger of overrunning the spot, for since logging had begun in this particular section there had been much more travel along the top of the range, and the footway of the trail was much more in evidence.

Shortly after leaving the top of Mt. Collins we passed and recognized the site of one of our camps in 1919. Here Walter and I had lain side by side in our little "sleeping sock", our shoulders touching but each in a different state.

For a short time we passed through an area of scorched brush, traces of the fire that had swept through the slash the year before. Then just before starting the climb up the first of the Sawteeth, we saw indications that water might not be far from the top. It was yet early in the afternoon, but discretion prompted us to stop here, rather than attempt the traverse of the Sawteeth, where we would have to drop a long way down a steep slope to find any spot suitable for a camp.

Water in plenty was really there, for a wonder, hardly a hundred feet down, the topmost spring of the Board Camp Prong of Oconaluftee River. Close by this spring was a fairly level spot for the tent and all the good, springy browse one might want for a bed. A bountiful supper, the pipes were lit, and we settled down to yarn away the hours of dusk, and to enjoy the life of Riley.

August 10, 1925

Rare indeed are the times when the camper in the high Smokies is fortunate enough to start on his way in the morning without prefacing the day's journey by a stiff climb of hundreds of feet from the night's bivouac back to the divide, a heartbreaking start for the day's work ahead. This time our good fortune in finding water so close to the top saved us all the additional climbing, just as we were about to start the up-and-down traverse of the Sawteeth, rugged enough in itself. Many times had we argued as to just how many separate peaks there were in this stretch of mountains. Now we determined to keep a strict count to settle the question. The answer proved nineteen.

Wonderful though it is, taken all in all, the scenery as viewed from the Sawteeth is not as awe-inspiring as that from Le Conte. Yet the Sawteeth stand unrivalled in their claim to furnish the most spectacular travelling in all the Smoky country.

A backward look at Mt. Collins

The night before Walter had been telling the boys that here one might often sit astride the state line, as in a saddle. They hadn't voiced any definite doubts, but we could see they were accepting the story with some silent reservations. Now that they were on the ground, they realized that the old adage that truth is sometimes stranger than fiction still held good. Soon each one was straddling the ridge, so that he might tell the folks at home that he'd sat astride the mountain top, with one foot hanging down in North Carolina, the other in Tennessee.

Le Conte, as seen from the lowlands at its base, is widely famed for its majesty and beauty, and justly so. In my own estimation, it doesn't compare in grandeur with the view we had this morning, looking back at it across the deep valley at the head of Porters Creek.

Up to now, the trail had been fairly open, showing evidences of considerable use, but as we neared Porters Gap and beyond, the signs of travel dwindled away. The way was overgrown by brush of every description, blackberry briars in particular. The long pull up Laurel Top, where we halted for the noon lunch and a much needed rest, was not too bad, but the next, an unnamed peak, was pure hell—steep, rocky, brush-choked, as rugged a kind of traveling as one could well imagine. Here our speed was a very slow snail's pace. The boys, who had wanted to see just how rough the Smokies could be, were getting a glorious example this day. To give them full credit, they were taking it like real men, without a single complaint.

Our morning idea had been to make the night camp a little east of the end of Hughes Ridge. A late start, frequent stops to enjoy the scenery and the hard going had slowed us down. Late in the afternoon, after a dry march—one canteen of water apiece—it was evident we would never make our destination before dark. The summer had been one of the driest in years. The vegetation on the heights was parched and withering, and we began to fear we would have difficulty in finding enough water for a camp. So it proved.

Anxious survey of both sides of the mountain brought conviction that the chances were somewhat better on the north—Tennessee—side. Down we went, twelve to fifteen hundred feet, on a brushy, tree-covered slope. So steep it was that our feet wouldn't hold well in the soft earth of the forest floor. At times we were virtually forced to swing from tree to bush to keep from tumbling and sliding down, out of control. To make it worse, there were scattered patches of rhododendron through which we had to shove our way. Here the added weight of our packs helped us gain passage—when they did not hang us up in the dense, tangled branches. Finally we struck the faint rudiments of a trail and started following it, believing that a trail must go somewhere and knowing that it afforded a little better footing and less brush.

Where the path crossed the ravine we normally would have found water, but now the pockets of sand among the rocks were dust dry. On we pushed rapidly, for it was getting late and in a deep valley like this one night comes soon, with no twilight. Finally, a mile and a half from the top and fully two thousand feet down, we located a tiny waterhole in the dry creek bed, and immediately set about making camp.

Dusk was upon us before all the firewood was cut, and the other chores of camp-making were sketchily done. The menu was cut to essentials, all easily prepared, and the beds spread on the bare earth. Lack of browse for a mattress was no bar to sound slumber, for we all were well nigh exhausted. This day's march, by and large, was much the most rigorous of the whole trip.

Ailes takes a sun bath

August 11, 1925

It would have been a terrible job to try to push our way back up to the state line, with no trail to follow, and certainly not worth the effort. If one main object of the trip had been to show the boys some of the majestic scenery of the Smokies, and to let them know at first hand just how rugged the terrain become, it had already been achieved along the way from Indian Gap to the point where we left the divide.

After a late breakfast, with no particular plan in mind, we started slowly down the stream bed. In no time at all it began to hold a surprisingly large flow of water, very low for times of normal rainfall, it is true, but in an amazing volume for the short distance since the stream bed was dry, too dry for us to uncover even a trickle of water by the usual method of moving a few boulders and digging into the damp earth beneath. This manner of water-finding, at which Walter was an adept, had saved us from a dry camp many times before.

Trout were visible in all the pools, a most enticing prospect. We were in no great rush to leave the mountains, so decided to pitch camp in the first open glade and do a little fishing. Walter started up the stream and I down, with the boys slowly coming along behind.

Dry weather decided the issue. The water was too low and too clear, and the wary trout weren't having any of our bait. When we gathered at the camp, there wasn't a single fin to show for all our efforts. Appetites in no wise dampened by lack of fish on the menu, in the middle of the afternoon we observed a time-honored custom for the last night out, by cooking and consuming a magnificent meal. Then, with a cold water shave, a dip in the creek to wash away the sweat and grime of hard packing, a change to lighter clothing from the heavy woolen we had been wearing for protection from the cold air on the high tops, we were ready to start out to civilization in the morning.

August 12, 1925

A few hundred yards down the stream we picked up a trail of sorts, little used and in places almost too dim to follow. Growing plainer as we went along, it stayed well out from the creek, an unusual thing for a wood's trail in a deep valley. Possibly the explanation is that it was not a happen-so trail, but one marked for the use of the rangers of the Champion Fiber Company, owners of thousands of acres of virgin timberlands in this area. We saw a number of their "No Trespassing" signs and passed one possession cabin.

The way wound through the most beautiful mixed hardwood forest one could imagine, trees of a score of different varieties, all approaching maximum size. As usual in such a forest, there was an absence of brush and a few small trees, the massive trunks of the giants going up and up, ramrod-straight and unmarred by a single branch, to the forest crown a hundred feet above our heads. The sun was shining brightly, with an occasional ray breaking through, but the heavy canopy aloft was so dense that the light around us was dim and subdued, as under the arches and in the aisles of a great cathedral.

The trail grew plainer and more used, the valley broadened and the grade lessened. In a couple of miles or so, we reached the tiny settlement of Greenbrier, where we chartered a rattley Ford truck to haul us over the rough, rocky road to Gatlinburg. Here our ways parted. They, enthusiastic over their experiences, got other transportation to Elkmont, while Walter and I continued our truck ride down the Little Pigeon River to Sevierville for the night.

August 13, 1925

Sevierville's bus service to Knoxville was of the best, and by 8:30 A.M. we were at the Southern station, waiting for the train home.

Waiting there, also, were Col. D. C. Chapman, Chairman of the Tennessee Park Commission, Harlen Kelsey, of the Southern Appalachian National Park

Trail's end – Greenbrier

Commission, and G. Freeman Pollock, owner of Skyland, Virginia, and an enthusiastic promoter of the proposed Shenandoah National Park. All of the group had just returned from a visit to the top of Le Conte. Pollock, who had never been there before, was duly impressed by what he had seen of the Smokies and conceded that our mountains outclassed the Shenandoah section of the Blue Ridge as a scenic area.

Kelsey and Pollock were returning to the East. We enjoyed a very pleasant visit with them en route to Jonesboro, filling in Kelsey, in particular, with data on the Smokies for the use of his Committee.

Grub List – four men, ten days

Bacon	6 lb.	Dehydrated vegetables	1 lb.
Ham	6 lb.	Navy beans	1 lb.
Egg Powder	8 oz.	Sweet chocolate	3 lb.
Erbswurst	3 lb.	Sugar	8 lb.
Canned cheese	3 lb.	Coffee	2 lb.
Powdered milk	1 lb.	Tea	8 oz.
Shortening	8 oz.	Evaporated apricots	2 lb.
Flour	7 lb.	Evaporated apples	2 lb.
Corn meal	4 lb.	Evaporated peaches	2 lb.
Rice	3 lb.	Prunes	1 lb.
Oatmeal	3 lb.	Raisins	2 lb.
Dried beef	1 lb.	Salted peanuts	12 oz.
Bouillon cubes	4 oz.	Hard candies	1 lb.
Baking powder	4 oz.	Salt, pepper, etc.	8 oz.
		Total	65 lb. 4 oz.

Approximately 1 pound 10 ounces per man per day.

DATE: JULY 20-26, 1927

DESTINATION: CENTRAL PORTION OF THE GREAT SMOKIES.

OBJECT: EXPLORATION.

WEATHER: CLOUDY, SHOWERS.

PARTY: WALTER S. DIEHL, PAUL M. FINK.

The high mountains were calling us again. In fact, they seldom ceased calling, and we were always willing to answer whenever we had a few free days. This year we wanted to spend a few days in the high Smokies, but for some reason or other didn't have the yen to visit again the rougher, wilder portion of the range, where we had gone several times in the past few years. Nor did the easier travelling in the more open tops of the Western Smokies offer just what we were wanting. All that remained was the central portion, from Indian Gap west, crossing Clingmans Dome and on to Silers Bald. Neither a long nor a hard trip, our packs would be reasonably light.

July 20, 1927

A mid-afternoon start from Jonesboro by car brought us to Gatlinburg via Greeneville, Newport and Sevierville, in time for supper at the bountiful table of Andy Huff. His Mountain View Hotel, a modest building as yet, was only beginning to draw a trickle of the visitors that were to flood it in the years ahead. The delicious fried country ham that was to make his hostelry known all over the country was on the table in plenty, and we were never ones to overlook such noble fare.

July 21, 1927

The wagon road had been slowly inching its way further up the valley of the Little Pigeon River. Andy took us in his car to the Sugarlands, a big lift on what was to be a long, hot march to Indian Gap. His kindness, no surprise to anyone who knew Andy, set us on our journey hours earlier than otherwise would have been possible.

Ahead of us as we came out of the timber into the Upper Beech Flats we saw a man gathering blackberries. To our astonishment, it proved to be Bob Dulaney, long a next door neighbor of mine in Jonesboro and my companion on many a mountain excursion near home. He, with a group of fellows from Chattanooga, were spending a few days in camp at Fort Harry, fishing and exploring the neighborhood.

There was all the time in the world for us to gain our planned camp site, Indian Gap. We leisurely followed the old wagon road built during the Civil War, now washed out and impassable to any vehicle. Anytime the notion struck us, we stopped to rest and talk. Frequent showers caught up with us, to make us "hole up" under any convenient ledge or leaning tree we could find. Even so, we were more than merely damp by the time we had pitched our tent close by the topmost spring, rustled enough near-dry firewood and gotten supper under way.

Here, as at many another time before and since, we proved the truth of Horace Kephart's saying that rhododendron was a godsend to the southern mountain traveler. In the first place, the hard, white wood is top grade fuel under any circumstances, burning with a hot, smokeless flame and leaving long-lived coals. With rain falling and all the forest wet, one can always find a few dead branches in every clump, so twisted and gnarled that a part at least has stayed clear of the earth and not sodden by the pervading moisture.

Somewhere we had read that by one account of the wandering of De Soto's Spanish expedition in 1541, he had led his little army of hardy adventurers across the heights of the Smokies at Indian Gap and down into Tennessee along the ages-old Indian trail. Observing the roughness of the terrain and recalling that De Soto was supposed to be driving a herd of some three hundred hogs as a sort of commissary on the hoof, we wondered if he really had passed this way. If so, our regard for his hardihood and ability as a drover rose to greater heights than before.

July 22, 1927

The usual Smoky mist was all about us as we rose, ate a hearty breakfast and packed up for the day's march, over and beyond Clingmans Dome.

Several years before we had waded through ankle-deep muck along the top of the well-named Miry Ridge. A mile west of Indian Gap travelling conditions were even worse. A little foot travel and abundant rain had turned the soft woods-earth into a thick, sloppy black mire in which we often sank halfway to our knees. In a trice our whole outfits, and us, were spattered and smeared with it. A time or two we essayed to help matters by walking to one side of the regular footway, but soon found that beating down bushes and clambering over down timber made for even rougher going, and we came back to the sloppy trail.

The hardest shower yet caught us suddenly just as we topped the last high point on Meigs Post. Before we could open our packs and break out our rain-shirts we were well wet again. No novelty to us and as always unpleasant, it did serve at least one good purpose, washing off at least a part of the coat of muck we had accumulated.

While the loose fitting skirts of a rain shirt give much needed ventilation and don't sweat the wearer like a tighter fitting garment, when he is wet through already it isn't much help. We left them in our packs and plodded on, now and then stopping for a few minutes shelter under some leaning, larger-than-ordinary balsam tree. Near the summit of Clingmans Dome was a rude cabin by the trailside, evidently hurriedly thrown together for the use of some surveying party. The door was inhospitably locked, and there was no shelter there for us.

The top of the Dome bore as heavy a stand of spruce and balsam as we had ever seen. There was not a single spot from which to see out. The absence made little difference to us just then, for the cloud was still down around us, and even had the top been entirely bare, we couldn't have seen the length of a rifle shot.

A more pelting rain than those gone before drove in as we reached the very top. This time the packs went down, the rain shirts out and on, and we huddled down to ride it out. The knitted navy watch-caps we wore were fine as head cushions when packing with a tumpline and comfortably warm for night head covering, but they were less than no use as protection from a hard rain.

All things must have an end, and this rain was no exception. As the downpour slackened there was a little lifting of the cloud, and we decided to follow Forney Ridge to the southward, to take a look at Andrews Bald. Tucking our packs away under the protection of a thickly foliaged balsam tree, we started.

Had we had the least premonition what the trailless ridge would be like, we would have dismissed the idea without much thought. A quarter of the way down we ran full into the marks of a terrific wind storm of some years before, a "blowdown" where trees by the hundreds had been blown up by the roots by the tornado and pitched around like jackstraws. The smaller twigs had long since rotted away, and now the bare, sharp ends of the larger branches stuck out like a gigantic *cheval-de-frise*, over many acres.

For a hundred yards or so, we pushed and clambered through it, endangering our eyes and tearing our clothes on the sharp snags. With no end in sight, we gave it up as not worth the effort, regardless of how beautiful Andrews Bald itself or the view from it might be. Slowly we fought our way back out of the tangle, retraced our steps to the top of the Dome, picked up our packs, and started west along the state line.

The constant and dense cloud kept us from checking our position with any degree of accuracy, so when we found a likely spot some three miles beyond the Dome we thought it best to make camp, rather than go further in search of a better spot. Well enough we did, for another driving shower caught us and we were thoroughly soaked once more before the tent was up.

Good or even fair fuel was hard to come by, but the fire was finally started, kept alive by fresh kindling at intervals and free use of the "inspirator." This little gadget, a foot-long piece of copper fuel line, at the end of two feet of rubber tube, is a godsend to every camper. By it, air can be blown to just the exact spot needed to boost a lagging blaze, and a brick fire speedily coaxed into being. Otherwise, one might blow and blow until his eyeballs bugged out and never get his fire under way.

Supper, of sorts, over, as good a fire as possible was built up in an attempt to dry out our sodden clothes. The job was only a moderate success, the wet wood giving off considerably more smoke than heat we were still damp when we finally rolled into our blankets. Sleeping in wet clothing was by no means a new experience to us, for we had done it many times before. With all wool clothing, inside and out, it isn't nearly so unpleasant and chill-provoking as if one were clad in cotton.

Sometime during the night, we were visited by some sort of wild animal we could hear moving and snuffling about our camp. It didn't sound big as a bear, probably a fox or a coon, so we didn't take the trouble to roll out and investigate.

July 23, 1927

The patter of another shower on the tent roof waked us at the first faint light of dawn. As usual, the cloud was still around, so we went back to sleep, not

Snug haven on Silers Bald

to come to life until nearly the middle of the morning. Leisurely a big meal, breakfast and lunch all in one, was cooked and eaten, camp broken and packs made, and about noon we were on our way west again. A hundred yards down the trail we met a skunk and did not argue the right of way with him. Possible he was our visitor of the night before. If so, it was well enough we didn't get up to hunt for him.

Half a mile further we came to what would have made us an excellent camp site had we gone a bit further the night before—Double Spring Gap, a small, open grassy spot in the timber. Here, on opposite sides of the clearing, are two free-flowing springs, about seventy-five yards apart and within ten feet elevation of the crest. From one, the water runs south into North Carolina, down Forney Creek and the Tuckaseegee River to the Little Tennessee. The other, flowing northerly, goes by the Fish Camp Prong into Little River and on to the Tennessee. The waters, rising so close together, do not unite for a hundred miles.

In the vicinity of Double Spring Gap, the spruce and balsam forest through which we had been travelling disappeared giving way to a dense stand of small beech, evidently second growth reforestation after the original hardwood forest had been cut off, either by the Little River Lumber Co., or the Ritter Lumber Co., operating in North Carolina.

The rest of the way to Silers Bald, reached about 2:00 P.M., was a delightfully easy walk on an open trail through beech woods. There were no decent lookouts. Had there been, they would have been of little service to us, for the weather stayed cloudy all day. Fortunately, there were no more showers. On the way we chanced upon two small snakes and a rabbit, both infrequently see at that altitude.

Choice camp sites, with everything a wilderness camper would ask, are easy to find on Silers Bald. We chose ours in the edge of the timber, not far down on the Carolina side. Our damp clothes had dried out on our backs during the day; this was the first time we were not wet since shortly after we started the long climb to Indian Gap. With all the time we needed, we set about preparing a gargantuan feast, to match the appetites developed by hard physical exertion in the open air. Replete at last, almost too full to move and certainly too full to bother with washing up the supper dishes, a time was spent smoking, yarning and deliciously loafing around the fire before we turned in to enjoy the best night's rest yet.

July 24, 1927

Middle of summer though it was, a light frost was showing on the grass as the sun rose for the first clear morning we had seen on the trip. Walter had decided he wanted to investigate the trout situation on the head waters of Hazel Creek, and after digging a few worms in the mucky soil started off down the mountain. Climbing back up had no appeal for me and I stayed in camp, cleaning pots and pans and setting things to rights in general while catching up on my loafing. Housekeeping chores completed, I moved out into the sunshine, to recline on a big flat rock and enjoy Nature in solitude.

The overflow from a tiny spring trickled lazily across the clearing, turning the rich black soil into a swampy quagmire. Here a clump of brightly hued bee-balm or horse mint had taken root, its flaming red blossoms set off by contrast with the clear rich yellow of the marsh sunflowers interspersed among them. A cloud of yellow and black butterflies fluttered in the air above.

All was quiet and serene, and I sat still as the rock on which I rested. Birds were calling in the timber behind me, and as I watched a ruby-throated hummingbird flashed through the air, to hover like a gleaming jewel over the bee-balm, probing with his long beak into the depths of the blossoms.

The faintest of rustles at my feet, and a tiny gray-brown shrew crept from a cranny beneath the rock and began exploring about in search of some tasty bug or worm. Soon he scuttled back to his den, never aware of my presence within arm's length. It had been a treat to watch tiny birds and beasts going unalarmed about their affairs in so beautiful a setting.

After lunch I strolled to the open top of the mountain for a good look at the central portion of the Smokies. The rains had cleared the haze from the air more than usual and the scene was wonderful, with a scope of view embracing Clingmans Dome—with Le Conte in the far back ground—Andrews Bald, Forney Ridge, the deep valley of the Tuckaseegee River and on to the Blue Ridge far away to the southeast, a vast tangled maze of mountains and valleys.

From the particular lookout a trail led some seventy-five yards through a dense thicket of young beech to a jutting rock on the north side of the summit. Here I could gaze over the headwaters of the Little River, mostly cut over within the past thirty years, but with a lusty growth of new timber beginning to cover the scars of logging. To the west and only four miles away was Cold Spring Knob, at the head of Miry ridge, where we planned to spend the next night. Beyond this, ranked one behind the other as I looked down the range, were Hemlock Knob, Briar Knob and the massive bulk of Thunderhead. Past the long, level tops of the Chilhowees, northward toward where the haze merged into the horizon, I could catch a misty glimpse of the flat lands of the East Tennessee Valley.

Walter was already back at camp when I returned, reporting poor fishing but with a string of sixteen speckled trout seven to eight inches long. That size was about average for speckles in the small, headwater streams. There is not much meat on such small fish, but fried over an open hardwood fire they are delicious and proved a welcome starter for the big feed we consumed that night.

July 25, 1927

We were making a leisurely trip of it, with only a short, easy march ahead of us this day. Half the morning we lazed about camp, eating a series of breakfasts, before we started for Cold Spring. This is one of the easiest portions of the Smokies to traverse; it is on an open trail through the young beech forest. The grade was good, with almost no climbing before the final little pull to the Knob. Our camp was close to the spring, whose icy water gave the name to the spot, where we, with Henry Patton, had spent a couple of nights five years before, en route to Thunderhead.

With all afternoon at our disposal, we made a really ship-shape camp, pre-

Sunset from Cold Spring Knob

paring to spend the night in luxury. Our bed was of woodsferns, piled three feet deep. Then, along toward evening, we observed a fixed rite for the last night out, cooking and eating everything we could possibly hold. After packing that food all over the mountains, we certainly weren't going to carry it home.

Near the top of Cold Spring Knob, we found another snake, and had seen a thirty inch brown one at the spring on Silers, a total of five along the state line. Never before had we seen so many so high.

July 26, 1927

There was much less evidence of travel along the top of Miry Ridge this year than when we had passed along five years before. In some spots the way was almost overgrown with weeds and small bushes. We were at a loss to account for this, unless the slackening of timber cutting by the Little River Lumber Company might have been responsible.

After passing the ever-present mucky places that gave the name of Miry Ridge and beyond the Ben Parton Lookout, we began to see some traces of recent forest fires. Beyond Pearsons Improvement, an old clearing atop the ridge, everything was burned over. This fire must have been shortly after our last visit, for firecherry and thick briars were springing up everywhere.

An old, abandoned logging road was far below us; we dropped straight down the mountain side to it. Using shortcuts through the brush at switchbacks, we followed it to Jakes Creek and Elkmont. There we caught a car to Gatlinburg and thence home in our vehicle.

Grub List – two men, five days

Bacon	4 lb.	Baking powder	2 oz.
Powdered eggs	4 oz.	Dehydrated vegetables	1 lb.
Erbswurst	1 lb.	Sweet chocolate	1 lb. 8 oz.
Cheese	1 lb.	Sugar	3 lb.
Powdered milk	4 oz.	Coffee	1 lb.
Shortening	4 oz.	Tea	2 oz.
Flour	2 lb.	Evaporated apples	1 lb.
Corn meal	2 lb.	Evaporated apricots	1 lb.
Rice	1 lb.	Raisins	1 lb.
Oatmeal	1 lb.	Onions	2 lb.
Dried beef	8 oz.	Salt, pepper, etc.	4 oz.
Bouillon cubes	2 oz.		
		Total	25 lb. 6 oz.

Approximately 2 pounds 8 ounces per man per day. A little bit on the heavy side, but all consumed.

DATE: AUGUST 9-14, 1929

DESTINATION: EASTERN PORTION OF THE GREAT SMOKIES.

OBJECT: EXPLORATION.

WEATHER: FAIR - RAIN.

PARTY: WALTER S. DIEHL, BILLY DIEHL, PAUL M. FINK.

After years of promotional work and land acquisition, a National Park in the Great Smokies was at last an assured thing. In a short time an essential part of the proposed area would be turned over to the National Park Service for development and administration. Motor roads and graded trails would be built deep into the mountains. People by the thousands would be visiting remote spots that hitherto few persons had ever seen. Already a trans-montane motor highway was under construction, pushing up the West Prong of the Little Pigeon River, through the Sugarlands, to the state line where a similar road on the North Carolina side would meet it.

At first, this highway was planned to reach the main divide at Indian Gap where an ages-old dim Indian trail and later a wagon road of sorts had crossed. More detailed surveys had shown an easier and more feasible route could pass through Newfound Gap, a couple of hundred feet lower and a mile further east.

Before all this wilderness was, to our way of thinking, ruined by roads and people, Walter and I wanted to tramp over at least a part of it again. For this year's trip we laid our sights on that part of the state line between Newfound Gap and Mt. Guyot, a section we had visited several times before. This time we added to the party Walter's brother, Billy, who had never before done any backpack camping.

August 9, 1929

Individual loads already apportioned, packs made and ready to hit the trail, we left Jonesboro in Walter's car bound for Gatlinburg. To our great surprise, the Mountain View Hotel, our usual stopping place, was chock-full of guests, and we were quartered in one of the cottages on the hill behind the main building.

At supper our host and old friend, Andy Huff, introduced us to Major Ireland, head of the U.S. Geological Survey party engaged in making a new and accurate map of the proposed park lands. Well enough it was, for the existing map, admittedly a reconnaissance map only, was so full of errors that it could not be depended on, even in a general way. As someone so aptly remarked, it was only good enough to get lost by.

Our conversation, most interesting to us, lasted on into the evening. We were not in any wise surprised to hear the Major say that the extreme ruggedness of the terrain was rendering his topographic work very difficult, indeed. When he was telling of his many troubles, I little thought that in less than a year I'd be having a hand in some of the nomenclature on that map.

August 10, 1929

With a man from the hotel along to take back our car, we drove over the new highway to Bear Pen Hollow, the end of safe motor transportation, making in a few minutes time what was formerly a long, hard day's march. Heavy grading for the roadway was in progress, pointed toward Newfound Gap, and we plodded along the rough footing of the rocky grade to Newfound Gap Branch. Here an old rudimentary trail, seldom used and hardly blazed, struck straight up the mountain side, growing steeper the further we went. It was a long, strenuous pull for men not yet trail-hardened. In spite of frequent stops to rest, pant, and catch our breath, we were well nigh exhausted when we finally topped the divide.

The familiar trail eastward toward the top of Mt. Collins was neither rough nor steep, but considerably overgrown with briars and bushes, and showed little signs of much travel since we had last been here in 1925. Logging operations had ceased, the timber cutters had gone their way, and the approach was too long and hard to let in enough visitors from outside to keep the trail open.

We might have expected it, for it seldom failed. As we neared the top of Mt. Collins, tag ends of clouds began to drift through the balsam trees around us. At the Jump-off the great bowl, as usual, was filled with mist to the brim, denying us the awesome look into the depths. Even the nearby trees were shrouded in fog.

With nothing to be seen and little indication of the cloud lifting any time

Newfound Gap, before the road

Le Conte, from east of Newfound Gap

soon, there was no point in lingering, so we pushed on toward the head spring of the Board Camp Prong, the planned campsite for the night.

Here, too, weeds and briars had sprung up to choke the dim trail, and we were forced to drop further down the top than previously before we could find a spot halfway decent to make camp. At that, it wasn't feasible to pitch the tent. When a tiny spatter of rain started falling in the night, we pulled it over us propping up a little space over our heads for breathing room.

State line, with Mt. Collins in background

August 11, 1929

It's a good deal harder to pull back up a hill under pack than it is to come down. We had ample proof of this axiom long before we reached the top of the ridge this morning. The growth became heavier, thicker, and more troublesome the further we pushed our way through it. Blackberry briars and huckleberry bushes had sprung up following the devastating fire two or three years previously, to make the going about as tough as anything we had ever encountered. There was little if any footway, the briars caught in our clothing, and the thick, woody stems of the bushes tripped us and held our feet as we shoved our way along by sheer strength and weight.

On the second and third peaks of the Sawteeth, we found evidence of a terrific wash on the Tennessee side, forcing us to leave the usual way along the crest and keep a little below it on the southern slope. The cloud had closed around us again, blocking the view and depriving us of the opportunity to see the devastation wrought by the great cloudburst of earlier that year, sweeping away all timber and soil, down to the bare, rocky frame of the mountain, for hundreds of feet down to the headwaters of Porters Creek.

With the cloud had come a high gusty wind, bending the trees and driving a pelting rain before it. There was no shelter; in a moment we were soaked to the skin.

The hard going and almost constant cloud had already disheartened us and now, wet, weary, and disgusted, we gave up the idea of pushing on to Mt.

Looking out into the fog

Guyot right there, and decided that when we came to Porters Gap we would drop down a couple of thousand feet into Tennessee. Then we would fish for a day or two and afterward, if the weather cleared, climb back up to the top. Or maybe we would just loaf deliciously the rest of the time at our disposal.

Following along the state line in the Smokies in a dense cloud, particularly in those almost trailless days, was a troublesome thing. The divide winds and twists first one way, then another, in a most confusing fashion. Unable to see out to get a compass sight on some prominent landmark, the map is useless and one has to depend on dead-reckoning. To still befuddle the traveler further, some of the buttressing ridges have a very distressing habit of being a little higher than the main chain. If one depends on keeping to the highest ridge for his true course, he can easily fall into sad error.

So it was with us. Shortly to the west of Porters Gap, we took the wrong

Mt. Collins, from the Sawteeth

lead in the dense cloud. After a while, when every vestige of a trail vanished, we realized that we were completely lost. So long as we had our packs that made no great difference. For a while we plodded on in the steady rain, then in mid-afternoon turned to the left down a steep, laurelly slope, broken by occasional rocky cliffs to make the descent more difficult. A couple of thousand feet of slipping and sliding down the mountainside followed, and just as the rain stopped we came to the bottom of a ravine with a stream big enough to have holes for trout. Sodden as we were, we were not inclined to be choosy.

At the first half-way decent spot, we halted and set about getting ready for the night.

Building a fire in rain-soaked woods is far from the simplest thing in the world, a real test of woodmanship. No luck on the first try, but we finally made it.

If one looks closely, in every forest are saplings, crowded out in the struggle for existence, dead but still standing, and sound, not yet filled with moisture. Several of these were split into kindling, half inch or smaller, with a double handful of long, thin shavings, all carefully sheltered from falling rain and contact with the wet earth. A few strips of birchbark, if available, is fine starting tinder, for it contains an oil that burns freely, wet or dry.

Then, if rhododendrons are at hand, cut an armful of the dead branches found in every clump. Its availability and value as fuel is often overlooked. Lacking rhododendron, cut several beech or birch saplings big as one's wrist and cut into fifteen-inch lengths, some split into quarters, some halved. Black or sweet birch will burn as well green as when seasoned.

Start the fire by laying a base of halved sticks, flat, to hold the fine kindlings from the wet ground. Around and above the fine stuff set up a teepee of pencil-sized sticks first, then medium, then larger, being careful not to pack too close, leaving plenty of space between for free draft. Should the rain be still falling, shelter the operation under a poncho, and touch a match to the fine stuff. Rising flames will ignite the progressively larger stuff, and in a few minutes there will be a fire that only a downpour will quench.

When at all available, use only hardwoods for fuel—hickory, birch, beech, maple, oak, ironwood, etc. Split sticks take fire more quickly than round. Keep a good supply ahead, under shelter. Put aside some dry kindling at night, even in the pack sack if necessary, to keep off dew and dampness. There is little fun hunting up fresh kindling in a drizzling, chilly dawn.

Fortunately, good firewood was in plenty at this camp site. Supper over, we set about drying out, a task that consumed a couple of hours or so, even around a big fire. Sapling racks were put up and all the clothes we could spare were hung close to the blaze as we dared without scorching, while we slid into our blankets to keep warm.

August 12, 1929

There was a great deal of doubt in our minds as to just where we were, even

Ridges are steep near the Sawteeth

what state we were in. The clouds were still down, not far above our heads. Maps and compass were of no value in locating our position. It really made very little difference, for we were in no hurry to get out, and our packs held all we needed for food and shelter.

Leaving Billy in camp, Walter and I set out to see what the stream offered in the way of fish. They were there all right, for we could see them, but they were in no mood to cooperate. When we came back to camp in mid-afternoon, the combined string was only ten. Walter was almost invariably the better fisherman, but this time I beat him, six to four.

My prize was the largest brook trout I'd ever caught, just a hair under a foot long. Usually a speckled trout hits a fly or worm with a bang, and there is no question whether or not one has a strike. This time it was different. The pool was rocky and deep, the hook near the bottom, and I never felt him take it.

In fact, I didn't know there was a fish on until I moved the lure and found resistance. Even then I reeled him in, he put up little fight, but nothing like the vicious tugging and darting about one might expect a trout half his size to put up.

Six separate showers had fallen during the day. Billy had taken shelter under the tent, but Walter and I, fishing, were well wet down once more. Between showers Billy had gotten in an abundant stock of firewood, so cooking the evening meal, under the protection of the tent awning, wasn't the unpleasant chore of the evening before.

The Campfire Council, after giving full consideration to the weather, unanimously decided to start downstream in the morning on the way out, no matter where it might lead.

August 13, 1929

The same cloud was still hanging low on the mountainside when we broke camp and started, perforce keeping to the creek bed in the absence of any trail or other sign of man. After a mile we did find some faint signs of previous visitors, so indistinctly we kept following the stream.

Some three more miles of rock-hopping and riffle-splashing, and we came to a fire warning sign, nailed to a tree by the North Carolina Forest Service. Now for the first time in a couple of days we were sure what state we were in. A little reflection and study of the map made us decide we had come off the state line onto one of the head branches of the Bradley Fork of Oconaluftee river. Smaller creeks coming in from either side soon made it a sizable stream with a plain trail beside it. All the way we found traces of extremely high water, more evidence of the ravages of the terrific cloudburst along the top the year before. Several miles upstream from Smokemont was the end of steel for the logging operations.

At Smokemont I found Mark Squires, head of the North Carolina Park Commission, then engaged in negotiations for the purchase of this large tract of land for National Park purposes. He very kindly gave us a lift in his car to Cherokee.

Hunting up Jack Gloyne, a friend of some years, we were most hospitably invited to spend the night at his home. The offer we felt compelled to decline; after some days on the trail, dirty, unshaven, with clothing strongly redolent of woodsmoke from drying out over an open fire, we were not in condition to stay in anyone's house. We did agree to make our camp that night in his barnyard.

After supper, Jack and his wife, the former Lula Owl, paid us a very enjoyable visit. She was a full-blooded Indian, with a Cherokee father and a Catawba mother. The Owl family has long been a prominent one among the Eastern Band of the Cherokee and are superior people by any standard. One of Mrs. Gloyne's brothers had received the M.A. from the University of North Carolina, another had attended Dartmouth College, yet another had been a student at Syracuse University, while a fourth had been an instructor at the YMCA Training School at Springfield, Massachusetts. She was herself a trained nurse and was doing public nursing among her people.

Mrs. Gloyne told us many interesting things about the Cherokee customs, beliefs and superstitions. For example, if in the course of her duties she should visit a house where a death had just occurred, she would call off the remainder of the day's visits, for she would not be welcomed at any home where she might subsequently call. Knowing from my correspondence with Jack of my deep interest in the ancient ways and crafts of the Cherokee, she brought me a gift, a copy of the New Testament, printed about 1860 in the characters of the Cherokee alphabet.

August 14, 1929

The trip home was uneventful. A Ford car chartered at Cherokee took us a far piece above Smokemont. From there it was a long, uphill but not hard pull along the old road to Indian Gap, then around the end of Mt. Mingus to Newfound Gap.

Down the steep mountainside we went, slipping and sliding, a far easier descent than the heartbreaking pull up four days before. Walking was rough for a mile or two along the road grade to Bear Pen Hollow, end of the then negotiable road. Here we begged a ride back to Gatlinburg, and our own car took us home to Jonesboro shortly after dark.

Grub List – three men, six days

Bacon	4 lb.
Ham	2 lb.
Erbswurst	12 oz.
Cheese	1 lb. 8 oz.
Powdered milk	4 oz.
Crisco	4 oz.
Flour	3 lb.
Corn meal	3 lb.
Rice	1 lb. 8 oz.
Oatmeal	1 lb. 8 oz.
Dried beef	2 lb.
Bouillon cubes	2 oz.
Baking powder	4 oz.
Sweet chocolate	2 lb.
Sugar	4 lb.
Coffee	1 lb.
Tea	2 oz.
Evaporated apples	1 lb. 8 oz.
Evaporated apricots	1 lb. 8 oz.
Raisins	1 lb. 8 oz.
Onions, fresh	2 lb.
Salt, pepper, etc.	4 oz.
Ovaltine	4 oz.
Chocolate malted milk, powdered	1 lb.
Total	35 lb. 4 oz.

AUGUST 11-16, 1930

DESTINATION: EASTERN PART OF THE GREAT SMOKIES.

OBJECT: EXPLORATION.

WEATHER: FAIR, RAIN.

PARTY: MYRON H. AVERY, WALTER S. DIEHL, PAUL M. FINK.

Myron H. Avery, Chairman of the Appalachian Trail Conference, had been long familiar with the mountain regions of Maine and New England. Now he wanted an opportunity for an intimate view of the Great Smokies, admittedly the wildest and most primitive country through which the Appalachian Trail would pass. Walter and I seldom needed any urging or excuse for planning a trip there, so we volunteered to give Myron a personally conducted tour of the eastern half of the Smokies. I had gotten together the most of the outfit at Jonesboro, so when Myron and Walter arrived by car there was little left to do but apportion the loads each one had to carry.

August 11, 1930

A pre-dawn start from Jonesboro put us in Gatlinburg in time for breakfast at the Mountain View Hotel with Rangers Phil Hough and John Needham, the first representatives of the National Park Service sent down to keep an eye on the Great Smoky Mountains National Park, then in the process of being created.

Arranging to leave our car at the hotel, with them to send it to pick us up where and whenever we sent for it, we took aboard a driver to bring it back, and drove around the northern flank of Mt. Le Conte to Greenbrier Cove, the end of motor transportation. In all our previous trips to Mt. Guyot we had started at either Newfound Gap or Indian Gap and travelled eastward. This time we wanted to reserve the route, to go to Guyot first and then proceed west.

Greenbrier Cove was a beautiful spot; before the creation of the Park it was dotted with the homes of the natives. Over it and to our left as we started up the Middle Prong of the Little Pigeon River, hung the lofty Greenbrier

The party, Fink, Diehl, Avery

Pinnacle, with the steep declivity of the Cat Stairs, so well named, at its end. The going was easy, the trail showing much evidence of travel and many Geological Survey bench marks, the work of survey crews compiling data for the new map then being made of the area.

Just above the spot where the Ramsay Prong and the Buck Fork unite to form the Middle Prong, whom should we meet striding down the trail but Andy Gregory, of Townsend, a native, self-trained surveyor. He had formerly done a great deal of work, surveying and mapping, on the western end of the Smokies for the Little River Lumber Company, and now was employed by the Tennessee Great Smoky Mountains Park Commission. Walter and I had known him for years; now we sat down to renew the acquaintance.

His soft voice and manner of speech fascinated me, and I could have listened to him by the hour. Naturally, he spoke the mountain patois, but seldom bothered himself with such little items of speech as prepositions, articles and such. Well I do remember his reference to Robert Lindsay Mason, the complete accuracy of whose book, "The Lure of the Great Smokies," had been questioned in some places. Speaking slowly and softly, Andy said,

"Mason—Robert Lindsay Mason—just a leetle grain wrong - times."

All the way to the Cherry Orchard, a magnificent stand of wild cherry trees, the grade was easy. Past there the ridges began to crowd in on both sides and the trail grew steep and rocky. At a creek crossing half a mile above the Orchard was a beautiful level campsite, too good to pass by, and we decided to call it a day.

August 12, 1930

After a long search, Myron had discovered, in the dusty, almost forgotten files of the U.S. Coast & Geodetic Survey, the long-lost map of the Southern mountains, drawn under the direction of Arnold Guyot, as a result of his explorations in the 1850's. With no names existing for them, or if so not known to him, Guyot had exercised an explorer's prerogative and affixed names of his own choosing to the physical features. His list of the peaks of the Smokies had been long known, but the current U.S. Geological Survey maps were so inaccurate and sketchy in detail that it had been very hard to make positive identification of all the names in the list. We three, and others, had been working on it for a long time. One of the objects of this trip was to look carefully over the area on the ground and see if we couldn't complete the identification.

The trail ascending along the creek reached the top of the mountain in the low gap just east of Mt. Guyot. Shortly before we came to the gap, we spied a peculiar log structure to one side; on closer inspection it proved to be a log bear pen or trap, with its "figure-four" trigger set but unbaited.

Such bear traps are made in two styles, one a deadfall weighted with heavy logs that, when the bait is taken, falls on the unfortunate bear and crushes him to death. This was the other type, a pen of lighter but strong timbers, roofed with poles. One side was propped high, so the bear could walk under to reach the bait, usually a piece of meat or a honey comb. Taking the bait tripped the trigger that dropped the whole pen down around the bear, holding him captive until the trapper visited the set.

Hiding our packs under bushes in the gap, we walked on to the summit of the high knob at the corner of Cocke and Sevier Counties (now Old Black). Normally we could have seen little or nothing from this point for the heavy timber, but fortunately for us, high wind two or three years before had levelled several acres of spruce, leaving an open spot for our benefit.

Observations taken from here showed our USGS map sadly off in this immediate sector. By it, the big mountain we were on (called Mt. Henry by Arnold Guyot) did not exist; Mt. Guyot was the county corner, at the head of the Pinnacle Lead; and the Pinnacle Lead, coming from the northeast, and the Balsam Range, from the south, joined the main divide less than a half mile apart. In reality, the point on which we stood, and not Mt. Guyot, was the county corner and the head of the Pinnacle Lead. The Balsams were nearly two miles from us, with the gigantic bulk of Mt. Guyot, several hundred feet higher than either, standing between.

Only a short distance from the gap where we had left our packs we found a good spring and campsite. With half the day gone, we decided to spend the rest of it exploring and to spend the night there. Re-hiding our packs after lunch, safe from marauding bear or chance, passer-by, we set out for the top of Mt. Guyot.

Here a rustic tower had been built, probably during some of the surveys incident to the purchase of the area for National Park purposes. The atmosphere was a little clearer than usual, and from the top of the tower we were able to get the real lay of the land in our minds, and to locate correctly Tricorner Knob, Thermometer Knob, Old Black (now Mt. Chapman) and other prominent points. The view was superb, and the country rough and wild enough to satisfy anyone. Myron was suitably impressed, continually exclaiming as the beauty or ruggedness of some new feature caught his eye.

Just before dark, as we sat talking around the fire in our camp at the gap, two natives, crossing from Pittman Center to North Carolina, came by. After a little chat, they ate their frugal meal, augmented by some of our supplies, and with no shelter bedded down for the night close by the spring.

August 13, 1930

The creation of the Park and the great amount of surveying incident to land purchase and mapping operations had resulted in a well-beaten trail along this portion of the state line. We followed it around the shoulder of Mt. Guyot rather than climbing back again across the summit on to Tricorner Knob. A little searching on the highest point here, and I found the big balsam tree where I'd cut my name and date back in 1921. Further on, we passed one of the campsites we'd used on that particular trip.

The pull up the circus-tent-shaped peak of Old Black (now Mt. Chapman) was long but not hard, and the trail fairly open. After passing the present Mt. Sequoyah, the country grew much rougher and steeper, particularly on the south (North Carolina) side.

Some months before the Tennessee Great Smoky Mountains Park Commission had had this section mapped from the air by the Aerotopograho Corporation, for use in the condemnation suit filed against the Champion Fiber Company, owners of nearly a hundred thousand acres of mountain timber lands within the proposed Park boundaries. I had been shown this map, the first attempt to map the area by aerial photography, though it was still somewhat of a secret document. From my memory of the terrain I did not agree with it, contending that it did not correctly show the steepness of the slopes, an important item, as the value of the land might be affected by the difficulty and cost of getting out the timber.

Before we started, we had been furnished a copy of this map to check on its accuracy as we went over the country afoot. Right here, and until we reached Mt. Collins (now Mt. Kephart), we found my suspicions confirmed; the map did not show many of the slopes nearly so steep as they really were. Our findings were reported to Col. D.C. Chapman, Chairman of the Commission, and as a result another and more accurate survey was made. A good part of the present map of the Smokies, showing this immediate section, is based on the aerial survey.

There was little of great interest to record as we pushed on toward Hughes Ridge (now Pecks Corner). Due to increased usage the footway of the trail was in general plainly marked and we did not have to keep so constantly on the alert to avoid straying from it. Having been along the way before, this time there was no need to climb trees to "look out" the country ahead, as we had done before. No actual construction, clearing, or maintenance had been done on any of the trail—simply increased use had kept it open. In some spots the brush was almost as bad as before.

The Carolina side, at the junction of Hughes Ridge and the state line, tends toward a more moderate slope, and the timber is a little more open than usual. Some grass was growing around here, and grazing cattle had left a labyrinth of paths, that started nowhere in particular, and ended the same way.

Water was not to be found just where we had expected to locate it, and we

Walter takes his ease

The lean-to at Hughes Ridge

scattered in search. Walter and I, with the heavier packs, laid them down by the side of the trail while we looked around, but Myron, carrying an easier-riding Bergan's pack, with a lighter load, kept his on. Every little hollow showed signs but no water, and we wandered further than we thought before we saw a rude pole lean-to, roofed with bark, evidently the work of some hunting party. Water in abundance was right at hand. Myron was left building a fireplace and getting the fire going while we went back for the packs.

No dice. In the maze of cowpaths everyone looked the real trail and like each other. No packs were to be seen. Not anticipating any such confusion, we hadn't taken the precaution of marking down some landmark where we had dropped the packs.

Separating, we cast about further and further, continually calling to one another and back to Myron, to keep from getting lost. At first we laughed at the joke on us, but as time passed and the sun set, the humor of the situation evaporated. Dark was close at hand, and a bleak night camp loomed ahead, for our tent, sleeping bags, cook kit and food were all in the missing duffle bags. The tent we could get along without, but food and sleeping gear we must have.

Finally, after more than an hour's search and when gathering dusk was making it hard to see, we stumbled on the packs, in plain sight by the side of the trail. Several times in our search, we had passed within thirty feet without seeing them.

August 14, 1930

A cloud, one of the thick, water-charged kind for which the Smokies are famous, was resting all over the mountain in the morning. By ten o'clock there was not the least hint of it lightening, and we decided to give over the idea of moving on, and to loaf for the rest of the day. At no time did we get more than a few yards from the shelter. Well enough it was that we didn't, for several hard showers blew over during the day. We would have been drenched every time had we been on the trail.

But we had snug shelter, reasonably good firewood, plenty of water and food, and congenial companionship. What more could any camper wish?

August 15, 1930

During the night the mist had blown away, and we were on the trail early, bound for Laurel Top. Here, too, the aero map was in error, many small but sharp points not being shown. The trail in the neighborhood of Laurel Top was much overgrown, and the country rough enough to suit anyone. It was all old stuff to Walter and me, but Myron kept exclaiming over and over, "Magnificent!", "Marvelous!", "I never saw anything like it!", etc. We had no difficulty discerning that he was enjoying the trip to the utmost.

The exact location of Porters Gap, where a steep, seldom used trail once crossed the mountain, had long been in question. Different people had placed it in various places between Laurel Top and Sawteeth. We had determined this time to settle the matter beyond any question. After carefully observing the topography and everything we considered pertinent, we pegged it down, so we thought. We even chopped a blaze in the first deep gap about a mile west of Laurel Top, and marked it "Porters Gap." The surveys of the next year showed us to be wrong; the real Porters Gap was nearly a mile further west, and in the most unlikely spot for a gap to be almost on top of a high ridge. Whether our erroneous marking misled anyone and brought about the present name we never knew. At any rate, it is now shown on the maps as False Gap.

Not far from our version of Porters Gap, in a tiny clearing in the brush, we found a beautiful clump of Gray's lily, the only instance I can recall of having seen it in the Smokies.

The year before, when Walter, his brother Billy and I had passed this way eastbound, we decided that the Sawteeth had more, bigger and tougher huckleberry bushes, kalmia and other shrubs than any we had ever seen before, but this year it was worse. With great difficulty we battled through it until we came to Dry Sluice Gap, then gave up for the day and turned down into North Carolina, to our campsite of the year before.

August 16, 1930

The way past the spectacular rock point of Charlies Bunion and the rest of the Sawteeth was rougher and even more brush-choked than what we had pushed and literally swam through the day before. We were trail hardened now, though, and our loads were not so heavy, so we made light of the difficulties. One thing we had not anticipated was the steepness of the end of Mt. Collins. Always before, when we passed that way, we had been eastbound, and in going *down* that slope we hadn't realized just how long and how steep that descent had been. Now the five hundred foot climb *up* it brought it very painfully to our attention.

The previous year, when we had stood at the Jump-off on the end of Mt. Collins and looked into the great gulf below, it was totally filled with mist, and we could not begin to tell how great a change in the face of the mountain had been wrought by the cloudburst early in 1929.

Before this debacle, the whole mountain side, precipitous though it might have been, had been wholly mantled with vegetation and little trace of the rock beneath could be seen. When the deluge came, an unprecedented volume of water descended in so few minutes that the water soaked earth lost its grip on the stone core of the mountain and slid into the abyss hundreds of feet below carrying with it trees, bushes, and every vestige of vegetation, leaving nothing but the sheer bare rock behind.

The name by which the site of this landslide is now known, Charlies Bunion, was given it a few days afterward, according to Horace Kephart, present at the christening. When torrents of water and great quantities of driftwood came down the swollen Oconaluftee River at Bryson City, a party, including Kephart and Charlie Conner, climbed the mountain to see what had been the damage done by the downpour there. Conner, a native of the Lufty Valley, had long been afflicted with a protruding bunion on one of his feet. All of the party were familiar with the region; they were awestricken by the terrific destruction wrought by the falling water. Looking at the now bare cliff and commenting on one particular outstanding rocky pinnacle, one of the party remarked,

"That sticks out like Charlie's bunion!"

And so a new name had been born.

From Mt. Collins to Newfound Gap was like riding on a gravy train. Compared with what we had been forcing our way through and climbing over during the past few days, an open trail on a gentle down grade was sheer joy and delight.

The trans-mountain highway linking the two states had by now reached Newfound Gap from the Tennessee side, but the Carolina portion was as yet uncompleted. The heavy road cutting in the Gap (nothing like so extensive as today) and the raw scars on the side of the mountain were a great change from when we had last seen the untouched Gap a year before. The roadway was not paved, only gravelled, but tourists and mountain lovers were already beginning to drive along it to reach the crest of the Smokies, something cars had never before been able to do. By the first one returning to Gatlinburg, we sent a message to the hotel asking that our car be sent up for us.

There was little to do and nothing new to see in the Gap, so after a little rest we started walking down the road, which we had never seen, to meet the car en route. In some way our message had been delayed, and we had gotten all the way to the Grassy Patch before the car came into sight.

Walter had brought from Washington a pair of soleless moccasins for me. Around camp I'd found them a delightfully restful change from heavy tramping boots and had put them on again after stopping in Newfound Gap. Believing we would meet the car any minute, I didn't change back to boots when

Myron works, Walter supervises

starting down, a very sad error indeed. One can hardly imagine the condition of my feet, after packing five miles in soft-soled, heelless moccasins.

We ate one of the big dinners for which the hospitable Mountain View Hotel is famed, and then started our car toward home. Myron acknowledged that the eastern end of the Smokies was as beautiful and challenging as we had claimed; it was easily the choicest portion of all the eastern mountains.

Horace Albright on Le Conte

By 1930, the creation of the Great Smoky Mountains National Park was assured, but as yet the land had not been turned over to the Government for protection and development. Horace Albright, Director of the National Park Service, was of course well informed of all that was within the proposed boundaries, but had not yet seen it in person. All former visits and other details had been handled by Arno B. Cammerer, Associate Director.

Mr. Albright now desired a personal acquaintance with the Smokies, and made the trip down from Washington bringing with him Dr. Roy Sexton, a brilliant young surgeon of the city. Dr. Sexton was a great lover of the outdoors and thoroughly familiar with the Blue Ridge Mountains in Virginia, where the Shenandoah National Park, a companion project, was beginning to take shape.

Arrangements were made by the Great Smoky Mountains Conservation

Association to take Mr. Albright to a number of the chief points of attraction, to each of which he was to be escorted by men familiar with it. Dr. H. M. Jennison, head of the Botany Department of the University of Tennessee, and I were asked to accompany him on his visit to Mt. Le Conte. John T. Moutoux, feature writer of the *Knoxville News-Sentinel*, represented the press on the excursion, while Bill Ramsay, a native of the Gatlinburg area, served admirably as guide.

The following account of the trip is that appearing in the *Knoxville News-Sentinel*.

> Horace M. Albright, director of the National Park Service, went to the top of Le Conte and came back as enthusiastic about the region as the most ardent member of the Smoky Mountains Hiking Club.
>
> But his enthusiasm was more significant than that of the average visitor on Le Conte. For Albright, as head of all the national parks in this country and for a number of years superintendent of Yellowstone, has seen all the wonder spots of this country; and in comparing them with the views he got from the top of Le Conte, he said:
>
> "This is truly wonderful country. It would have been a national calamity if this had not been preserved in a national park. It is essentially of national park grandeur and is as important as any of them—and that is saying a lot, for our national park system is an exclusive collection of the finest scenery in the country."
>
> He was particularly impressed with Le Conte. "This is a gorgeous mountain," he said. "It has character. When its name becomes known over the country, it will be added to the list of outstanding peaks. It will take its place beside Pikes Peak, Mt. Whitney, Ranier and others of classic beauty."
>
> He was also happy over the name Great Smokies. "It will be the most beautiful name in our whole park system," he said. "Its name alone will bring thousands to this park."
>
> The national park chief saw Le Conte and the Smokies under the most favorable conditions. The weather seemed made to order. Not a drop of rain all along the way during the two days. And his companions were of the finest. There was Dr. Roy Sexton, a brilliant young Wash-

ington physician, active in the Potomac Hiking Club and a friend of Director Albright; Paul Fink, the banker-naturalist of Jonesboro; Dr. H. M. Jennison, the U-T botanist; and Bill Ramsay, who knows that a guide is expected to be useful rather than entertaining.

The party left Mountain View Hotel at Gatlinburg Tuesday morning on horseback. Director Albright was astride Joe, the horse that rode Jack Huff to the top of Le Conte. Dr. Sexton led the way, so that he might take movie shots of the party fording Roaring Fork Creek, passing through the big tree country just beyond Clabo's place, and at other scenic spots.

One of the fallen trees was so big that Albright and Dr. Sexton dismounted to take movie and still shots of each other standing beside the tree.

"This is a gorgeous country," said the park chief, and before he got back to Gatlinburg again he almost wore out that and several other adjectives.

Dr. Sexton, who knows every foot of the Shenandoah Park in Virginia, said: "The Shenandoah does not begin to compare with this in vegetation. It is the heaviest I have ever seen."

The top of Brushy Mountain was reached at noon, and while Ramsay and two helpers built a fire to boil coffee, the party rode out on Grassy Gap. The view was magnificent.

We left our horses on Brushy and, after lunch began the climb up Le Conte. We had ridden about eight miles and had about two and a half miles to go on foot.

The journey on foot was taken with extreme leisure. Dr. Jennison had been asked to go along to identify the flora for the park director. The U-T botanist shared his job with Paul Fink, and between the two, Albright learned the name and characteristics of every tree, plant, flower, fern and moss on the mountain.

"We call them" so and so, Ramsay, the guide, would add, giving the names used by the natives.

"Just look at the long frond on this moss," he would shout to Jennison and Fink. He seemed as eager over his find as a child over a new toy. A moment later, again stooping over and examining some more moss, he would say, "Just look at this. It looks like small pine trees."

"The flower that struck Albright's fancy most was the trillium, and it so happened that they were the most numerous. "I think this ought to be called the Trillium Trail," suggested the park chief. Dr. Sexton rather favored "The Mossy Trail," but Albright's name was adopted and called that during the remainder of the trip.

Frequent stops were made to give Jennison and Fink time to go into detail about the plants and flowers they were finding. Fink, who is quite a student of the history of this region, dipped into that, too, much to the delight of the park chief.

As we were nearing the top, clouds began to roll in on us. The guide was the first to notice it. "That means we will have rain in a couple of hours," Bill predicted, but his weather forecast was wrong. There was not a drop.

"The rareness of the atmosphere was by this time quite perceptible and, with clouds all around, it seemed as if we had passed into another world. This feeling became more pronounced when at last we reached the top of the last knob and found ourselves in a forest of spruce so thick that the trunks of the trees blocked one's view a few hundred feet ahead.

"A few minutes later we emerged from the black forest into a clearing. We had reached the opening Jack Huff had cut out for his camp. Several men had gathered around an oven, apparently cooking supper." The fire looked comfortable, for the air was chilly and damp and the fog thick.

"We went into Jack Huff's newest cabin. He and Dick Holt of Knoxville were sitting on a bench in front of an open log fire in the grate. A radio was on, and the first thing we heard was an announcer saying that the program was being broadcast from the Manhattan Hotel, New York. The contrast was striking.

The party gathered around the fire, Jack Huff brought in another armful of wood, the radio was softened, and the park chief, the amiable young doctor and the banker-naturalist from Jonesboro took turns in telling stories and jokes.

Soon there were several blasts of a whistle outside. It was the supper bell. Bill had set a table beside the outdoor kitchen, and on the table were plates of scrambled eggs, ham biscuits—but the guide did the best he could by toasting some of the bread.

After supper the party went back into the cabin, and for two hours and a half it was just one story after another. Albright, out of his park service, had a wealth of experiences to draw from. When we came in from supper the clouds still enshrouded the mountain top. Later in the evening Jennison walked to the door, looked out and to his surprise saw a clear sky.

So it was decided to go to bed early and get up to see the sunrise from Myrtle Point. The alarm dock was set for 3.

Story-telling ceased the moment the light was blown out, but probably because no one in the crowd was used to going to bed at 9:30, it was several hours before the last quit tossing about in bed.

However, everyone seemed to be asleep when the alarm went off. Jennison, nearest the mantel, jumped out and had a time shutting off the alarm. Then he went to the door, looked out and announced the sky was as clear as crystal. It was quite cold. Everyone put on all the clothes he had, then threw an army blanket over his shoulders. By 3:30 the tramp to Myrtle Point began.

By the light of the moon we went to see the sunrise. Myrtle Point was reached a few minutes before 4:00—just as the rising sun cast its first glow over Mt. Guyot. The air was clear, and the view so wonderful it took one's breath.

There were row on row of peaks, in all directions, and as far as the eye could see. Dr. Sexton shot several rolls of movies while Fink pointed out the peaks to Albright. The park chief had a topographic map in his hands, and the information furnished by Fink was in corroboration of that which Albright read from the map.

DATE: SEPTEMBER 17-20, 1938

DESTINATION: ROAN MOUNTAIN.

OBJECT: OUTING.

WEATHER: FAIR, STORMY, COLD.

PARTY: WALTER S. DIEHL, PAUL M. FINK.

As the time for a camping trip in the Southern Appalachians, September can hardly be beaten. The weather is generally settled with a small chance of rain. The days are not so hot as earlier in the summer. The night air has a little nip that makes for better sleeping and calls for extra cover. Sometimes the nights can get real chilly.

Walter and I had done a lot of strenuous back-packing in the last twenty-five years, preferably in the rougher parts of our mountains. Now we were growing older, fatter and lazier, and inclined to take our outings a little less vigorously. As he phrased it, "It makes no difference to me how rough the country or how heavy the pack, just so I don't have to get more than a hundred yards from the car."

Guided by such a trend of thought, we settled on Roan Mountain as the spot to visit this year; it was easily accessible by car which allowed us to carry our gear right up to the campsite. Too, the Roan is without equal as a place to loaf around for a few days. There is an abundance of beautiful campsites among the rhododendrons and the balsams, the best of water, and plenty of good firewood.

The restrictions imposed by backpacking had always made it obligatory to fill our travelling larder with condensed, light-weight and water-free foods. No such privation this time. We were going to fare deluxe this time. Walter had brought along a small auto ice-box, that we stocked with steaks, ham, country sausage, and the like. Then there were canned peaches, figs, nectarines, grape fruit, fruit juices, fancy cheeses, and such delicacies.

We wanted to use still the same old tent that had served so well for years, but there was to be no rolling up in blankets on the bare ground. Each of us had his own "blow-bed," and Walter had brought two down sleeping bags,

Our snug haven

which we were to test for an Eastern manufacturer. Just in case, we took along some extra "long johns." We were all set for the life of Riley.

September 17, 1938

Two hours from home, we were on top the mountains searching out just the right spot to set up woods housekeeping. On the edge of the rhododendron gardens, we found it, a tiny bit of deep grass snugly hidden away among the rhodos where no chance passerby would be likely to stumble on it. The car was parked Walter's specified distance, a hundred yards away. He hunted about a bit at the border of the spruce to find a little spring running liquid ice. When our teeth ceased chattering, we tested the temperature of the water and found it only eight degrees above freezing, by far the coldest spring we had ever seen. Now we were all set, sheltered from wind and weather and safe from intrusion. It couldn't have been better. Our supper was equally tops—soup, broiled steak, reflector-baked hot biscuits, nectarines, etc. We couldn't have fared better in town and did full justice to it.

Walter looks over the menu

September 18, 1938

Orange juice, fried country ham, more hot biscuits, stewed figs, coffee and doughnuts—no hardship there. We'd come prepared to live like kings and intended doing it, even if we made hogs of ourselves in the bargain.

Eastward from Carvers Gap to the Hump, the mountain is a broad, open bald top that we had never explored before. A few pleasant hours were spent wandering over it, as far as the Big Yellow. The whole mountain was ours. Not another person was in sight, not even the livestock usually grazing on the lush grass of the high meadows. As we sat eating our lunch in the lee of a rocky outcrop, a pair of questing ravens winged over, almost at arm's length. They were even more startled than we, emitting loud squawks and flapping up top speed as they speedily put distance between us.

Walter had brought along an air pistol with plenty of ammunition. It was a

Target practice

weapon of precision, and we spent the rest of the afternoon in target practice. Everything from tin cans to grasshoppers served as fair marks.

Our supper was almost a replica of that of the night before with another big steak as the main course. And for the record, a steak broiled over hardwood coals has a flavor no other method of cooking can impart.

September 9, 1938

The sky was overcast, a fair breeze making the air perceptibly cooler as we put away the morning grapefruit, ham with red gravy, and hot biscuits. It was not threatening enough to cause any worry.

The time not spent loafing around camp was devoted to exploring the western end of the mountain, the Roan High Bluff, with its wonderful view of the valley of Rock Creek and the high range of the Black Mountains, with Mt.

Strange how luxuriantly one's whiskers grow in the open

Mitchell in the center. On the sky line to the west were the outlines of Unaka Mountain, Big Bald, Big Butte and Camp Creek Bald, all peaks we'd camped on in years before.

After noon the temperature was still dropping and the wind freshening. While our campsite was well sheltered, it seemed the point of wisdom to put a storm rig on the tent. Gusts of wind catching under the front awning made it belly out like a storm-driven sail, so it was thrown back, stretched tight over the top of the tent and guyed down tight.

Before dark the wind was blowing almost a gale, the trees whipping and bending almost flat before its force. Though our fire was in the lee of some large boulders, it was a trying task to cook supper, the sudden hard gusts blowing the flame and heat out to the side. We could see no possibility of keeping a night fire going to ward off the increasing chill. We had additional heavy

Ooh! Fried ham!

woolen underwear in the car; while it was yet light we put it on, as well as all the other clothing we had.

Cold as the air was, and with no fire to help warm us, there was no point in sitting around shivering. We slid into our sleeping bags early and were comfortable enough, even if the storm was howling a few yards above our heads. Soon we were asleep.

We didn't hear the supreme blast coming about midnight. Its arrival brought us back to consciousness with a jerk, though, when tent, poles and all came piling down on top of us. Fortunately, the tent cover was securely lashed to the poles, or it would have gone sailing away like a ghost across the mountain. There was nothing we could do in the middle of the night but untangle the mess, pull the tent over us for extra shelter, tuck it in snugly all around us and, shivering in our down bags, go back to sleep again as best we might.

September 20, 1938

The wind had largely spent itself by morning, but cold ------! Our thermometer stood between 15 and 20 degrees; the water bucket frozen over. A brisk fire thawed us out somewhat, but it took no time at all for us to see we were not outfitted to stay on the Roan long in that temperature. Our time was about up anyway, so we gathered together our gear and started down the mountain, wondering just what might have brought about so abrupt and severe a change in the weather.

The newspapers soon cleared up that question. A terrific hurricane, the worst in many years, was going up the East Coast, to smash into New England, taking 600 lives and causing $500,000,000 damage to property. It had been the fringe effects of this vast atmospheric disturbance that we had received. We congratulated ourselves that there had been no rain with it.

The sleeping bags we had been testing had been designed for use at moderate temperatures, down to 40 degrees. We sent them back to the manufacturer, with the suggestion that he add another pound of down if he wanted them to serve down to freezing.

WATCH THAT AXE

This sketch is not the account of any single camping trip. It is written simply to recount two incidents, unconnected in themselves, but directly connected as affecting the same person. They occurred within a distance of half a mile, though a couple of years intervened. It is written to point out an ever present hazard of camping, one that under different circumstances might well have had serious results in each case. It also tells of an outstanding display of intestinal fortitude. The hero in both occasions was Henry Patton. I just happened to be along.

Late one Fall day, about 1916, we were starting to make camp at the mouth of Devil Fork on Clark Creek. Henry was an excellent camp cook and firemaker and enjoyed those phases of camping so much I always left them to him. My own efforts would be devoted to pitching the tent, getting in browse for beds, cutting night firewood, and caring for the multitude of other small camp duties.

Rigging up the tent, my back was turned to Henry as he started the fire. With no change from his usual tone of voice, he asked:

"Where is your first-aid kit?"

Without turning, I answered,

"In the top of my pack. Get it if you want it."

"You'll have to get it."

Turning, I saw his knee, from over which he had drawn his pants, covered with blood. Chopping an ironwood sapling into firewood, the axe had slipped, the corner of the keen blade cutting a three-inch gash deep into the hollow beside the kneecap. Fortunately, there were no important tendons or blood vessels just there. Though it bled profusely at first, we put a compress on it and soon the flow stopped.

Naturally, I did the rest of the firemaking and cooking that night. He didn't sleep too well, I'm thinking, but the next morning he was chipper as usual, only grunting occasionally when some sudden move brought a twinge of pain. The crotch of a maple sapling close at hand made a dandy crutch. After noon when time came to travel down the creek to meet his father's car, he hobbled along with no great trouble. At home a doctor looked at the wound but did nothing except change the dressing. In a week or two he was walking about as usual, without even a limp.

The wounded warrior rests

Henry soon entered upon his pre-medical studies. We had always carried first-aid kits containing bandages, compresses, adhesive tape, antiseptic, pain-killer and a few simple medicines. He now made up a more elaborate one, adding a scalpel, surgical needles and thread and a few more medicines.

Some two years after the first incident, we were again on Clark Creek, with our camp at Sill Branch, about half a mile from the scene of the knee cutting. We had planned to arise and make an early start for the Big Falls in the morning. During the night a severe electrical storm with a dashing rain awaked us. Before going back to sleep, we decided to give up the idea of going to the falls and spend the morrow loafing around camp.

Henry rolled out first in the morning, telling me not to get up; he'd cook the breakfast and call me when it was ready. I immediately went back to sleep. The next thing I knew he was crawling back into the tent. When I asked if breakfast were ready, I was told that if I wanted anything to eat I'd have to fix it for myself; he had cut his foot chopping wood.

This time the axe blade had shorn through the side of his shoe and into his left foot, between the ankle bone and the heel, just missing the big tendon. Had it not been that the heavy leather of the counter of his shoe was partial protection his heel might have been cut half off, crippling him for life.

Staunching the bleeding and saying not a word to me, he finished building his fire, put water on to boil and sterilized his needles and thread. Then hobbling a hundred feet up the trail away from camp so, as he said, I couldn't hear him if he should cry out, he sewed up the gaping wound without benefit of anesthetic, dressed it and came back to the tent to awaken me. A greater display of hardihood and superiority over pain I've never seen.

This time, like the other, the cut healed speedily, with no trace of infection, and before long he was walking about as good as new.

Two narrow escapes from serious in jury were enough. Henceforth, when we were camping together, by tacit agreement he was allowed to build the fires and cook the food, but if there was any wood to be chopped, I did it.

OUTFITTING

Over the years many friends have shown great interest in our mountain trips for various reasons. Some, while not so frank about it as one man, may mentally have had similar ideas. Every time I'd return he would have a multitude of questions. How many miles had we walked? How much our packs weighed? Had we been rained on? Were we ever lost? He left town, and I didn't see him for several years. When we finally met again, he asked,

"Are you still going into the mountains, like you used to do?"

"Sure. Every chance I get."

"I was thinking of you just a little time ago."

"Thinking of what?"

"What a heck of an idea some people have of pleasure."

Others looked and listened with a doubtful, quizzical air, as though they deemed us slightly off the beam mentally, not tending to become violent, of course, but maybe just a little "tetched." Anybody that would voluntarily undergo all that labor and hardship when he could be comfortable at home—well, there certainly must be something wrong with him.

Then there were others, genuinely interested, with scores of questions. How did we outfit for long trips? What sort of clothes did we wear? How were we sheltered? Should anyone of like mind chance to have read these accounts, it might not be amiss to include a little information of these matters, what and why.

With us, logistics was a very simple problem—either we carried it or we didn't have it. There was no means nor place of getting additional supplies after we shoved off. Our clothes and other gear had to last the whole trip; there were no repair shops in the woods. Hanging over all our planning was the ever present problem of weight; if everything was to be carried on our backs, it must be pared to the last ounce. There was no sense in carrying needlessly heavy articles, yet they must be sturdy enough to take the bumps and knocks of packing. It took much reading, hours of talking and planning, and a lot of trial and experimenting in the field. Our outfits were never the same from trip to trip, for between each time something new had been seen, heard of, or devised that seemed to offer promise of improvement. The perfect outfit was ever an elusive goal to be sought, but never reached.

CLOTHING

One trip showed me the fallacy of wearing ordinary clothing, particularly shoes. When at last I limped home, I had more blisters and abrasions on my feet than one would think could be contained in a single pair of shoes. Heavier, more roomy workshoes, with woolen socks to cushion the feet, cured most of that trouble. About that time the U.S. Army was developing the famous Munson last for all its footwear, one of the most comfortable ever devised. The issue garrison shoes, well soaked in neatsfoot oil, served us for years. To give a firm grip on slick rocks and the like, heels and the margins of the soles were studded with hobnails.

During the First World War, the Red Cross enlisted civilian help in knitting wool socks for trench use. Like everything military, elaborate specifications were laid down as to how every stitch should be knitted. Some of the old ladies, individuals all, decided they had been knitting socks all their lives and no young squirt could tell them how to knit. As a result, when the war was ended, the local Red Cross Chapter had quite a few pairs on hand, beautifully done, but rejected by the inspector. These we bought, and for years we were wearing soft, warm wool socks, superior to anything the stores had to offer.

Likewise, it didn't take long for us to realize the great superiority of wool, inside and out, for trail and camp wear. Even in the heat of summer, light wool underwear is a little hotter than cotton. When one tops out on a high ridge soaking wet with sweat (one doesn't perspire at such times) to meet a cool breeze face to face the cotton-clad tramper will be shivering with a chill in no time at all, while his partner, dressed in wool, is damp but comfortable. So it is with the rain that inevitably descends before one has been on the trail long. When at night, with never a chance to dry out, one perforce must sleep in his sodden garments, he who is clad in wool can rest in relative comfort. When we could, we carried extra wool shirts, socks, and underwear. Even so, in showery weather it was never possible to keep entirely dry.

We learned, too, that army issue clothing, shirts and breeches, were designed for comfort as well as the ability to take hard punishment. At the end of World War I, they were available in plenty in the salvage stores, and we stocked up. All branches of the service wore breeches then, with leggins. Of these, we found the woolen wrap puttees best, though inclined to be vulnerable to attack by briars and stiff brush.

Knitted navy watch caps served triple duty—head covering by day, cushion for the head against the rub and pull of a tumpline and as a very warm nightcap to ward off the evening chill.

SHELTER

It's all romantic and fascinating to think of sleeping under the stars with only the sky for a canopy. Reality is something else again, and one needs more protection over him than just his blanket, at least in our mountains. Heavy dews can have his blanket soaking wet before dawn, and there is always the chance that, clear as the sky may be at nightfall, a pelting shower may blow up across the next ridge without any warning. So some sort of protection is essential for one's well-being.

On my first few trips we depended on an old-style army pup tent but soon found the weight excessive and the accommodations rather crowded. Both ends open, one always got either head or feet wet, depending on which way the wind blew.

About 1919 I bought a Compac tent, a very light weight model weighing about five pounds, giving shelter for two, though a bit crowded. Walter dubbed it a "sleeping sock" and claimed we put it on rather than crawled into it. Four feet high at the peak, the sewn-in floor was kite shaped, and all well waterproofed. One attractive feature was that in foul weather the door could be buttoned tight, a couple of screened windows providing ventilation. Like the pup tent, this had one great drawback for a wilderness trip, of providing no shelter for one's outfit, or where he could cook, eat, loaf and carry on his various activities in comfort, on those not infrequent times when the rain keeps falling all day.

Walter put his inventive genius to work and came up with the plan for a new model. Next, he salvaged the remains of the first balloon to use helium for an inflatant, and sent it, with the plans, down to me for processing. Numerous long sessions at the sewing machine, and the finished job was ready for use when we, with Frank Bain, started for Le Conte in June of 1921.

The material was a very strong, finely woven balloon silk, waterproofed with something like airplane dope. The style was very much like that of the old favorite, the Baker model, differing mainly in that the top and rear wall were both triangular in shape and met at a point, thereby saving much material and weight, and losing little usable space. The rope ridge was about six feet high. Projecting forward from it was a six-by-six awning that could be guyed out to make a front porch. Under its protection a small fire could be built, all the outfit sheltered, and the party could carry on all its woods housekeeping in dry comfort without crowding. All this was supported by a pair of sheer poles on either side, or else suspended between convenient trees. (Note: This was theoretical only. Convenient trees were never found.) Pictures of the tent in use are to be found illustrating the account of the 1921 Le Conte trip and later excursions.

In actual use the Diehl model tent proved all we had hoped for it, the best type we have ever seen for the kind of shifting wilderness camping we most enjoyed. Designed for two men, it was not overcrowded with three. By lowering the ridge and spreading out the sides, it could handle four, with another one or two under the awning. This tent served us the rest of our camping days.

SLEEPING COMFORT

Sleeping peacefully, rolled in one's blanket on the bare earth may sound just as romantic as slumbering under the canopy of the stars, but it is no wise conducive to a good night's rest—and rest is what one needs most after a hard day's packing. Bare earth is a poor substitute for a Beauty Rest mattress. On occasion we had to put up with it, but whenever possible we made use of such wildwood materials as were at hand to soften the bed. At the lower levels we cut grass, weeds, ferns and the like, and piled them down to lie upon. At a little higher elevation we used hemlock boughs. Above 5,500 feet we generally were fortunate enough to find the best of bed material, the smaller branches of the balsam trees. Laid down a foot or two deep, shingle fashion, these make a soft, springy, aromatic mattress whose superior isn't to be found in the open. Incidentally, these small branches of hemlock, spruce and balsam are spoken of as browse.

Along toward the end of our camping days, we discovered the value of a new bit of equipment, new to us at least, the air mattress or "blow bed." We had heard of such things, but had laid aside the idea, thinking them too bulky and heavy for our specialized, streamlined type of camping. One trial convinced us that maybe we didn't know quite as much as we thought we did, and that the labor of packing a very few more pounds would be more than compensated by the saving of time and labor in making camp at night, to say nothing of the joy of restful sleep on a far more comfortable bed.

In the beginning we carried simply wool blankets, generally army surplus. These are harder woven, not so fluffy and consequently not quite so warm as those intended for home use. They wear better in the woods and are not so inclined to gathering burrs, sticks and leaves.

No matter how carefully one tucks himself in his blanket when he lies down, before long, turning and twisting in vain search of a softer, more comfortable spot, his feet creep out and the chilly night air blows in where his cocoon has come open down the back. We soon began folding our blankets in half lengthwise, then sewing across the bottom and halfway up the side, making a sleeping bag.

Some time later I made an improvement on that idea. Using light but strong balloon silk (also called airplane cloth) for a cover and lamb's wool batting as filler, I made a wool quilt, folded and sewn like the blanket bag, with a zipper closing the rest of the side. The lower or foot end was slightly tapered to save weight. Sleeping in wool clothing, this bag was warm enough for any ordinary summer weather on the high tops, where one is not surprised to see frost any month of the year.

When Walter and I were outfitting for a few day's stay on Roan Mountain in 1938, he brought with him two down filled sleeping bags, offered us by the manufacturer at a reduced cost in consideration of our running some field tests on them. They proved warm enough down to about freezing but, when the temperature dropped fifteen degrees below that, we decided to return them and tell the maker to pluck another duck and add its feathers to the filling.

FOOD

Compiling a grub list for a long trip called for a lot of thought and calculating. How much per man per day and how many days, allowing a margin of a day or two for unexpected delay by unfavorable weather. Everything would have to be carried; barring some fish there was no hope of getting any game or living off the country. Hence everything must be as condensed and waterfree as possible, to pare down bulk and weight to the last ounce. There was no point in carrying water in our food when it could be easily restored in cooking. The foods must be such as would not spoil or mold en route under either hot sun or the dampness of the woods. It must be palatable and not too difficult to prepare, with enough diversity to give a balanced and varied diet. One *can* live indefinitely on nothing but bacon, beans and bannock, but it grows monotonous after the second day.

Several specimen grub lists have been given following the accounts of various trips; from them the reader can gain an idea of how sumptuously we fared. Possibly a bit of explanation of a few items will help.

Few campers were as fortunate as we with one item. When we would begin getting our supplies together, Walter's father would cut one of his incomparable hams and give us a goodly portion of the center cut. Nothing is more delectable in camp than fried country ham with red gravy. I'm confident the aroma of it cooking, bourne on the breeze, lured in every bear and other forest dweller for miles around. Unfortunately for us, ham will not keep too many days after cutting, and we were forced to make-do the rest of the trip with bacon.

All the ingredients for breadmaking were carried unmixed, so we could vary the kind at will—cornbread, flapjacks, loaf bread, bannock or biscuits. Often oatmeal or rice served as a substitute for bread.

Dehydrated foods were only beginning to show up on the markets and were in no wise as palatable or as easily prepared as they are today. Powdered milk was hard to re-liquify and had a peculiar taste, so it was used only in cooking and not alone. The same went for powdered eggs. Vegetables, such as potatoes, green beans, corn, soup vegetables, etc., were entirely waterfree, hard as rocks and required several hours of soaking and boiling to restore the natural consistency, though not always the natural flavor.

One thing we did find very satisfactory was dried soup of several kinds. Earliest of these was erbswurst, the celebrated "iron ration" of the German army before and during World War I. A green pea and black bean meal, with bacon crumbs and salt added, it came in a roll about the size and general appearance of a stick of dynamite. It kept indefinitely in any climate, and even mice and weevils paid it no mind. Other brands of soup were soon on the market, more palatable and more easily prepared, and we made full use of them.

With so concentrated a diet, one always developed a craving for fruits and acids. This we satisfied with dried fruits, generally apples and apricots. The tartness of the apricots was most welcome.

The woodsman of the Far North is very partial to tea as a beverage, and we very early found its value as a pick-me-up or quick stimulant at the end of a hard day's march. With the fire's first blaze, a pot was brewing, drunk black and scalding hot, with plenty of sugar, to give energy to finish the job of campmaking. Often hot tea would be brewed in our canteen cups at the noonday halt.

For these noon lunches, we carried high-energy foods that required no cooking—cheese, dried beef, raisins and sweet chocolate, perhaps adding a bit of bread left over from breakfast. Another lunch, between meals or emergency food was rockihominy, an article unknown to most present-day campers. This is much the same as the parched corn that was the trail ration of the Indians and early woodsmen. Dried corn was roasted to a golden brown, then ground to a very coarse meal, almost like hominy grits. It has amazing food value. A couple of heaping tablespoonfuls, taken dry and washed down with cold water, or mixed with water in a cup and drunk, will carry a man all day long.

For convenience in packing, everything possible was carried in waterproof cloth bags; the cooking fats, baking powder, salt, powdered milk and eggs in friction top tins.

At first, we undertook to assemble our cooking kit from various pots and pans abstracted from the home kitchen or bought at the dime store, but this proved unsatisfactory. The several items would never nest together compactly and generally were of such light material that they failed to stand up under the rigors of back-packing. An Abercrombie & Fitch steel kit was bought—two cooking and one coffee pot, four cereal bowls and four cups and four plates, all fitting compactly into the larger pot and covered by the folding-handled frying pan.

Bread was baked in the frying pan, but someone devised the very successful plan of using an aluminum army mess kit as a dutch oven. A pone of dough laid in the bottom, the cover snapped tight and the whole thing covered over in the hot ashes and embers. Many a loaf of bread in the mess kit did we eat and enjoy.

Later the mess kit was replaced by an aluminum folding reflecting baker, bulkier and more inconvenient to pack but far more versatile. With it one can bake any kind of biscuits or bread, pies, cakes, roast meats or about any kind of cooking done in the oven at home. All this adds greatly in varying the camp diet.

MISCELLANEOUS

For light at night we relied most on the blazing camp fire, but always carried a small miner's carbide lamp with extra carbide in a friction top tin. Used only an hour or so a day, a pound of carbide was ample for a week's trip. It was sturdy and dependable, not temperamental as electric flash lights are inclined to be at times. When all the firewood was damp, it did double duty coaxing it to blaze. Some times, but not always, a small flash light went along.

Once in a while we carried a half-size or boy's axe. Generally a small Marble belt axe (never carried there) with a seventeen-inch handle was sufficiently large for our needs. Had we been doing winter camping, calling for more and bigger firewood, the larger axe would have been essential. Each of us carried a sheath knife and a sturdy pocket knife.

Only a very few times did we carry firearms, and then nothing larger than a .22 rifle or pistol. We had no fear of predatory animals and felt that the possibility of getting game was small, unless we devoted much time to hunting. The extra weight of gun and ammunition would not likely be compensated for by fresh meat in the pot.

On most of our trips into the Smokies, we did take telescopic rods and fishing tackle; we knew that the streams fairly swarmed with speckled trout, not large but delicious in the frying pan. We could not depend on them sufficiently to make any allowance in our grub list, for sometimes the fish wouldn't listen to reason and we didn't do so well. When they were in the mood, it was no trick at all to catch as many in a morning as we could possibly eat in a couple of days.

Also there was a first aid kit, with an assortment of bandages and adhesive tape, antiseptics and a few simple medicines; and a waterproof bag of small stores—spare hobnails, cords, thongs, coil of copper wire, handful of assorted nails, whetstone, spare stock of matches and other odds and ends. Each of the party carried a small pouch of personal articles—shaving gear, fly-dope, pipe and tobacco, notebook, etc.

One or more cameras and spare film was always along, often with ray filters and tripod. Sometimes an aneroid barometer and binoculars were added to the outfit.

"How was all this lot of gear carried?" we were sometimes asked. On my first trip, I wrapped everything and carried it in a blanket roll across my shoulder. One time using that method was sufficient. A blanket roll couldn't hold enough, was hot, bulky and uncomfortable. I soon graduated to an old issue—Spanish-American War knapsack, with my blanket rolled in a waterproof bag and strapped on top. That arrangement was fairly good, but hardly commodious enough for a long trip. When loaded past thirty pounds, the straps cut into the shoulders unmercifully.

Finally, after some experimenting, our packs became almost standardized. All the gear was stowed in heavy canvas seabags. These were carried by pack-straps of our own planning and manufacture, combining the conventional pack-strap with the tumpline, getting many of the advantages of each.

The tumpline, widely used by the packers and guides of the north, is a broad leather band going over the crown of the head, with a long strap attached to each end. By these the load is suspended, and rests against the back just above the hips. Using the tumpline, one can carry a tremendous weight with less discomfort than with any other method. But as the bearer plods along, head down, unable to raise his eyes far above the trail before him, he misses seeing the scenery or whatever else may be about. He is simply a pack animal. A sudden slip or stumble can instantly throw the wearer off balance on his back, with the possible chance of a twisted neck.

Any sort of shoulder straps will cut painfully or chafe when the load weighs over forty pounds. An outfit and supplies for a long trip will considerably exceed that figure. Several times we have started out carrying sixty-five pounds per man. A combination of shoulder straps and tumpline seemed the answer. Each type could be used separately, alternately resting each set of muscles, or jointly, spreading the load.

Walter and I each built our harness on a combined pattern, varying slightly in detail but over all about the same. These we used successfully for years.

Myron Avery introduced us to the Bergan's or Norwegian-type pack, its commodious sack attached to a frame of metal tubing. Most of the weight is supported by a broad webbing band resting on the hips, all held in place by conventional shoulder straps. For short trips, where food supplies do not make too bulky a load, and up to forty pounds, it has no superior for ease of packing. The current U.S. army pack is closely designed after this era.

Another type of carrier we used at times is the pack frame or pack board. To this frame the duffle bag or other load was lashed, the whole supported by combined shoulder straps and tump. The chief virtue of the pack frame is that the load carried never touched the back, hence anything that can be tied or can be carried, no matter how many sharp edges or protruding corners it may have can be taken. Nor is there any limit to bulk, just so long as it can be lashed, strapped, or hung on the frame.

No outfit is perfect, nor did we ever make two trips with exactly the same gear or supplies. There was always the effort to improve some article previously used or a change made to suit specific conditions expected to be met. The study of camping equipment, supplies, and procedure was always a fascinating, never-ending search for us.

"Who knows no toyle can never skill of rest,
Who alwais walks on carpet soft and gay
Knows not hard hills, nor likes the mountain way."

Thomas Churchyard (c. 1660 A.D.)

www.ingramcontent.com/pod-product-compliance
Lightning Source LLC
Chambersburg PA
CBHW031135160426